Silver Burdett Ginn Science
DISCOVERYWORKS

 HOUGHTON MIFFLIN

Boston • Atlanta • Dallas • Denver • Geneva, Illinois • Palo Alto • Princeton

Authors

William Badders
Science Resource Teacher
Cleveland Public Schools
Cleveland, OH

Lowell J. Bethel
Professor of Science Education
The University of Texas at Austin
Austin, TX

Victoria Fu
Professor of Child Development
Virginia Polytechnic Institute and
State University
Blacksburg, VA

Donald Peck
Director, Center for Elementary Science
Fairleigh Dickinson University
Madison, NJ

Carolyn Sumners
Director of Astronomy and Physics
Houston Museum of Natural Science
Houston, TX

Catherine Valentino
Senior Vice President for
Curriculum Development
Voyager Expanded Learning
West Kingston, RI

Consulting Author

R. Mike Mullane
Astronaut, retired
Albuquerque, NM

Acknowledgements appear on page H46, which constitutes an extension of this copyright page.

ISBN: 0-382-41638-4   ISBN: 0-382-33385-3

14 15 16 17 18 19-RRD-05 04 03 02 01

CONTENTS

UNIT C Energy, Work, and Machines

UNIT E

The Solid Earth

THEME: CONSTANCY AND CHANGE

UNIT
G Movement and Control

THEME: SYSTEMS

UNIT A

PLANTS

Theme: Systems

GET READY TO

OBSERVE & QUESTION

How are plants adapted to different environments?

Plants are found growing in nearly every environment on Earth—from sandy deserts to woodland ponds. Explore how different plants are adapted to life under widely differing conditions.

EXPERIMENT & HYPOTHESIZE

What are the stages in the life cycle of a seed plant?

Have you ever followed the life cycle of a plant from the time you plant the seed until the time the plant produces its own seeds? It usually takes several months—or even years—for a plant to pass through its life cycle. But with the amazing Wisconsin Fast Plants™ you can see a plant pass through all the stages of its life cycle in just a few weeks!

INVESTIGATE!

RESEARCH & ANALYZE

As you investigate, find out more from these books.

Why Save the Rain Forest?

- **Why Save the Rain Forest?** by Donald Silver, Illustrated by Patricia J. Wynne (Julian Messner, 1993). From this beautifully illustrated book, find out about the wide range of exotic plants living in the layers of the rain forest.

- **The Blossom on the Bough**, written and illustrated by Anne Ophelia Dowden (Ticknor & Fields, 1994). More than just a pretty picture book, this book is filled with information on how plants survive in a variety of climates.

- **A Pocketful of Goobers: A Story About George Washington Carver**, by Barbara Mitchell (Carolrhoda, 1986). Read the fascinating story of how George Washington Carver, a former enslaved person, discovered more than 300 uses for the common peanut.

WORK TOGETHER & SHARE IDEAS

How can you create an arboretum—an exhibit of trees and shrubs— in your classroom?

Working together, you'll have a chance to set up a mini-arboretum of native plants, display plants you've grown from seed, and create an exhibit of local crops. You'll even learn how to prepare a soil mix so that your local plants will have the best mixture of nutrients to grow in.

1

PLANTS—
INSIDE AND OUT

You probably have a favorite animal. But do you have a favorite plant? Think about the plants you have seen in gardens, flower shops, and other public places. Is there one that you like more than the others? In this chapter, you'll learn that plants are unique and interesting living things.

A Time to Explore

Before Hurricane Andrew hit Florida in 1992, thousands of unusual plants lined the paths of Fairchild Tropical Gardens. These plants had been collected from the tropics. Then ferocious winds blew the plants upside down and inside out.

The toppled plants provided an opportunity for botanist Jack Fischer, an expert on tropical plants. He could examine parts of trees normally hidden from view. He discovered growing buds at the tops of palm trees, and he studied the exposed roots of tropical trees.

As research director for the Gardens, Jack Fischer decided to keep an acre of land in its natural state. People could see the effects of the hurricane, and they could witness the regrowth of plant life.

Coming Up

Jack Fischer, research director of Fairchild Tropical Gardens (*far left*); trees toppled by Hurricane Andrew (*near left*)

WHAT ARE THE PARTS OF A FLOWERING PLANT?

When you look in a full-length mirror, what do you see? Your arms, legs, torso, and head make up several distinct parts of your body. A flowering plant has several distinct parts, too. Each part carries out an essential job needed in the life of the plant.

Activity

Take It Apart

Have you ever met General Sherman? General Sherman is a giant sequoia tree that's over 80 m (262 ft) tall and wide enough for a car to drive through. Yet this huge tree has the same basic parts as a geranium. Examine a plant and get to know its parts.

MATERIALS

- potted plant, such as a geranium
- metric ruler
- newspaper
- plastic knife
- cut flower
- hand lens
- *Science Notebook*

Procedure

1. With other members of your group, **observe** a potted plant. In your *Science Notebook*, list all the plant parts you can see. **Infer** what parts might be hidden from view.

2. **Examine** the leaves. **Describe** and **record** their shape. How does a leaf's width compare to its length? How thick is the leaf? How are the leaves attached? **Record** your observations. **Draw** a leaf.

3. **Observe** the stem. **Record** whether the stem has branches. Is the main stem stiff, or is it flexible? **Record** your observations.

Step 2

4. Carefully hold the pot upside down over a newspaper. Tap the bottom of the pot gently until the plant and soil come out. If the soil is stuck to the pot, use a plastic knife to loosen it. You may remove some of the soil so that you can observe parts that were hidden. **Record** your observations.

5. Does your plant have a flower? If your plant doesn't have a flower, **examine** a cut flower. Use a hand lens to **observe** the structures in the center of the flower. **Record** your observations. **Draw** the flower, showing all of its structures.

Analyze and Conclude

1. What are the main parts of a flowering plant?

2. On the drawing of the leaf and the flower, label any parts that you can identify.

3. In what ways is your plant similar to a tree such as General Sherman? In what ways is it different? On what do you base your conclusions?

4. If you have ever examined other plants, how were these plants different from the plant you observed in the activity? How were they the same?

Step 4

Activity
Putting Down Roots

A tiny radish seed doesn't look like much. But with a little water, its roots really get "absorbed" in their work! Examine radish roots in this activity.

MATERIALS
- blunt scissors
- blotting paper
- shallow dish
- water
- soaked radish seeds
- plastic wrap
- hand lens
- food coloring
- *Science Notebook*

Procedure

1. Cut a sheet of blotting paper to fit inside the bottom of a shallow dish. Sprinkle enough water on the blotting paper so that it is damp but not soggy.

2. Sprinkle four to six soaked radish seeds onto the blotting paper. Cover the dish with plastic wrap and set it in an undisturbed spot that is not in direct sunlight.

3. Examine the radish seeds each day, using a hand lens. Record your observations in your *Science Notebook*. Add water when needed to keep the blotting paper damp.

Step 2

4. On the third or fourth day, add a few drops of food coloring to the damp blotting paper. **Predict** how this will affect the seedling. **Discuss** your predictions with other members of your group.

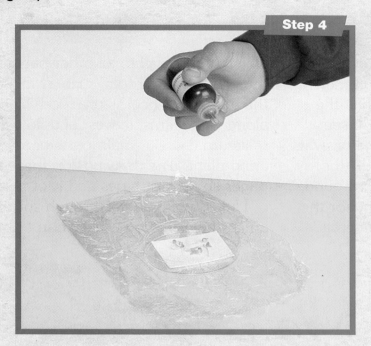

Step 4

5. After ten minutes, **observe** the seedlings again. **Record** your observations. Wait another ten minutes and then **observe** the seedlings again and **record** your observations.

Analyze and Conclude

1. What changes took place in the seeds from the first day to the fourth day?

2. The threadlike structures extending from the growing root are called root hairs. How did the root hairs change when you added food coloring to the dish?

3. Based on your observations, **infer** the role of a plant's root hairs.

4. Suppose two plants were the same except that one plant had many healthy root hairs and the other had many damaged root hairs. **Predict** which plant would be able to take in water faster. **Compare** your prediction with that of other group members.

INVESTIGATE FURTHER!
....
EXPERIMENT

Like a radish, the carrot is an edible root. A carrot plant has one main root called a taproot. Carefully cut off the lower tip of a carrot and place the cut end in a cup of colored water. Observe any changes after 15 minutes and again after 30 minutes. Then remove the carrot and make another cut 2 to 3 cm above the cut end. What do you observe? Record your observations. What can you conclude about the function of a carrot?

Roots

Did you know that when you sit under a shady tree on a hot summer day, you are seeing less than half the tree? For all of the tree that you *see* above ground, there is an equal or even greater part of it below ground—the roots. The **roots** are the underground foundation of a plant. They anchor the plant and absorb water and minerals,

which then travel to all other parts of the plant. Some roots, such as those of the carrot and beet, store food. Roots, along with stems, leaves, and flowers, make up the four main parts of a flowering plant. The drawings on these two pages show root types and root parts.

Unless you burrow through soil like an earthworm, you usually don't notice

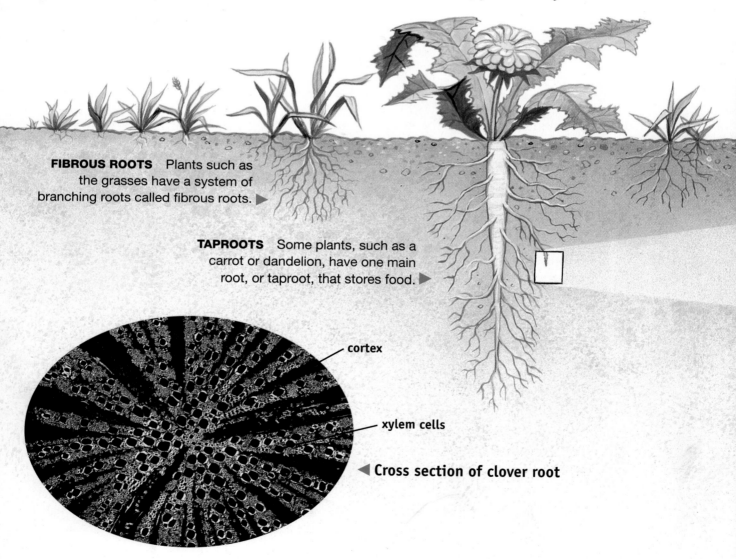

FIBROUS ROOTS Plants such as the grasses have a system of branching roots called fibrous roots. ▶

TAPROOTS Some plants, such as a carrot or dandelion, have one main root, or taproot, that stores food. ▶

cortex

xylem cells

◀ **Cross section of clover root**

roots. But the roots are there, keeping a plant firmly anchored in the soil. Even plants that live in water have roots. Roots of floating water plants hang down from the plant just under the water's surface. Roots of anchored water plants grow in the soil along the shores of streams, rivers, lakes, and oceans. Roots of water plants also keep the plant anchored or store oxygen to help the plants float. ■

epidermis   cortex   phloem   xylem

TRANSPORT IN A ROOT The red and blue arrows show the paths of water and minerals into a root. *Blue* represents water; *red* represents minerals. ▶

root hair

water
minerals

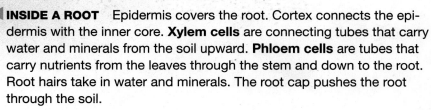

epidermis
cortex
phloem cells
xylem cells
root hairs
root cap

INVESTIGATE FURTHER!

EXPERIMENT

Make your own model of a root. Staple several small strips of paper towel so that they hang down from one large strip. The model should look like a section of root with root hairs coming down from it. Place your root model over a jar half-filled with water. Dip only the lowest edges of the small strips in the water. What happens to the rest of your "root"?

◀**INSIDE A ROOT** Epidermis covers the root. Cortex connects the epidermis with the inner core. **Xylem cells** are connecting tubes that carry water and minerals from the soil upward. **Phloem cells** are tubes that carry nutrients from the leaves through the stem and down to the root. Root hairs take in water and minerals. The root cap pushes the root through the soil.

Stems

Have you ever heard the expression "as sturdy as an oak"? Or have you ever heard someone described as "as slender as a reed"? Both comparisons refer to plant stems. The trunk of an oak tree is its stem. The reed is the stem of a grasslike plant. The **stem** is that part of a plant that connects its roots and its leaves. It is the plant's main support above the ground.

The most obvious job of a stem is to hold up a plant's leaves and flowers.

Stems of many flowering plants, such as buttercups, marigolds, beans, and reeds, are green and fairly stiff. They will wilt if they're deprived of water for too long. These kinds of plants die after one growing season. Stems of most larger flowering plants, including roses, oaks, basswoods, and maples, are woody and don't die after one season. A woody plant such as a tree can live for hundreds—sometimes thousands—of years!

CUTAWAY VIEW OF NONWOODY PLANT STEM This stem has thick walls and fibers running through it. The fibers give the stem its strength. This view shows the xylem and phloem cells that make up the transport system of the stem. ▼

xylem

phloem

◄ A buttercup, a nonwoody plant; at the end of the growing season, this plant dies.

◀ **Basswood, or linden tree; this is a woody plant that can live many years.**

▲ **Young basswood stem as seen through a microscope**

Transport in Stems

Inside stems are tubelike cells that carry water up from the roots and food down from the leaves. One kind of tubelike cells forms a tissue called xylem. Recall that xylem carries water and minerals up from the roots and then through the stems.

Another group of tubelike cells forms a tissue called phloem. Remember that phloem carries sugars produced in the leaves down through the stems to other parts of the plant. Xylem and phloem tubes in the stem connect with xylem and phloem tubes in the root. All the xylem and phloem cells, taken as a group, form the transport system of a plant. ■

phloem

growth layer

xylem

bark

heartwood

sapwood

▲ **CUTAWAY VIEW OF WOODY PLANT STEM** The trunk, which is actually a woody stem, is formed of many layers of cells. These layers have an outside protective covering called bark. This view shows the transport system of xylem and phloem. Each year the xylem cells form new layers of growth called annual rings.

Leaves

In autumn in some parts of the country, you will find enormous numbers of falling red, yellow, and brown leaves. Why do plants have so many leaves? What do leaves do?

Look at the pictures of leaves on this page. A **leaf**, which is a plant part that grows out of the stem, is the food-making factory of a plant. Many leaves are thinner than a knife blade. In fact, the thin, flat part of a leaf is called a blade. The leaves of broad-leaved plants are shaped so that the greatest amount of leaf can be exposed to the sun. Sunlight is an essential part of the process of photosynthesis, or food-making in plants. The leaves of needle-leaved plants, such as pine and spruce, also carry on photosynthesis.

VEINS Along with the petiole, the veins form the transport system of the leaf. Water enters the leaf through the veins.

BROAD LEAF Plants such as maple and oak are called broad-leaved trees and have broad, flat leaves. ▶

BLADE The blade is the broad, flat part of a leaf.

PETIOLE The petiole is an extension of the xylem and phloem tubes of the stem.

◀ **NEEDLE LEAVES** Plants such as pine, spruce, and fir have leaves shaped to reduce water loss.

UPPER EPIDERMIS Cell layer that protects the leaf from drying out

PALISADE LAYER Columnlike cells where food making occurs

SPONGY LAYER Loosely-packed cells where food making occurs and where veins are located

VEIN Bundle of cells that contain xylem cells for the transport of water and phloem cells for the transport of sugar and other nutrients

LOWER EPIDERMIS Cell layer that protects the leaf and allows for the exchange of gases

Inside a Leaf

A typical leaf may be very thin, but it's also crammed full of cells, as shown above. If you cut across a leaf, producing a cross section, you'll find several layers of cells. Since the leaf's main function is to manufacture food for the plant, its cells are designed for food making.

Photosynthesis takes place in the two middle layers of cells. The top and bottom layers protect the leaf and keep it from drying out. Another function of the bottom layer is to allow for the exchange of gases needed in food making. A leaf also contains many veins, which allow for the transport of water and manufactured food. ■

▲ The pointy spines of a cactus do not make food. They protect the stem from animal intruders. Cactus spines are modified leaves.

▲ In pea plants some leaves function as tendrils. They twist around objects and support the plant.

Flowers

The most colorful part of a plant is its flower. The **flower** is the reproductive part of a flowering plant. It is inside the flower that seeds are produced. Some plants, such as sunflowers, have big showy flower heads. Other plants, such as grasses, have tiny green flowers that you hardly notice. Flowers come in all shapes and sizes and in a great variety and range of colors. Some plants have tall spikes filled with flowers; others have small flowers with covered hoods. Flowering plants grow wild in

nearly all regions of the world, except where the ground is always covered by snow and ice.

Looking Inside a Flower

Many plants have large showy brightly colored flowers that are attractive to insects, birds, and even bats! The flower's beauty is an adaptive feature: It draws animals toward the plant, encouraging them to dip into the flower to draw out the sweet nectar. While the animals remove the nectar, they are

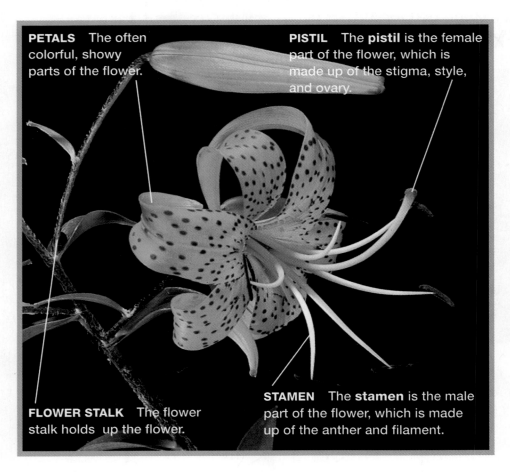

PETALS The often colorful, showy parts of the flower.

PISTIL The **pistil** is the female part of the flower, which is made up of the stigma, style, and ovary.

FLOWER STALK The flower stalk holds up the flower.

STAMEN The **stamen** is the male part of the flower, which is made up of the anther and filament.

Snapdragon

A16

POLLINATING A FLOWER The tiny hummingbird sticks its long tongue into the flower tube to remove nectar. The bird accidentally removes pollen, which is passed on to the next flower. Inside the female part of the flower, the pollen joins with egg cells, and a seed begins to develop. ▶

also accidentally removing pollen. Pollen grains contain the male sex cells. These pollen grains are in turn carried to the next flower, where they are brushed off on the female part of the flower. Without intending to do so, the animals—insects, birds, or bats—pollinate flowers. Pollination sets in motion the process of seed production. A flower can form one to hundreds of seeds. ■

◀ **VARIETY IN FLOWERS** All these flowers have the same basic parts, even though they look so different.

Black-eyed Susan

Ladyslipper

Lily

Plants in Our Lives

Where in the world is your breakfast from? Plants provide many essential parts of your life—from the house you live in to the furniture you sit on; from the foods you eat to the clothes you wear. Even many medicines are made from plants.

Plants on the Move

Where did you eat your breakfast today? Perhaps you sat at a kitchen table made from the wood of pine or oak. While you were eating, in a sense you were really taking a trip around the world. Some of the breakfast foods that you ate come from plants that originally grew in different parts of the world.

Did you eat corn flakes? Corn was first grown in South and Central America. The ears of corn were very small. After each growing season, farmers saved the corn kernels from the largest ears to plant the next year. Over

WHEAT One of the two oldest cultivated food plants, wheat was brought from the Mediterranean region to the U.S. in the 1600s.

CORN First grown in the New World by the Incas, Aztecs, and Mayas, Columbus brought corn to Europe in 1493.

POTATO Grown first in South America, the potato was brought to Spain in 1570 from Peru. It was brought to the U.S. from Ireland in 1719.

COFFEE Africa was the first home to the coffee tree. Ethiopians used the beans to make a hot drink around 1000 A.D. Coffee spread to Europe in the 15th century.

hundreds of years, farmers grew larger and larger ears of corn.

Your breakfast might have included a cereal made from rice or a piece of bread made from wheat. Wheat was probably first grown as a food for people about 7000 B.C. in the Near East.

How did crops travel so far around the world? When people traveled or moved to new lands, they took seeds for their crops with them. So over time, crops that were first grown and used by people in one part of the world came to be grown in more distant places.

Food from Plants

Corn, wheat, and rice are examples of seeds that are eaten. These seeds, called grains, are often ground up to make flour. Flour is then used to make bread, tortillas, or pasta.

▲ **Wheat stalks contain grains of wheat that are processed into the flour used to make loaves of bread.**

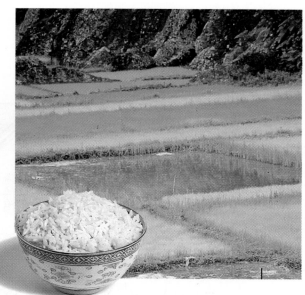

▲ **Rice plants are harvested from paddies and processed to remove the grains of rice used in cooked rice.**

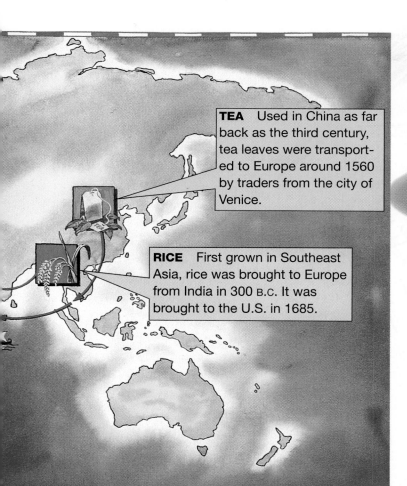

TEA Used in China as far back as the third century, tea leaves were transported to Europe around 1560 by traders from the city of Venice.

RICE First grown in Southeast Asia, rice was brought to Europe from India in 300 B.C. It was brought to the U.S. in 1685.

◀ **Map of worldwide journey of foods over the centuries**

You are probably familiar with many other plant parts that you eat. For example, apples, pears, oranges, and other common fruits develop from the ovary inside a flower. Lettuce, cabbage, and spinach are leaves that you may eat. But did you know that you also eat stems, roots, flowers, and seeds? For example, celery and asparagus are two stems that people often eat. Carrots, radishes, and beets are commonly eaten roots. An artichoke is really the flower of a plant. Flowers from the coral tree, or erythrinas, are a popular food in the southeastern part of Mexico. In Costa Rica, cooks use the flower of the yucca plant in soup.

▲ **SPINACH** Like lettuce and cabbage, spinach is an edible leaf.

▲ **QUININE** From the bark of the cinchona tree comes quinine, used to treat malaria.

Whenever you eat peas or beans, you are eating the seeds of plants. You may also eat sprouting seeds. You do so whenever you eat bean sprouts or alfalfa sprouts.

The cinnamon you might sprinkle on toast at breakfast comes from the bark of a laurel tree, which grows in Asia.

SCIENCE IN LITERATURE

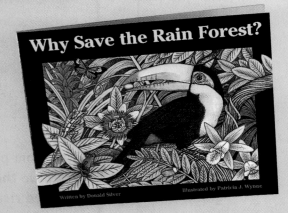

WHY SAVE THE RAIN FOREST?
by Donald Silver
Illustrated by Patricia J. Wynne
Simon & Schuster, 1993

Now you know that breakfast foods come from all over the world. If you were to look at a world map showing ecosystems, you'd find that most of these plants come from tropical rain forests. There is such a map on pages 44 and 45 of *Why Save the Rain Forest?* by Donald Silver. The book will give you an idea of how much land was covered by rain forests thousands of years ago, when many of these plants were discovered. Then read pages 12 and 13 to learn about the ways the rain forest is a part of your life.

By now, everyone has heard about saving rain forests. But why should they be saved? Read pages 22 and 23 to find out some ways that rain forest plants could save our lives in the future.

▲ **CORN** Like wheat and rice, corn is a grain and a staple of life. It has fed billions of people in vast regions of the world for thousands of years.

▲ **COTTON PLANT** After the cotton plant produces flowers, its seeds are held in a ball of fluffy white fibers. These fibers are separated to make cotton fabric.

Bananas are from a tree first found in Southeast Asia. Grapes and apples were probably first grown and eaten thousands of years ago in the river valleys of the Middle East.

What's your favorite breakfast drink? Orange juice comes from fruit that was first grown in Southeast Asia. Do you drink hot cocoa? The Aztecs of Central America began making something they called *chocolatl* from the seeds of the cocoa plant.

Plants Are Lifesavers

When Europeans came to South America hundreds of years ago, some became ill with malaria. Malaria is a tropical disease that is carried by a certain type of mosquito. The Europeans learned that the native South Americans used the bark of the cinchona tree to cure the fever produced by malaria. The powerful chemical from the tree bark is called quinine (kwī′nīn). Quinine is still used as a treatment for life-threatening malaria.

From a tree that grows in the Pacific Northwest comes a drug that can treat people with some forms of cancer. The drug, called taxol, is from the bark of the Pacific yew tree. Today, quinine and taxol are synthesized, or manufactured, in a laboratory. But they were first discovered in plants. ■

INVESTIGATION 1

1. Imagine that you are a drop of water in the soil below a maple tree. Trace your path as you move into the roots of the tree and up through the plant. Name the structures you pass through.

2. Make a chart of the main parts of a plant and the role of each of these parts.

WHAT DO PLANT CELLS LOOK LIKE?

The roots, stems, and leaves that you examined in Investigation 1 are basic parts of all plants. But there is a plant part that is even more basic. In this investigation, you'll investigate plant cells.

Activity

Observing Plant Cells

The part of the onion you eat may grow underground like a root, but it's actually a ball of leaves called a bulb. Onions may not smell very pleasant, but they show the structure of plant cells very well.

MATERIALS
- slice of onion
- tweezers
- microscope slide
- red food coloring
- toothpick
- cover slip
- microscope
- *Science Notebook*

SAFETY
Be careful when handling glass slides.

Procedure

1. Take a section of a quartered onion and snap it in half, as shown. A thin piece of skin should separate from the section. Peel this piece off with the tweezers.

2. Place the onion skin on a microscope slide. Cover it with a few drops of food coloring. Use a toothpick to smooth out the wrinkles. Cover the onion skin with a cover slip.

3. Observe the onion skin under a microscope at low power and draw in your *Science Notebook* what you see. Repeat your observations under high power.

Step 1

4. The small circle that turned red inside the onion cell is called a **nucleus**. Label the nucleus in your drawing.

5. The boundary of the cell is called the **cell wall**. Label the cell wall in your drawing.

Analyze and Conclude

1. Like all living things, plants are made of cells. Describe the appearance of the cells that you observed.

2. A cell wall is found only in plant cells, not in animal cells. What job do you think the cell wall has?

3. Suppose you looked at a microscope slide taken from a living thing that you had never seen before. How could you tell whether you were looking at a plant cell or an animal cell?

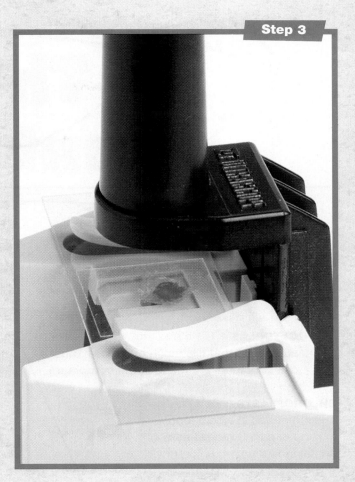

INVESTIGATE FURTHER!

EXPERIMENT

Use a dropper to add two drops of water to a microscope slide. Place a single *Elodea* leaf in the water and cover it with a cover slip. Observe the leaf under a microscope's low power. Then study the leaf under high power and make a sketch of what you see. Describe any structures that you see in the leaf cell that you did not see in the onion cell in the activity. Infer what the functions of such structures are, based on the leaf's role in a plant.

The Plant Cell

When you get up close to a plant—with a microscope, for instance—you can see its cells. The **cell** is the basic unit of all living things. Cells are tiny compartments that are equipped with several basic structures to carry on life activities. The drawing shows the main parts of a plant cell.

CYTOPLASM (sīt′ō plaz əm)   The jellylike substance that fills much of the cell; other cell structures are found in the **cytoplasm**.

CHLOROPLASTS (klôr′ə plasts)   The structures in which food making occurs; **chloroplasts** contain the pigment chlorophyll.

CELL WALL   The **cell wall** is the tough outer covering of a plant cell that gives it a rigid shape; it is made of cellulose.

CELL MEMBRANE   A thin layer that surrounds all cells; the **cell membrane** allows water and dissolved materials to pass into and out of the cell.

NUCLEUS (nōō′klē əs)   The **nucleus** controls all the cell's activities and is very important in cell reproduction.

VACUOLE (vak′yōō ōl) A **vacuole** is a large storage area filled with fluid that hold various substances, including food.

The Story Tree Rings Tell

The stems and leaves of many small flowering plants die in cold weather. Many trees lose their leaves in cold weather, but their stems, or trunks, remain standing and begin growing again in the spring. If you've ever looked at a cut tree stump, you can see that the trunk has a story to tell. Each spring and summer new growth of xylem and phloem cells occurs in the trunk. Generally the size of the cells varies with the amount of rain. For example, if the spring has been rainy, the xylem cells will be very large. This ring of cells appears light in color.

In the drier summer months, new xylem is also formed, but the cells are smaller and closer together. This ring of cells appears darker in color. So during one growing season layers of transport cells are laid down. The rings that are formed are called annual rings.

ANNUAL RINGS   The rings are the result of growth each season. By counting rings scientists can tell the age of a tree.

SAPWOOD   Living xylem cells that give the tree support and strength; most of the tree's wood is sapwood.

CAMBIUM   The thin growing layer of living cells; it produces phloem cells near the trunk's outer part and xylem cells toward the trunk's center.

OUTER BARK   The protective covering of the tree; just like your skin, it protects the tree from disease and from drying out.

HEARTWOOD   The innermost part of the tree is made up of old, dried-up layers of xylem. If the heartwood gets rotten, the result is a big hole in the trunk.

Year after year these rings form. So you can tell the age of trees simply by counting the annual rings. The size of the annual rings tells a story about weather conditions that the tree survived. During periods of drought, rings tend to be very narrow. During wet periods, rings tend to be wide.

Several kinds of trees, including cedars from Japan, cypresses from Mexico, and pines from the United States, live for thousands of years. An environment's history can be read in the rings of such trees.

Most trees increase their trunk size by about 2.5 cm (1 in.) each year. But some large trees have interesting ways of growing. The banyan tree, which grows in Asia, appears to have a huge number of trunks. The baobab tree actually stores water in its swollen trunk. In times of drought, the trunk shrinks. ■

The banyan tree develops thick air roots from its branches. They drop to the soil and take root. ▶

◀ The baobab tree stores water in its swollen trunk.

Bamboo trees are the fastest-growing trees on Earth. Their trunks have been known to grow 2.5 cm (1 in.) in an hour! ▶

INVESTIGATION 2

THINK IT WRITE IT

1. Draw a plant cell and then label and explain the role of all the main cell parts.

2. Explain how scientists might learn about changes in climate in a region by reading the annual rings of very old trees.

REFLECT & EVALUATE

WORD POWER

cell	phloem cells
cell membrane	pistil
cell wall	root
chloroplast	stamen
cytoplasm	stem
flower	vacuole
leaf	xylem cells
nucleus	

 On Your Own
Write a definition for each term in the list.

 With a Partner
Write each term in the list on one side of an index card and the definition on the other side. Use the cards to quiz your partner.

BUILD YOUR PORTFOLIO

Draw and label the parts of a flowering plant. Briefly describe the function of the stem, flower, vein, root, leaf, xylem, and phloem.

Analyze Information

Study the drawing. Then use the drawing to describe the main parts of the leaf.

Assess Performance

Design and carry out an activity to see how light affects the growth of a plant. Compare your results with those of others. What do the results tell you about how a plant functions?

Problem Solving

1. While walking through an indoor garden, you come upon a huge room where rain forest plants are growing. Some of the plants have leaves more than 1.8 m (6 ft) long. Explain why rain forest plants need such big leaves.

2. You go to a restaurant and one of your friends says she wants to eat a flower, a fruit, a leaf, a stem, and a root. What could she order from the menu to satisfy her wish?

CHAPTER 2

PLANT PROCESSES

Plants are Earth's food factories. They spend their days busily making food. When they have made enough food for themselves, they store what's left over, which animals then get to eat. And as if that were not enough, plants even give us much of the oxygen we breathe. Maybe we should call them Earth's superheroes!

cattails

fireweed

The Wild Supermarket

The plants you eat probably come from your local supermarket. But the supermarkets of fields and forests are stocked with good things to eat, too.

- In the southern United States, the wild kudzu is considered a pest. Its monstrous leafy vines can grow a foot a day. They cover trees, houses, and power lines. In Asia, however, kudzu is a valuable food. People eat its leaves, roots, seeds, and its beautiful purple flowers.

- A wild plant called the groundnut helped the Pilgrims survive their first winter in North America. Native Americans showed the hungry settlers how to find and cook the potatolike roots.

- Another plant eaten by Native Americans is the cattail. The bottom third of its stalk tastes much like asparagus.

Read on to find out more about Earth's green superheroes.

Coming Up

◄ A supermarket basket full of Earth's green superheroes

HOW DO PLANTS MAKE THEIR OWN FOOD?

Imagine Earth as a barren wasteland with no plants. Do you think you could survive? Well, think again. Your life depends—either directly or indirectly —on the food that plants produce. In this investigation find out how plants make this food.

Activity

In the Dark

A sugar called glucose is food for plants. To make this food, plants need some basic ingredients and an energy source. In this activity you can experiment to see what might provide this energy source.

Procedure

1. Pour potting soil in two plastic cups so that each cup is two-thirds full.

2. Place three soaked pea seeds in each cup. Cover them with a thin layer of soil.

3. Water each cup until the soil is damp but not soaking wet.

4. Place one cup in a sunny spot or near a bright light. Put the other cup in a dark closet or under a box that will keep out the light. With the members of your group, **predict** which plants will grow better when the seeds sprout. **Observe** the cups daily until the seedlings have developed their first leaves.

Step 1

5. After the first leaves develop, **compare** the heights and colors of the two sets of seedlings. **Record** your observations in your *Science Notebook*.

6. To find out whether food has been made in the leaves, do an iodine test for starch. Your teacher will prepare a leaf from each cup for the test. Place the leaves in a dish. Add several drops of the iodine solution to each leaf and allow the iodine to soak in for 10 minutes. If the leaf turns dark purple, it means that sugar (glucose) has been made in the leaf and has changed into starch. If you cannot tell whether the color has changed, ask your teacher for help.

Step 6

Analyze and Conclude

1. How do the stems of the two groups of plants compare in height and color?

2. **Hypothesize** the reason for the differences you observed.

3. Which plants are best able to make food?

4. Based on the results of your experiment, what things do you think plants need to make food?

5. What was the variable in this experiment?

INVESTIGATE FURTHER!

RESEARCH

Do plants make the same amount of food in all kinds of light? If you have ever used a prism or seen a rainbow, you know that sunlight is made of many different colors. Design an experiment in which you control the color of light that is received by a plant. Grow the same kinds of plants under different colors of light by placing colored cellophane or plastic wrap between the light source and the plants.

PHOTOSYNTHESIS

Sun

sunlight

Plants trap light energy from the Sun during photosynthesis.

Carbon dioxide enters the leaf through holes in its surface.

Oxygen, a waste product of photo-synthesis, is released.

light energy

carbon dioxide + water ⟶ glucose + oxygen

Chloroplast

Food is made in the chloroplasts.

water from roots

Water enters roots through root hairs.

▲ Radishes store starch in the roots.

In addition to glucose, photosynthesis produces a "waste" product that humans and other animals need to survive: oxygen. This oxygen and any leftover water leave the plant through the same tiny holes through which the carbon dioxide enters.

Plants cannot produce food all the time. Because photosynthesis requires sunlight, the process of trapping sunlight can't take place at night or on very cloudy days. Although carbon dioxide is almost always available, water may be scarce at times. So plants must produce

Lettuce stores starch in its leaves. ▼

food when light energy, carbon dioxide, and water are all available. Then plants can store the food—generally in the leaves but sometimes in the roots, stems, or other plant parts.

Most plants store extra glucose in the form of **starch**, a chemical that is a chain of sugar molecules. In the activity "Making Food . . . and Storing It!" you found that plants store starch. This starch might be stored in the plant leaves (lettuce), in leafstalks (celery), in roots (carrots), or in underground stems (white potatoes).

▲ Celery stores starch in its leafstalks.

Plants use the energy in glucose to grow, to produce seeds, and, in fact, to carry out all their life functions. They use the energy from glucose in much the same way that we use the energy from the foods we eat. Both plant cells and animal cells use oxygen to release the energy found in food. This process is called **cell respiration** (res pə rā'shən). You'll learn more about this process later in the chapter. ■

INVESTIGATION 3

HOW DO PLANTS REACT TO LIGHT AND GRAVITY?

Have you ever planted a garden? If you have, did you worry about placing each seed so that the roots would grow down into the soil? Why isn't this a problem? In this investigation you'll explore the adaptations plants have for growing in the right direction and for getting as much sunlight as they can.

Activity

Ups and Downs

Imagine that you are doing plant experiments aboard a space shuttle. You want to know how a plant grows where there is no up or down. To plan for your shuttle experiment, you need to know how a plant grows right here on Earth.

Procedure

1. Using scissors, cut two strips of blotting paper. Place the strips inside each of two clear plastic cups so that each strip snugly lines the inside of a cup. Fill each cup one-third full with water.

2. After the blotting paper is completely moistened, place four lima beans in a row, curved side up, in one cup. Make sure the beans are between the inside of the cup and the blotting paper. Using a grease pencil, write a letter (*A, B, C,* and *D*) on the outside of the cup above each lima bean.

3. In the second cup, place four lima beans—this time, curved side down—between the cup and the blotting paper. Using a grease pencil, write a number (*1, 2, 3,* and *4*) on the outside of the cup above each bean.

4. Place both cups in a sunny spot. **Predict** how the seedlings will look when they sprout. **Discuss** your predictions with your group.

5. **Observe** the growth of your seedlings every day for at least two weeks. In your *Science Notebook*, set up a chart to record your data. **Record** your observations every day.

Analyze and Conclude

1. At the end of two days, what did you **observe** in the cup with the lettered seedlings? What did you **observe** in the cup with the numbered seedlings?

2. **Hypothesize** how roots respond to gravity.

3. **Infer** how these plant responses help the plant survive.

INVESTIGATE FURTHER!

EXPERIMENT

How will different conditions affect seedlings? Set up two cups with blotting paper. Moisten the blotting paper. Place two lima beans curved side down in each cup. Place one cup in a sunny spot and the other in a cardboard box with a lid. Predict what will happen to the seedlings. Discuss your predictions.

Plant Responses

In the activity "Ups and Downs," you saw how seedlings respond to one condition of their environment—gravity. Plant responses to conditions in the environment are called **tropisms** (trō′piz əmz). The word *tropism* comes from a Greek word that means "a turning." The plant response that you observed was geotropism, or a turning toward Earth. (*Geo-* means "Earth.")

Growth Toward Gravity

Roots respond to Earth's gravity by growing toward the center of Earth. Growing toward the center of Earth is a geotropic response. This growth response ensures that the roots will grow down into the soil, the plant's source of water and nutrients. Leaves and stems have the opposite response to gravity. They grow away from Earth's center. This response ensures that leaves and stems will be exposed to the sunlight that the plant needs to make its food.

Growth Toward Light

Leaves and stems tend to turn, or grow, toward a source of light. Growing toward light is a phototropic response, or a turning toward light. (*Photo-* means "light.") You have probably seen the leaves of houseplants turn toward a window. Stems may bend toward that window or the nearest source of light. The plants are not just bending—they

▲ Roots show a geotropic response, or a growth downward, toward the center of Earth.

▲ The stems and leaves of these plants are showing a phototropic response, or a growth toward light.

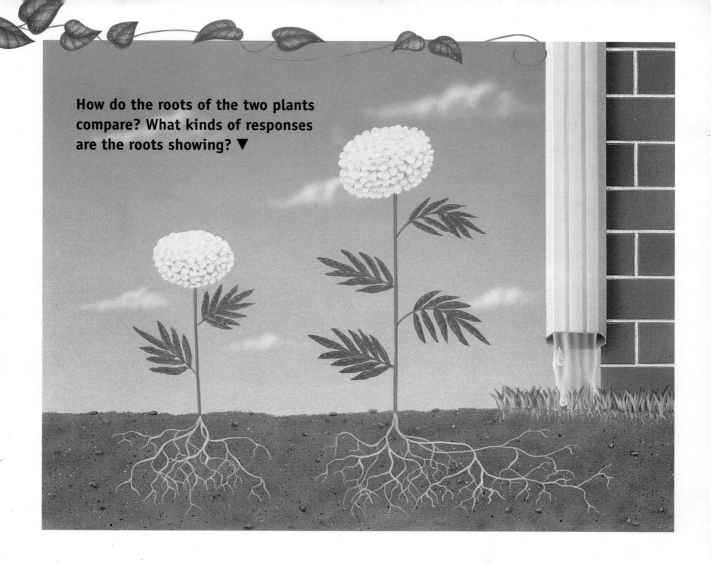

How do the roots of the two plants compare? What kinds of responses are the roots showing? ▼

are actually growing toward light. Such growth allows their leaves to capture the most sunlight for the process of photosynthesis.

Growth Toward Water

When plant roots are in soil that has lots of water, they grow toward the water. This kind of growth is a hydrotropic response. (*Hydro-* means "water.") However, roots do not "know" where the moisture is. They do not "try" to find the water. Instead, when roots come into contact with moist soil, they continue to grow toward the moisture. Roots touching only very dry soil may grow very slowly or not at all.

UNIT PROJECT LINK

Take a walk through a local park, woodland, or garden where there are plants that naturally grow well in your area. Bring along a field guide to identify the plants. List the plants that you find growing in bright direct sunlight. List also the plants growing in shade. Draw a picture of each plant and label each according to the best lighting conditions for that particular plant. Decide which plants from your list could grow in a terrarium.

The tendrils of (*1*) peas, (*2*) clematis, (*3*) morning glory, and
(*4*) sugar-snap peas curl and twine around other objects.

Hanging On

Some plants have tendrils—thread-like parts of a climbing plant—that respond to objects they contact. The tendrils wrap around these objects, using the objects to support the plant as it climbs toward sunlight. This response to touch is still another kind of tropism. It is called a thigmotropic response. (*Thigmo-* means "touch.") Cucumbers, peas, morning glories, and grapes put out tendrils that curl around almost any object they touch. Tendrils help support plants. ■

INVESTIGATION 3

1. On a sunny kitchen windowsill, several potted plants appear to be bending toward the window. Explain what is happening.

2. A group of students grew lima-bean seeds in a plastic cup. After the seeds sprouted, the students turned them so that the roots pointed upward. Explain how the roots would develop between the third and the tenth days.

REFLECT & EVALUATE

WORD POWER

chloroplast   producer
consumer   starch
decomposer   stoma
food chain   tropism
food web
glucose
cell respiration
photosynthesis
transpiration

On Your Own

Use each term in a different sentence that tells the meaning of the term.

With a Partner

Make a word-search puzzle. See if your partner can tell you what each hidden term means.

BUILD YOUR PORTFOLIO

Draw a food chain that includes food you eat. Then use the information in your food chain to draw a labeled diagram of an energy pyramid.

Analyze Information

Study the drawing on page A34 that explains photosynthesis. Then explain the way in which photosynthesis occurs.

Assess Performance

Design and carry out an experiment to show transpiration in a plant. Compare your results with those of other students. What do the results tell you about plant transpiration?

Problem Solving

1. People sometimes refer to fertilizer as "plant food." You have learned in this chapter that plants do not eat food—instead they make their own food. Explain why it is not correct to refer to fertilizer as *plant food*.

2. The rain forests of South America and Central America are rapidly being cut down. Why do scientists consider this a problem for every living thing on Earth?

3. Have you ever planted flower bulbs, such as daffodil or tulip bulbs, upside down? What do you think would happen if you did? Explain your answer.

CHAPTER 3

PLANT REPRODUCTION

Do you know the saying "Tall oaks from little acorns grow"? Since prehistoric times, people have wondered about these little giants of the plant world. How can an acorn, maple seed, or pine cone produce a towering tree?

The Secret at Wollemi Park

Imagine the excitement when, in 1994, a grove of prehistoric pine trees was discovered in Wollemi Park, Australia. Newspapers told the story around the world. Everyone wanted to see the ancient trees.

With only 39 trees in the grove, the Wollemi pine is one of the world's rarest plants. The ancestors of these trees had withstood the nibblings of dinosaurs. But one carelessly tossed match from a tourist could cause the pine to disappear forever. How could its survival be assured?

Under the guidance of Barbara Briggs, the scientific director of Australia's parks, the location of the grove was kept secret. Scientists were sent to the grove to gather seeds to grow more of the trees. With their help the Wollemi pine will survive.

◄ The Wollemi pine, one of the world's rarest plants

HOW DO PLANTS REPRODUCE?

An uncooked lima bean may seem lifeless. So does an onion. But perhaps you've planted bean seeds and watched them grow. Or you may have noticed that after several weeks, green leaves and roots begin to grow from an onion left in a paper bag. In Investigation 1 you'll find out where these new plants come from.

Activity

The Secret of a Seed

You put a seed in soil and keep it moist. In a few days a tiny new plant with roots, a stem, and leaves appears. How can a new living plant come from a seed that seems lifeless? Find out what secrets a seed holds!

MATERIALS

- soaked lima bean seeds
- soaked corn kernels
- plastic knife
- hand lens
- toothpicks
- *Science Notebook*

SAFETY

Use care in handling the knife.

Procedure

1. **Examine** and **compare** a lima bean seed and a corn kernel, which is actually a corn seed. **Record** your observations in your *Science Notebook*. **Make drawings** of the seeds.

2. Carefully peel off the thin outer covering of a lima bean and a corn kernel. **Observe** the covering with a hand lens. **Record** the differences and similarities you see.

3. Gently split open the bean seed with either your fingernail or a plastic

 Step 3

knife. Spread open the two halves of the bean seed and **examine** each half with the hand lens. **Draw** what you observe.

4. **Predict** what you will find inside the corn kernel. Then, with the knife, carefully cut the corn kernel in half lengthwise through one side and lay the halves flat. **Examine** each half with the hand lens. **Compare** the inside of the corn kernel with the inside of the bean seed. **Draw** the inside of the corn kernel. **Discuss** what you have observed with other members of your group.

5. Use a toothpick to scrape off a bit of the material that fills up each seed. **Examine** the material with the hand lens. **Compare** the material from the bean seed with that from the corn seed.

Analyze and Conclude

1. How was the covering of the lima bean seed different from the covering of the corn kernel? How was it similar? What purpose do you think this covering serves?

2. What structures did you find inside each seed?

3. **Hypothesize** the function of the material that fills up each seed.

4. What can you **infer** about seeds from this activity?

INVESTIGATE FURTHER!

EXPERIMENT

Line two clear plastic cups with moistened blotting paper. Place two soaked lima bean seeds between the blotting paper and the inside of one cup. Place two soaked corn kernels between the blotting paper and the inside of the other cup. Set the cups in a warm, sunny place. Keep the blotting paper moist. Relate what you observe over the next few days to the observations you made in the activity.

Activity

New Plants From Old

Can a new plant be reproduced from parts of an old plant? Find out!

MATERIALS

- goggles
- plastic cups
- plastic saucers
- plastic sandwich bags
- measuring cup
- water
- soil
- toothpicks
- small onions
- carrot tops
- geranium or other common houseplant cuttings
- *Science Notebook*

SAFETY

Wear goggles while doing this activity.

Procedure

1. With the members of your group, decide how you can grow new plants from each of the plant parts you've been given. Should you use soil or water? Will the plant parts stand up by themselves, or will they need support?

2. With your group, decide how you will care for your plants. Will the plants need warmth? Will they need light and moisture?

3. Predict what might happen to each of the plant parts. Record your predictions in your *Science Notebook*.

4. Observe your plant parts over the next two weeks. Record your observations daily.

Analyze and Conclude

1. Describe what happened to each of your plant parts. How do your results compare with your predictions?

2. Compare your group's results with those of other groups. How could you account for any differences?

3. Classify the plant parts you used as *roots, stems,* or *leaves*. Why might a gardener want to grow new plants from plant parts rather than from seeds?

Step 1

RESOURCE

From Flower to Fruit

How would you encourage someone to come and visit you? You might prepare some food, put on your best clothes, and make sure you smell good. That's just what many flowers do to attract insects. When an insect visits a flower, however, the visit begins the process that produces seeds.

The flower is the reproductive organ of a flowering plant. Some kinds of plants have flowers that produce both male and female sex cells. Other kinds have flowers that produce either male or female sex cells.

When an insect, small bird, or bat visits a flower, that animal transfers the male sex cells from one flower to another. This transfer is part of the process of sexual reproduction in the flower. During **sexual reproduction** a male sex cell joins with a female sex cell to produce a fertilized cell. In flowering plants, this fertilized cell develops into a tiny plant enclosed in a seed.

In Chapter 1 you learned about the parts of a flower. The drawing below will help you recall the main flower parts. You may also want to refer to the flower on page A16.

THE PARTS OF A FLOWER

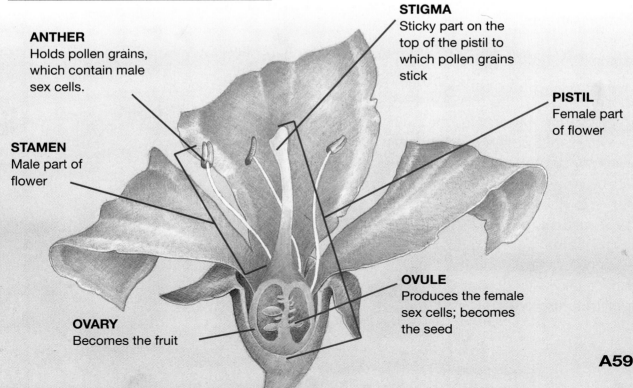

ANTHER
Holds pollen grains, which contain male sex cells.

STAMEN
Male part of flower

OVARY
Becomes the fruit

STIGMA
Sticky part on the top of the pistil to which pollen grains stick

PISTIL
Female part of flower

OVULE
Produces the female sex cells; becomes the seed

A59

◀ Pollen grains cling to a bee's body after it visits a flower. Pollen grains as seen with a microscope (*below*)

Some flowers are pollinated when wind or rainwater carries pollen to them from another flower. Most flowers that are pollinated by the wind or rain are not scented or brightly colored. They do not need to attract insects.

Producing Seeds and Fruits

Follow the pictures on these two pages to see how seeds and fruits are formed. The first step in producing seeds is the transfer of pollen grains from the male part of a flower (the stamen) to the female part of another flower (the pistil). The pollen grains contain the male sex cells. When an insect, a bird, or even a bat brushes against an anther, which contains the pollen grains, some of the pollen sticks to the animal's body. As the animal moves to the next flower, some pollen brushes off its body onto the stigma, which is at the tip of the pistil. This transfer of pollen grains is called **pollination** (päl′ə nā′shən). Even plants that have flowers with both female and male sex cells usually do not pollinate themselves.

1 Pollen grain lands on the stigma of the pistil.

2 A tube grows down into the ovary. **Fertilization** (fʉrt ′l i zā′shən) takes place when a male sex cell from the pollen grain joins with the female sex cell inside the ovary.

Pollination can take place only between plants of the same kind. If the pollen from an apple blossom lands on a tulip, for example, no pollination occurs. A tulip must be pollinated by pollen grains from another tulip.

Inside the ovule, the fertilized egg forms an **embryo** (em′brē ō), a tiny new plant. Other cells in the ovule produce a food supply for the embryo. The ovule then forms a protective **seed coat** around the embryo and its food supply, forming a seed. In the activity "The Secret of a Seed," you peeled the seed coat off bean and corn seeds. Inside each seed you found a tiny embryo and its food supply.

The ovary surrounding the seed or seeds enlarges and develops into a **fruit**. The fruit protects the seeds as they grow. Some fruits, such as plums and cherries, have only one seed; others, such as oranges and strawberries, have many seeds. Some fruits, such as tomatoes and apples, are soft

and moist; others, such as walnuts, wheat, and beans, are hard and dry. Some fruits, such as those on dandelions, have tiny parachutes that help spread the seeds over great distances. A bean pod and a corn husk look much different from the soft, moist inside of an apple, but the pod and husk are other forms of fruit that protect seeds as they grow. ■

③ Following fertilization, the ovary enlarges and begins to form a fruit.

④ The ovary continues to enlarge, and seeds begin to form.

⑤ The fruit has ripened and has split open, releasing the seeds.

Growing Plants
Without Seeds

STS
SCIENCE
TECHNOLOGY
& SOCIETY

When you plant seeds, you are planting the result of sexual reproduction—the joining of male and female sex cells from parent plants. However, you found in the activity "New Plants From Old" that you can grow new plants without using seeds. Such plants are produced by asexual reproduction. In **asexual reproduction**, offspring are produced from one or more cells of a single parent.

In the activity you produced new plants from parts of other plants through a type of asexual reproduction called vegetative propagation (vej ə-tāt′iv präp ə gā′shən). *Vegetative* means "growing." *Propagation* means "increasing in number." The new plants you grew are called **clones**. Clones are exact copies of the parent plants.

Tissue Culture

Another type of asexual reproduction is tissue culture. A group of cells that works together is called a tissue. *Culture* is another word for *growing*. Tissue culture involves growing new plants from the cells of healthy and disease-resistant plants in a laboratory.

Technicians preparing tissue culture in a laboratory (*below*) and a scientist observing the culture (*right*).

A62

To grow plants from a tissue culture, technicians must work in a germ-free environment. They carefully select a parent plant and remove some of its cells. Then each cell is placed in a mixture where it can grow into an exact copy of the parent.

Through tissue culture, as many as 1 million plants can be grown in a year from a small piece of a parent plant. In the near future one laboratory in India expects to grow 20 to 25 million plants a year this way.

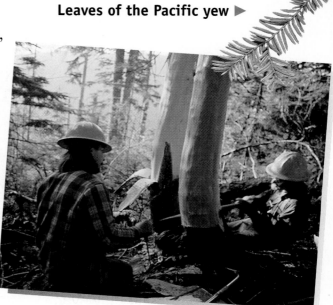

Leaves of the Pacific yew ▶

▲ Bark of the Pacific yew, which is used to produce taxol

Anticancer Drugs

Several laboratories in the United States are using tissue culture to try to create an anticancer drug called taxol. Taxol, which shrinks tumors in many patients and causes some tumors to disappear, is found only in the bark of the Pacific yew tree. These trees are becoming scarce because it takes the bark of three trees to produce the taxol for one treatment! Scientists are now trying to produce yew tree tissue through tissue culture. They hope to make taxol directly from this tree tissue without growing whole trees.

The Future

Tissue culture allows growers to raise valuable plants in a short time, year-round, and under disease-free conditions. Today the process is expensive. But farmers someday might be able to raise crops of potato, corn, or wheat that began with one perfect plant. It is hoped that these crops will be resistant to the diseases, insects, and drought that used to kill them. ■

INVESTIGATION 1

1. Describe how seeds and fruit form in a flower.

2. Describe two ways that plants can be reproduced asexually.

WHAT ARE THE STAGES IN THE LIFE CYCLE OF A SEED PLANT?

In Investigation 1 you saw how seeds were formed from male and female sex cells. But what happens after the seed falls from the plant? In Investigation 2 you'll find out the rest of the story of the life cycle of seed plants.

Activity

It's Just a Stage

Infant, child, teenager, adult: These are the stages of the human life cycle. In this activity you'll use Wisconsin Fast Plants™ to find out if plants have similar life cycle stages.

MATERIALS

- planter
- soil
- fertilizer pellets
- seeds of Wisconsin Fast Plants™
- water
- dropper
- good source of artificial light
- metric ruler
- red marker
- pollinating kit
- *Science Notebook*

SAFETY

Do not eat any seeds or soil!

Procedure

1. Follow your teacher's instructions and have each member of your group fill a planter with soil, fertilizer pellets, and seeds. Then water the plants.

2. Place the planter under a good source of artificial light. If possible, keep the light on 24 hours a day. Water as needed.

3. In your *Science Notebook,* **make a chart** for recording height as the plants grow. **Measure** and **record** each plant's height each day. **Make a line graph** that shows the growth of each plant. Also **record** your observations about the appearance of each plant. **Make drawings** of the plants as they grow.

Plant #	Height (cm)			
	Day 1	Day 2	Day 3	Day 4
1				
2				
3				

4. When the stems are 5 cm tall, use a red marker to make a dot on the stem just below the leaves. Each day, **measure** and **record** the distance between the soil and the dot.

Step 4

5. If your plants have flowers, follow your teacher's instructions for transferring pollen from the flower of one plant to the flower of another plant. **Record** your method of pollination.

6. Continue to **observe** your plants. If fruits are produced, open several when they are ripe and **examine** the contents. What could you do with the contents?

Analyze and Conclude

1. Seedlings are the tiny plants that first appear above the soil. How many days after planting seeds did seedlings appear? If you saw flower buds, how many days after planting did they appear? If your plants formed fruits, how many days did it take for them to ripen?

2. What can you **infer** about stem growth from the measurements you made using the red marker?

3. What stages in the life cycle of a plant did you observe? What was the length of this life cycle?

4. What stage in the plant's life cycle is similar to the life cycle stage you are in? Explain your answer.

The Story of a
Tree Seed

In the late spring the seeds of the red maple ripen and fall off the tree. The seeds are inside the fruit, connected in pairs. A paper-thin "wing" enables them to be carried by the wind.

As they fall to the ground, many seeds are eaten or hidden by small animals and insects. Some lie on the ground long enough for their fruits to open and release the seeds.

1 **GERMINATION** Water in the soil softens a maple seed. **Germination**, or sprouting, occurs. Inside the seed the embryo grows. As the root grows into the soil, it absorbs nutrients and water, and the rest of the embryo sprouts. The tiny plant uses food stored in the **seed leaves** that surround it.

2 **SEEDLING** As its stem appears above the ground, the plant becomes a **seedling**. True leaves develop in the familiar shape of the red maple. Then, with the cooler days of fall, the seedling stops growing. Chlorophyll in its leaves disappears, leaving behind the bright colors that were there all along.

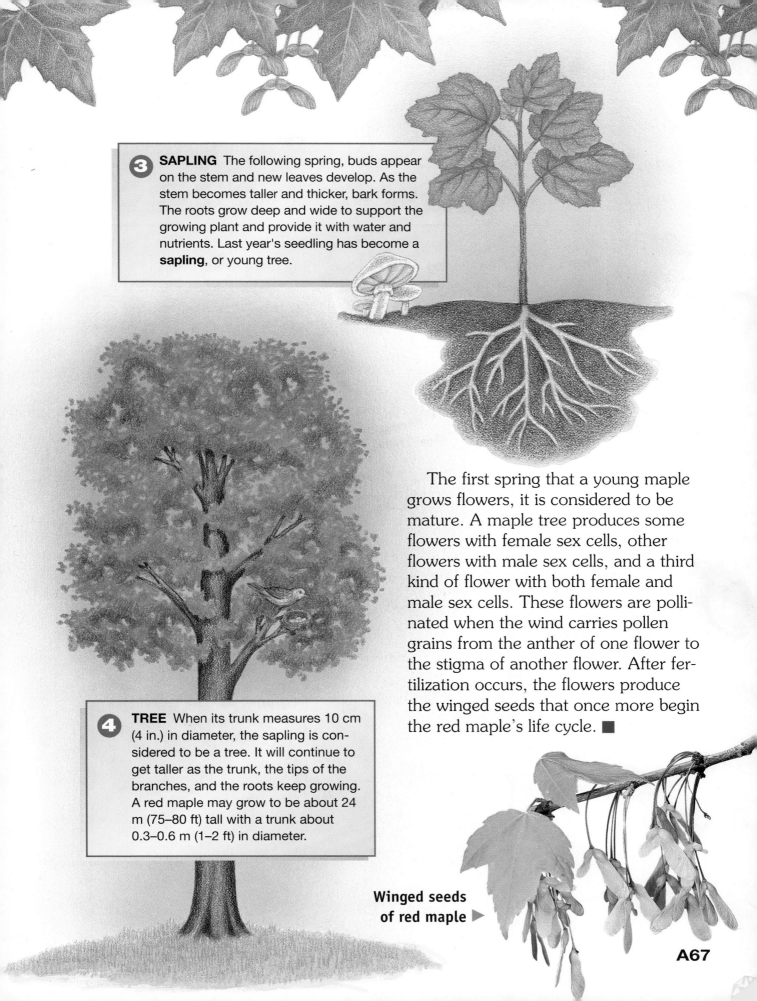

3 **SAPLING** The following spring, buds appear on the stem and new leaves develop. As the stem becomes taller and thicker, bark forms. The roots grow deep and wide to support the growing plant and provide it with water and nutrients. Last year's seedling has become a **sapling**, or young tree.

4 **TREE** When its trunk measures 10 cm (4 in.) in diameter, the sapling is considered to be a tree. It will continue to get taller as the trunk, the tips of the branches, and the roots keep growing. A red maple may grow to be about 24 m (75–80 ft) tall with a trunk about 0.3–0.6 m (1–2 ft) in diameter.

The first spring that a young maple grows flowers, it is considered to be mature. A maple tree produces some flowers with female sex cells, other flowers with male sex cells, and a third kind of flower with both female and male sex cells. These flowers are pollinated when the wind carries pollen grains from the anther of one flower to the stigma of another flower. After fertilization occurs, the flowers produce the winged seeds that once more begin the red maple's life cycle. ■

Winged seeds of red maple ▶

The Life of a Bristlecone Pine

One of the oldest living things on Earth is a bristlecone pine named Methuselah. Methuselah has lived in Great Basin National Park in California's White Mountains for about 4,600 years! If this twisted, wind-battered tree could talk, what might it tell us about our history?

Today only a small portion of Methuselah is still alive. We know how old Methuselah is because scientists have learned how to use a tiny hollow drill to bore into trees and remove a thin core of wood. They can count the annual rings on the core and don't have to cut down the tree. How many other trees will live as long as Methuselah?

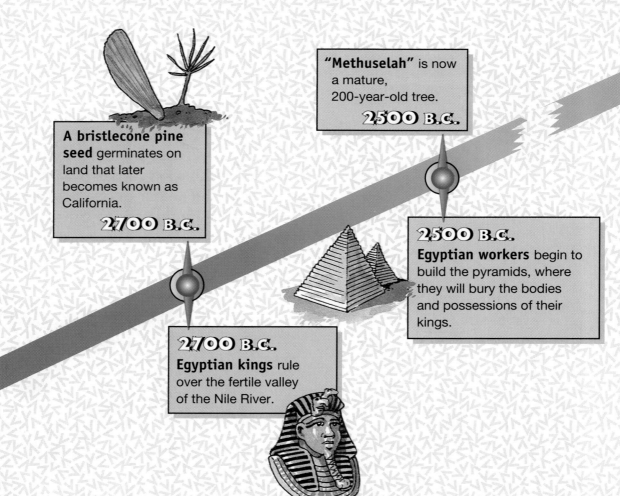

A bristlecone pine seed germinates on land that later becomes known as California.
2700 B.C.

"Methuselah" is now a mature, 200-year-old tree.
2500 B.C.

2700 B.C.
Egyptian kings rule over the fertile valley of the Nile River.

2500 B.C.
Egyptian workers begin to build the pyramids, where they will bury the bodies and possessions of their kings.

UNIT PROJECT LINK

Collect seeds for a green-house project. Use books or talk with people at local plant nurseries to find out the conditions needed for each seed to germinate. Keep a record of the conditions needed for germination.

Americans land on the Moon.
1969

PRESENT
Part of Methuselah still lives today.

1963
A tree older than Methuselah is cut down so that its age can be determined.

A.D. 1776
Thomas Jefferson writes the Declaration of Independence in Philadelphia, PA.

Methuselah today ▼

Timing Things Right

Why can't a cactus live in the Arctic? Why do pine trees have needle-shaped leaves, while water lilies have large flat leaves? The answer is that each of these plants is adapted for certain environmental conditions. An **adaptation** (ad əp tā′shən) is any trait that enables an organism to survive.

Cold Seeds

Seeds need the proper temperature to germinate. This temperature depends on the type of plant. Some seeds, such as those of the apple, peach, pine, and the ash tree shown here, need a period of cold before their seeds will sprout.

▲ Ash seeds must be exposed to cold before they can germinate.

Hot Seeds

Jack pines depend on forest fires for their survival. The life cycle of these trees is adapted to the fires. Their cones open and release seeds only after they are heated to high temperatures. The fire may kill the mature jack pine trees, but their seeds quickly germinate

▲ **Lodgepole pines growing 5 years after a forest fire**

in the charred soil. Lodgepole pines also produce cones that open after they are heated, but these trees also have a safety net. In case there are no fires, some of their seeds also sprout under ordinary conditions.

Blooming Desert

Some flowering desert plants have adapted to their dry, hot environment by developing very short life cycles. They sprout, burst into bloom, and produce seeds following a heavy rain. Many of these plants then die, but their seeds are ready to sprout during the next rain. In contrast to the ancient bristlecone pine called Methuselah, the desert bladderpod mustard plant sprouts from a seed, grows, blooms, produces its own seeds, and dies within as little as ten days.

▲ The bladderpod mustard plant's short life cycle is an adaptation to desert conditions.

SCIENCE IN LITERATURE

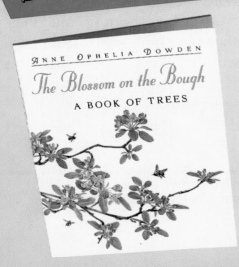

ANNE OPHELIA DOWDEN

The Blossom on the Bough

A BOOK OF TREES

THE BLOSSOM ON THE BOUGH: A BOOK OF TREES
Written and illustrated by
Anne Ophelia Dowden
Ticknor & Fields, 1994

Do you like to draw and paint? If the answer is yes, then you might become a botanical artist—an artist who draws flowers and trees. Anne Ophelia Dowden has created watercolor paintings that not only are beautiful but also teach science. In *The Blossom on the Bough*, you'll see paintings of trees from all over North America.

The paintings show you parts of trees that may not be near each other on the real plant, such as male and female cones. The paintings also compare parts of trees that cannot be seen at the same time of year. That's what makes looking at botanical illustrations a great way to learn about plants.

Water-Storing Stems

Other desert plants adapt by storing water in their thick stems. On a rare rainy day, a large cactus can absorb and store 1,000 L (260 gal) of water. A giant saguaro cactus can store 9,000 L (2,340 gal) of water in its stem—enough to survive even if there is no more rain for three years! The spines on many cactuses reduce the surface area exposed to the dry desert air. This adaptation reduces the amount of water lost through transpiration.

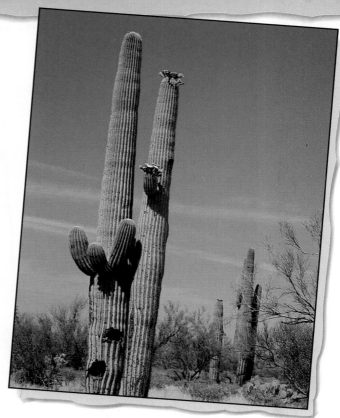

▲ A giant saguaro cactus can store enormous amounts of water.

▲ The longleaf pine is adapted to areas that are rocky or sandy, and it even grows well in poor soil.

Food-Storing Roots

Longleaf pine seedlings, which look like clumps of grass, hardly grow at all during their first six years. Instead these pines store food in their roots. In their seventh year, they shoot up much faster than other pine trees and develop a thick bark that is resistant to fire. This quick growth and protective bark increase the seedlings' chances of survival. ■

INVESTIGATION 2

THINK IT WRITE IT

1. Give examples of ways that plants could survive a forest fire.

2. What kinds of adaptations do plants need to survive in your region?

REFLECT & EVALUATE

WORD POWER

adaptation   fruit
clone   germination
embryo   pollination
fertilization   sapling
asexual reproduction
seed coat
seed leaves
seedling
sexual reproduction

On Your Own

Review the terms in the list. Then use as many terms as you can in a paragraph that tells about sexual and asexual reproduction in plants.

With a Partner

Mix up the letters of each term in the list. Provide a clue for each term and challenge your partner to unscramble the terms.

BUILD YOUR PORTFOLIO

Draw the stages in the life cycle of a plant of your choice.

Analyze Information

Study the drawing. Then use it to describe and explain the environment for which the plant is adapted.

Assess Performance

Design and build a model of a flower that will be pollinated by bees and a model of a flower that will be pollinated by the wind or rain. Compare the models and explain why they differ.

Problem Solving

1. Throughout the world, basic foods in the human diet are seeds, such as rice, wheat, corn, and oats. Based on your knowledge of what a seed is, explain why seeds are nutritious.

2. Compare sexual reproduction and asexual reproduction in plants.

3. Explain how the short life cycle of the desert bladderpod mustard plant helps that species of plant survive. Explain how a plant might use a long life cycle to adapt to a difficult environment.

A WORLD OF PLANTS

There are many kinds of plants. Some, like mosses, are tiny; others, like redwood trees, are huge. Some plants, like sunflowers, stand tall; others, like ivy, creep along the ground. In this chapter, you'll explore the rich variety of plant life.

Plant Animals

There's a leopard hanging around one of the gardens of the San Diego Zoo. Actually, the leopard is part of the garden! It is a piece of topiary (tō'pē er ē), or plant sculpture.

Linda Rodriguez is a topiary artist for the zoo. She makes some of her plant sculptures by allowing bushes to grow and then snipping them into different shapes. For faster results, Rodriguez designs a hollow mesh frame, packs it tightly with moss, and then roots ivy in the moss. The artist trains and cuts the growing plants to the shape of the frame.

Linda Rodriguez tries to make the sculptures lifelike. She knew she had succeeded when a strutting peacock at the zoo tried for days to get the attention of a topiary flamingo. What questions would you ask the topiary artist about her work with plants?

◀ Linda Rodriguez sculpts an ivy-covered animal. A lion with a spider-plant mane looms in the background.

All Kinds of Plants

All plants are members of the **plant kingdom**. The plant kingdom family tree on this page shows that all plants are related. But as you saw in the activity on pages A76 and A77, different types of plants have different traits. Scientists use such differences to classify plants. For example, they divide the plant kingdom into two major groups: nonseed plants and seed plants. The **nonseed plants**—plants that do not reproduce with seeds—include mosses, ferns, and other less-familiar plants. The **seed plants**—plants that reproduce with seeds—include plants that have flowers or cones.

Mosses and Liverworts

If you walk through a forest, you may notice a spongy carpeting underfoot. This carpeting is formed of mosses. **Mosses** are small nonseed plants that lack true roots, stems, and leaves.

Like other nonseed plants, mosses reproduce by means of spores. Spores are one-celled structures that grow into new plants. Mosses also reproduce sexually, producing sperm cells and egg cells. However, no seeds are produced.

Liverworts are nonseed plants that lack true roots, stems, and leaves. They grow in moist places, such as along the banks of streams.

THE PLANT KINGDOM

Dicots

Monocots

Liverworts

Mosses

ANGIOSPERMS

GYMNOSPERMS

SEED PLANTS

Conifers

Ferns

NONSEED PLANTS

Horsetails

COMMON ANCESTOR

▲ Mosses produce spores at the tips of tall leafless stalks.

▲ The liverwort *Marchantia* produces spores on stalks with umbrella-shaped tops.

Mosses don't have xylem cells for carrying water. Because mosses lack structures to carry water, water must diffuse from cell to cell throughout the plant. This is why mosses are small plants that grow only in moist places.

Ferns and Horsetails

Ferns are spore-forming plants that have roots, stems, and leaves. Before the dinosaurs lived, giant ferns covered much of Earth. Today, ferns are not so common. But they still grow in many places that are not too hot or cold and that have lots of moisture.

Like mosses, ferns reproduce by spores. Ferns also reproduce sexually without producing seeds. Unlike mosses, ferns have xylem tubes to carry water from the roots throughout the plant. The roots of ferns anchor the plant in soil and carry water to the scaly, underground stems. These underground stems are called rhizomes.

The most obvious parts of ferns are their leaves, called fronds. At a glance, some fern fronds appear to be made of many leaves attached to several stems. Actually, all of the leaflike parts form one large fern frond. Spore cases, which look like dots, are often produced on the undersides of the fronds. Spore cases contain spores.

Horsetails, shown on page A81, look more like paintbrushes than the tails of horses. There are about 30 species of horsetails living in marshes and swamps around the world. Horsetails share some traits with ferns. For example, horsetails reproduce by spores and have underground stems.

The spots on the undersides of fern fronds are clusters of spore cases. ▶

▲ A typical conifer

Conifers

Many plants, such as firs and the jack pine you read about in Chapter 3, produce seeds in cones. Cone-bearing plants are called **conifers** (kän′ə fərz). Like ferns, conifers have roots, stems, and leaves. However, conifers differ from ferns in the way they reproduce.

When conifers reproduce sexually, they form seeds. The seeds are located between the scales of protective cones. Unlike flowering seed plants, conifers do not form fruits.

Conifers may be small shrubs or tall trees. Huge forests of conifers blanket much of the northern part of the world. Unlike other kinds of trees, most conifers keep their leaves in autumn. Many conifers, such as pines, have needlelike leaves. Others, such as cedar trees, have leaves that look like overlapping scales.

Flowering Plants

Have you ever walked through a garden on a spring morning and been greeted by sweet odors and bright colors? The aromas and colors mean just

SCIENCE IN LITERATURE

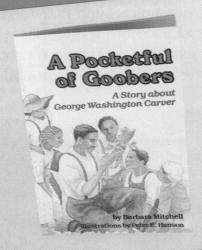

**A POCKETFUL OF GOOBERS:
A STORY ABOUT GEORGE
WASHINGTON CARVER**
by Barbara Mitchell
Carolrhoda Books, 1986

Honey-roasted peanuts. Peanut butter. Peanut oil. How many ways can you use peanuts? George Washington Carver, a plant scientist, discovered more than 300 uses for peanuts. He figured out how peanuts could be used to make milklike drinks, cheeses, shoe polishes, dyes, and even floor coverings.

To the poor farmers of the South at the beginning of the twentieth century, this former enslaved person was a hero. Find out how Carver's "goobers" saved the day when you read *A Pocketful of Goobers* by Barbara Mitchell.

◄ **Hibiscus, a flowering plant**

two groups—monocots and dicots. **Monocots** produce seeds with a single seed leaf, or food-storing leaf. A corn plant is an example of a monocot. Each kernel has one seed leaf used by the germinating seed for food. **Dicots** are plants that produce seeds with two seed leaves. A lima bean plant is an example of a dicot.

We couldn't get along without flowering plants. Each day, you eat parts of such plants—juicy oranges, dry grains made into bread and pasta, or corn made into oil or margarine—for breakfast, lunch, and dinner. On hot summer days, you cool off in their shade. You may sit on their wood either at a bench in the park or on a chair in your home. You might even use flowering plants as medicine when you are sick! ■

one thing—flowering plants are in bloom.

Most of the plants you are familiar with are flowering plants. **Flowering plants** are plants that have roots, stems, and leaves, and that reproduce by seeds formed in flowers. As the seeds are formed, a fruit develops to cover and protect them.

Flowering plants may be divided into

▲ **Water lilies, flowering plants**

◄ **Bird of paradise, a flowering plant**

Horsetails, nonseed plants ►

A81

Leaf Traits and
Classification

▲ **One species or two?**

Look at the flowering plants in the drawing above. Are the plants of the same, or different, species? If you said "different," congratulations! The plant on the top is a common dandelion. The one on the bottom is the prairie dandelion.

What clues suggest the dandelions are of different species? As you learned on pages A76 and A77, leaf traits help distinguish plant species. Different plant species have leaves of different shapes and sizes. The leaves are also arranged differently on the stems. Read on to find out how to classify broad-leaved plants.

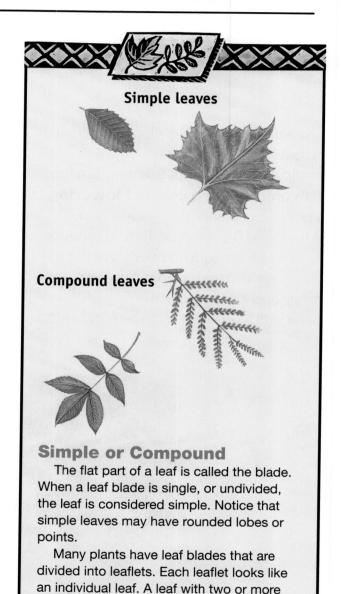

Simple leaves

Compound leaves

Simple or Compound

The flat part of a leaf is called the blade. When a leaf blade is single, or undivided, the leaf is considered simple. Notice that simple leaves may have rounded lobes or points.

Many plants have leaf blades that are divided into leaflets. Each leaflet looks like an individual leaf. A leaf with two or more leaflets is a compound leaf. The number of leaflets may be three, five, seven, or many. The leaflets may join all in one point, or they may be spread out. Sometimes even leaflets have leaflets!

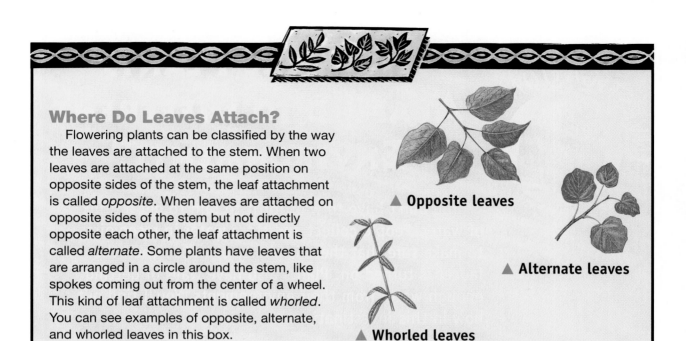

Where Do Leaves Attach?

Flowering plants can be classified by the way the leaves are attached to the stem. When two leaves are attached at the same position on opposite sides of the stem, the leaf attachment is called *opposite*. When leaves are attached on opposite sides of the stem but not directly opposite each other, the leaf attachment is called *alternate*. Some plants have leaves that are arranged in a circle around the stem, like spokes coming out from the center of a wheel. This kind of leaf attachment is called *whorled*. You can see examples of opposite, alternate, and whorled leaves in this box.

▲ **Opposite leaves**

▲ **Alternate leaves**

▲ **Whorled leaves**

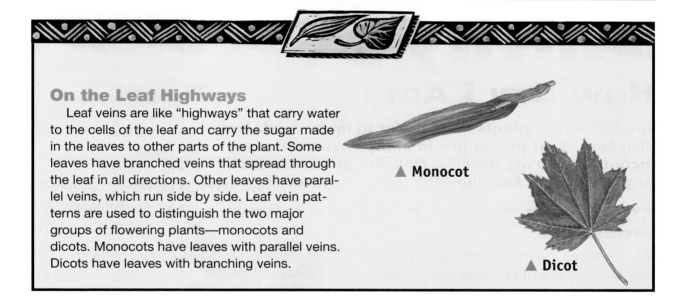

On the Leaf Highways

Leaf veins are like "highways" that carry water to the cells of the leaf and carry the sugar made in the leaves to other parts of the plant. Some leaves have branched veins that spread through the leaf in all directions. Other leaves have parallel veins, which run side by side. Leaf vein patterns are used to distinguish the two major groups of flowering plants—monocots and dicots. Monocots have leaves with parallel veins. Dicots have leaves with branching veins.

▲ **Monocot**

▲ **Dicot**

INVESTIGATION 1

1. What are two traits you would look for to identify an unknown plant as a moss?

2. How can you distinguish between the two main kinds of seed plants? Give one example from each group.

Plants and Water

All plants need water. However, some plants live in water, while others live where there is almost no water. How can plants live in such different environments?

Each kind of plant has structures or behaviors that help it survive in its environment. These structures or behaviors are called **adaptations**. The organism's adaptations are related to its habitat, or where it lives.

Root Adaptations

Most flowering plants absorb water through their roots. But not all root systems are alike. The mesquite (mes kēt′) is a scrubby-looking tree that lives in dry areas. Its roots reach deep into the soil in search of water. Unlike the mesquite, many desert plants have long roots that spread in all directions just beneath the soil's surface. These roots absorb any

dew that collects and sinks into the top layer of soil.

Some plants growing high in the rain forest are not rooted in the ground at all. Instead, these plants have air roots. In some of these plants, the leaves gather water that falls as rain. These leaves then funnel the water to the roots, where it is absorbed.

Plant Conservationists

Many plants have adaptations to conserve the water they take in. In the activity on pages A84 and A85, you may have observed the stomata on the undersides of leaves. Plants take in carbon dioxide and give off oxygen and water vapor through stomata. Plants lose a great deal of water through their stomata. Many plants have adaptations to control the amount of water lost through their leaves.

A mesquite tree ▼

An aloe is a succulent. ▶

During winter, water in the soil may be frozen and unavailable. Many trees lose their leaves, an adaptation that allows them to overcome this lack of water. Trees that drop their leaves in fall are called deciduous (dē sij′ōō əs) trees. Dropping leaves reduces water loss through the stomata. These trees also go into a rest period and don't need as much water for their life processes.

Many conifers have needlelike leaves, which have a small surface area from which water can evaporate. Cactus spines and conifer needles also have waxy coatings that seal in moisture.

Succulents, such as the aloe shown here, are plants with fleshy leaves or stems and usually live in dry areas. After a rain, the leaves or stems swell with water that is stored and used slowly. Many succulents have tiny leaves, which reduces evaporation. Waxy or woolly leaf coverings on succulents keep in the much-needed moisture.

▲ **Water lilies have stomata on the tops of the leaves.**

Too Much Water

Why doesn't a water lily floating on water drown? Aquatic plants have adaptations for surviving in wet places. Water lily leaves are waxy to keep out water. Also, the stomata are on the tops, rather than the undersides, of the leaves. Many underwater plants don't have stomata at all. Such plants carry on gas exchange directly through the outer layer of their cells. ■

Deciduous trees drop their leaves in winter, which helps conserve water. ▼

The Story of Seed Dispersal

In 1883 a series of volcanic eruptions tore apart the small Pacific island of Krakatoa. When quiet returned, the island was completely barren of life.

Three years later, scientists counted 24 plant species growing on Krakatoa. By 1933 the island was green with plants. How did all these plants cross kilometers of ocean and get to Krakatoa?

Recall that many plants produce fruits, the plant part that holds seeds formed in the flower. When ripe, fruit drops from the parent plant. If all fruit fell straight to the ground, the seeds would be crowded together. The seedlings, lacking space and shaded from the Sun by the parent plant,

would soon die. To survive, most seeds must be carried away from their parent plant. The scattering of seeds away from the parent plant is called **seed dispersal** (di spʉr′səl).

Most seeds cannot move by themselves. Instead, seeds have adaptations that allow other things to move them. Recall from Chapter 3 that agents such as animals and wind help pollinate flowers. As you can see from the photographs on this page and the next, these same agents help to disperse seeds. Seeds may also be dispersed by water or by being propelled from the parent plant much as a cannonball is shot from a cannon.

▲ Harvester ants disperse seeds by carrying them in their mouths.

▲ Burdocks, with their stick-tight hooks, are easily carried on animal fur.

▲ Birds that eat fruits may spread the seeds to new locations.

▲ Chipmunks often carry nuts far from the parent tree.

▲ The large seed of the coconut floats on water to a new location.

▲ Winged seeds of maple trees fly like helicopters through the air.

▲ The feathery seeds of milkweed are easily carried by the wind.

Plants of the Tundra

The tundra is a harsh environment with a cold, dry climate. Summer is very short in the tundra, but the number of hours of daylight is great, approaching 24 hours for a short time. Winter is cold and lasts up to nine months, with long nights for much of that time.

The short summer allows only the top few centimeters of frozen soil to thaw for a few weeks. Below this layer, the ground remains frozen. This permanently frozen soil is called permafrost.

Life in the Tundra

From a distance, the tundra appears barren and lifeless. However, during its short summers, the tundra comes alive. Large herds of reindeer and caribou wander the land. These large animals feed on small plants of the tundra.

Most trees and other deep-rooted plants cannot anchor in the permafrost layer. Trees that do grow, such as birch and willow, are severely bent and are small in size to withstand the high winds of the region. The black spruce creeps along the ground instead of growing upright.

The Arctic tundra is shown in violet. ▼

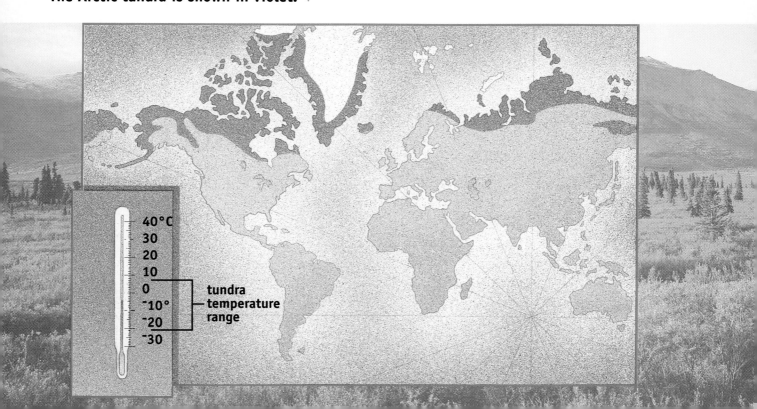

40°C
30
20
10
0
-10°
-20
-30

tundra
temperature
range

In terms of rainfall, the tundra resembles a desert. In this frigid land, the permafrost prevents melting snow from soaking into the ground. This water collects at the soil's surface to form bogs and puddles. In summer, these shallow pockets of water teem with plants such as sedges, grasses, and mosses. The puddles are also home to insects that serve as food for many migratory birds.

It's Been a Long Day

Recall that summer days in the tundra are long. The leaves of tundra plants are adapted to absorb the plentiful sunlight. The leaves are also small and grow low to the ground to help prevent the Sun from drying them out. Hugging the ground helps reduce evaporation. Many tundra plants also have tiny hairs or a waxy covering on their leaves to reduce water loss.

Tundra plants have many adaptations for staying warm. The petals of some flowers direct the Sun's rays inside the flower, keeping the air inside several degrees warmer than the surrounding air. Tundra plants, such as the cloudberry, grow low to the ground in dense mats. Air pockets between the leaves of these plants heat up like a greenhouse. These hardy plants of the tundra are well adapted to life in their harsh surroundings. ■

UNIT PROJECT LINK

Collect plants from your area and try to include all plant parts—from roots to flowers. Press these plants in a plant press that you build, following your teacher's instructions. Classify and label each plant with its name and traits. Hang the mounted plants in your exhibit.

More than 600 plant species thrive in the tundra by rooting in the thin layer of thawed soil. ▼

thaw layer	rock
permafrost	water
ice	

Buttercups ⋏

Cloudberries ⋏

Plants in Peril

STS
SCIENCE
TECHNOLOGY
& SOCIETY

You enter a time machine and zoom back to 360 million years ago. You find yourself in a forest of giant ferns and horsetails as tall as houses. There isn't a flowering plant anywhere to be seen!

The fern forests of the past are gone forever. Most plants that inhabited that ancient world have become extinct, or died out. These extinct organisms will never return to Earth.

Today many species of wild plants and other organisms are in danger of extinction. An endangered species is one with so few members that it is in danger of becoming extinct. A species that is declining in numbers is considered a threatened species.

Extinction is a natural process that has occurred almost since life began. However, human activity is speeding up the rate of species extinction. Some scientists warn that 680 endangered plants of the United States will be extinct by the year 2000. Worldwide, thousands of species face extinction.

Countdown to Destruction

A major cause of plant extinction is habitat destruction. Sadly, people have caused much of this damage. Each time land is cleared for roads and buildings, natural habitats are destroyed. When wetlands are filled to create more land, habitats are destroyed. More habitats are destroyed when farmers plow under sections of open land.

Extinction is a one-way street. Will these sixteen endangered plants survive? ▼

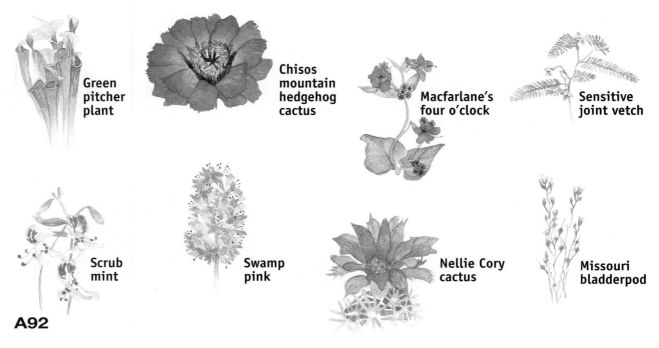

Green pitcher plant

Chisos mountain hedgehog cactus

Macfarlane's four o'clock

Sensitive joint vetch

Scrub mint

Swamp pink

Nellie Cory cactus

Missouri bladderpod

Of all Earth's environments, tropical rain forests are home to the greatest number of species. These forests, located in South America, Africa, and Asia, are disappearing. In 1950, 16 percent of Earth's land was rain forest. Then deforestation (dē fôr is tā'shən), or mass clearing of forest areas, began. By 1975, only 12 percent of Earth's land was rain forest. Scientists predict that only 7 percent of Earth's land will be rain forest by the year 2000. In just 50 years, more than half the world's rain forests will have been destroyed. Many plant species will be lost.

In North America, logging is destroying old forests faster than new trees can replace the old ones. Much of the wood becomes lumber. In some other countries, 50 percent of wood is used for heating and cooking.

▲ **Earth's rain forests are disappearing.**

Other Paths to Extinction

Many cactuses and orchids are rare, valuable, and exotic plants. Over-collecting poses a serious threat to these and other species. Daffodils once covered much of Spain and Portugal. When merchants paid high fees for the bulbs, collectors nearly wiped out these plants.

Food production also endangers plants. People who grow food crops often kill native plants in the process.

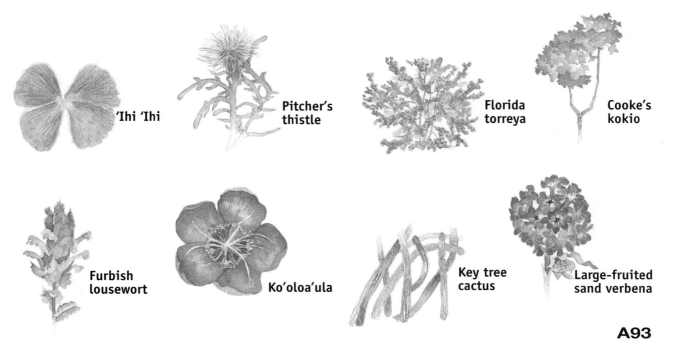

'Ihi 'Ihi

Pitcher's thistle

Florida torreya

Cooke's kokio

Furbish lousewort

Ko'oloa'ula

Key tree cactus

Large-fruited sand verbena

Grazing animals raised for food, such as sheep and cattle, can also destroy plants. These animals often nibble plants down to their roots.

Another danger is industrial pollution. Particles from smoke and exhaust block the stomata in plant leaves. When carbon dioxide and oxygen cannot be exchanged, the plant slowly dies. Rain falling through polluted air can become acidic. In North America and Europe, acid rain is destroying forests and turning lakes into lifeless pools of water. Excess use of fertilizers, insecticides, and other chemicals also harms plants and their habitats.

Saving the Green World

Governments around the world are beginning to take action to keep the world green. Some have passed laws prohibiting the collection or destruction of endangered plants. Laws have also been passed to protect habitats.

Governments alone cannot save endangered species from extinction. Through careful planning, developers can help prevent habitat loss while still providing land for homes and offices. Farmers can use natural enemies to kill insect pests and so reduce the use of insecticides.

People concerned about the environment may also take action to prevent species loss. Each time you recycle paper, you save trees. Each time you leave a flower unpicked, you save a wild plant. Each time you convince a friend to care about wild plants, you help to keep the world green. ■

The burning of rain forests threatens the survival of plants. ▼

INVESTIGATION 2

1. What are some adaptations of plants that enable them to survive in lakes and ponds, in deserts, and in the Arctic tundra?

2. Suggest some things a building developer might do to provide new office space in an area without destroying the habitats of native plant species.

REFLECT & EVALUATE

WORD POWER

adaptation
conifer
dicot
ferns
flowering plants
monocot
mosses
nonseed plants
plant kingdom
seed plants
seed dispersal

On Your Own
Write a definition for each term in the list.

With a Partner
Use the terms listed to make a word-search puzzle. See if your partner can find the hidden terms and tell what each one means.

BUILD YOUR PORTFOLIO

Make a poster that shows the main characteristics of mosses, ferns, conifers, and flowering plants.

Analyze Information

Study the drawings. Explain what adaptations each seed has for dispersal, and then identify the agent of dispersal.

Assess Performance

Using materials such as pipe cleaners, tissue paper, and construction paper, design your own plant. Make adaptations for your plant that will allow it to survive in a desert, a tundra, or a lake. Explain how your plant is adapted to the area you have chosen.

Problem Solving

1. Imagine you have discovered a new kind of plant. Explain how you could use the appearance of the plant's leaves to decide if your plant is a moss, fern, conifer, or flowering plant.

2. Wax repels water. Using this knowledge, explain how a wax covering helps prevent water loss from a leaf. How does a wax covering prevent a water plant from taking in too much water through its leaves?

3. Would you expect a plant living in the Arctic tundra to have smaller, or larger, leaves than a plant living in a deciduous forest? Why?

Throughout this unit you've investigated questions related to plants. How will you use what you've learned and share it with others? Here are some ideas.

Hold a Big Event
to Share Your Unit Project

Help restore native plants to your area. Contact an office of the Nature Conservancy, your state department of environmental conservation, a botanical garden, or a local environmental group. You might even help to change a vacant lot into a natural habitat. Invite students in other classes to join in.

Experiment

Obtain several live plants, both flowering and nonflowering. Carefully break apart each plant to separate its roots, stems, and leaves. Place each kind of plant part in a container of potting soil, labeling the container with the name of the plant and the plant part it contains. Water and observe each container, looking for growth once every week. Record what you observe. Which of the plant parts grew? Which did not? What can you conclude about vegetative propagation, or growing plants without seeds, from your observations?

Research

Since European settlers first came to North America, the landscape has changed greatly. Find out what plants once grew in your area but are no longer found there. Make a list of the plants you learn about. Choose one or two of the plants and create a mural that shows how the land looked when these plants grew in your area. Add to your mural a section that shows how the land has changed and add a caption explaining what caused the plants to disappear. Share your work with your classmates.

THE SOLAR SYSTEM AND BEYOND

Theme: Scale

GET READY TO

OBSERVE & QUESTION

How do the planets differ?

You can see several planets in the night sky with your unaided eyes. What does each planet look like up close? How big is each one compared to Earth? How far away is it? What is it made of? Does it have moons as Earth does—or perhaps even beautiful rings?

EXPERIMENT & HYPOTHESIZE

How do astronomers learn about space?

Astronomers use many different tools to study objects in space. In this unit you'll build your own telescope and observe distant objects through it. You'll also collect space dust, test the effects of weightlessness, and observe different colors that might be found in starlight.

INVESTIGATE!

RESEARCH & ANALYZE

As you investigate, find out more from these books.

- ***The Illustrated World of Space*** by Iain Nicolson (Simon & Schuster, 1991). From the nearby Moon to distant black holes, this book will tell you what's waiting to be explored in outer space.

- ***Stars, Clusters and Galaxies*** by John Gustafson (Julian Messner, 1992). How are stars born? How do they die? How is the universe organized? Find out by reading this book.

- ***The Wonderful Flight to the Mushroom Planet*** by Eleanor Cameron (Little, Brown and Company, 1988). What would a visit to an alien planet be like? This book presents one possibility.

WORK TOGETHER & SHARE IDEAS

How would you live on board a space station?

Working together, you'll have a chance to apply what you've learned. You'll turn your classroom into a simulated space station and explore what life might be like there in free fall. Look for the Unit Project Links for ideas on how to design your station.

EXPLORING THE NIGHT SKY

In the daytime sky the Moon, when visible, is a pale ghost. Seen on a clear night, it's round and full at times. At other times it's a curved sliver that looks like a comma. And what about the stars? On a dark, clear night you'll see hundreds and hundreds of them twinkling. Many, many objects are visible in the night sky. What could you see with a telescope?

Saving the Planet

From a hill in southern California, Carolyn and Eugene Shoemaker scan the sky with a 46-cm (18-in.) telescope. They search for huge space rocks called asteroids that pass close to Earth. So far they've discovered more than 300. Gene works for the U.S. Geological Survey. Carolyn is an amateur astronomer who has discovered 28 comets.

One night in March 1993, the Shoemakers and David Levy, another comet hunter, spotted a comet. It was on a collision course with the planet Jupiter! The comet contained 21 separate chunks that measured up to 4 km (about 2.5 mi) across. When these slammed into Jupiter, it was the greatest collision ever observed.

You too can explore the night sky. You can study craters on the Moon with binoculars. You may even find a meteorite in your rainwater!

Coming Up

◀ David Levy (*left*)
with Carolyn and
Eugene Shoemaker
(*center and right*)

HOW DO ASTRONOMERS LEARN ABOUT SPACE?

How can you learn about objects that are as far away as stars and planets? This is a problem that has puzzled scientists for centuries. Two solutions to this problem are to use telescopes and to collect material that has fallen to Earth from space. You can do these things, too!

Activity
Making a Telescopic Camera

Astronomers use many tools to help them study the sky. In this activity you'll build a simple version of one of those tools.

Procedure

1. Hold a lens above a table and directly below a ceiling light. Adjust the lens's height above the table until it forms an image of the ceiling light on the table.

2. Measure the distance between the lens and the table. Then cut a cardboard tube so it's about three fourths of this length.

MATERIALS
- lens
- metric ruler
- 2 cardboard tubes
- scissors
- tape
- wax paper
- *Science Notebook*

SAFETY
Never look at the Sun through a magnifying lens. Your eyes could be injured. Do not focus sunlight on anyone or on any flammable object.

B18

Step 1

3. Cut a second cardboard tube of the same length. Then cut this tube lengthwise. Overlap the edges and tape them so that this tube is slightly smaller in diameter than the other tube. This tube should slide smoothly inside the first tube, as shown.

Step 3

4. Using tape, attach the lens to the open end of the larger tube. You may have to make a cardboard ring to hold the lens.

5. Cut a square of wax paper to cover the open end of the smaller tube. Tape the wax paper in place. You have now made a simple type of telescopic camera—a device that projects a magnified image of distant objects onto film (or, in this case, wax paper).

Step 4

6. Aim the lens of your camera toward a bright area—perhaps out a window. Look at the wax paper at the other end of the camera. Slide the tubes until you get a clearly focused image on the wax paper.

Analyze and Conclude

1. Compare the image on the wax paper with the real scene. In your *Science Notebook,* make a list of ways in which the image is different from the reality.

Step 5

2. Astronomers and photographers place film where the wax paper is to create pictures. Make a list of other ways in which your cardboard-tube camera differs from a real camera on a telescope.

3. Is your image on the wax paper brighter than the real object? **Hypothesize** what astronomers might do to make their images of faint stars brighter.

UNIT PROJECT LINK

Astronauts often navigate by identifying stars through the windows of their spacecraft. You can do the same thing by creating a navigation pod for your space-station simulator. Draw windows for your station on large sheets of paper. Within the windows, draw the stars of several constellations that are near each other in the sky. Then use your telescopic camera to take sightings on particular stars.

Activity
Mining for Meteorites

Have you ever seen a "falling star"? Do you know what one looks like up close? Find out!

MATERIALS
- magnet
- clear plastic bag
- rainwater in a large pan
- hand lens
- tongue depressor
- microscope slide
- microscope
- *Science Notebook*

SAFETY
Clean up any spills immediately.

Procedure

1. Take a magnet and place it inside a clear plastic bag. Then run the covered magnet through the rainwater your teacher has collected.

Step 1

2. Use a hand lens to look carefully at the outside of the bag. If you find any small round balls there, use a tongue depressor to scrape them onto a microscope slide.

3. Observe the objects through a microscope. If they still look like round spheres, what you probably have are meteorites—pieces of space dust that came to Earth as "falling stars"!

Analyze and Conclude

1. Infer what material your meteorites are made of. What part of the activity provided you with this information?

2. Hypothesize what might cause most meteorites to be rounded in shape.

3. Hypothesize how small meteorites could wind up in rainwater. In your *Science Notebook,* draw a picture of Earth that shows where you think your meteorites were before they fell to the ground during a rain shower.

Step 2

Telescopes: How They Work

Imagine that you're living hundreds of years ago. All that you know about the stars and planets is based on what you can see with your unaided eyes. But you've just learned about a new device called a telescope—a viewing instrument that can magnify distant objects. After focusing this device on faraway buildings, mountains, and sailing ships, you think it might be interesting to look through it at the sky.

So you aim your telescope at the speck of light called Jupiter. Until now, Jupiter just looked to you like a very bright star. But what you see today astonishes you! Instead of appearing as a tiny point of light, Jupiter can now be clearly seen as a round disk. Not only that, but four smaller points of light—previously invisible to you—can now be seen close to Jupiter. As you watch through the telescope each night, it becomes obvious that the four smaller objects are moons that circle Jupiter, just as our own Moon orbits Earth. What an amazing discovery!

The person who actually made this discovery, in the seventeenth century, was the great Italian scientist Galileo Galilei. What he found revolutionized people's views of the universe. He made his observations using one of the most useful devices ever developed by human beings—the telescope.

The two main types of telescopes are pictured on the next page. A **refracting** (ri frakt′iŋ) **telescope** looks like a long, narrow tube, such as a sea captain might use. You look directly through the tube. Light from a distant object is focused by a large lens and then magnified by a smaller lens before it reaches your eye.

  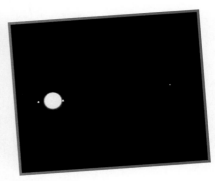

▲ **Galileo discovered four moons of Jupiter by viewing scenes like these through his telescope.**

A refracting telescope ▼

A reflecting telescope ▼

The camera you made in the activity on pages B18 and B19 used a simple single-lens refracting system.

A **reflecting telescope** gathers light in a curved mirror at the back of its tube. It then reflects and focuses the light on a smaller mirror near the front. The small mirror is often angled to send the image out through an eyepiece on the side of the tube. The eyepiece contains lenses that can usually be changed to give you different magnifications.

The largest telescopes in the world are reflectors, because it's easier to build large mirrors than large lenses. A mirror has only one surface that must be precisely made. A lens must be shaped per-fectly from top to bottom! Since a mirror reflects light, a mirror's bottom surface can rest on a supporting structure. Light must pass through a lens, so a lens has to be supported around the edge. The nation's largest reflecting telescope, at Mount Palomar, California, has a 5-m (200-in.) mirror. By comparison, the lens of the world's largest refractor, at Yerkes Observatory in Wisconsin, is only about 1 m (39 in.) in diameter.

Wonders in the Heavens

No one is sure who made the first tele-scope, although many historians believe it was a Dutch spectacle-maker named Hans Lippershey. Whoever was respon-

The observatory at Mount Palomar, California ▶

▲ **The Hubble Space Telescope, about to be released from an orbiting space shuttle**

sible, the Dutch had learned by the early 1600s how to line up two curved lenses in a tube and look through them to make faraway objects appear closer.

As soon as Galileo heard about the Dutch invention, he immediately set out to make his own telescope. Soon he built another, and then another, each one more refined and more powerful than the last. Then he did something no one else had ever done. He took his most powerful telescope outside and looked up.

Galileo's telescope could bring the heavens only 30 times closer, yet what he saw astounded him! The Moon became an alien wonderland covered by deep craters and towering mountains. And there were many more stars than he had ever imagined, some gleaming with newly visible colors.

Called "Galileo's ladder" for many years, the telescope was soon improved. An important advance came from the English scientist Sir Isaac Newton. The simple lenses of his day distorted color, but a mirror did not. So he designed a reflecting telescope that would collect light in a mirror before passing it through a lens.

Since Newton's time, astronomers have learned new ways to use telescopes to see things the human eye cannot see. For example, by attaching a camera to a telescope's eyepiece and exposing the film for long periods of time, astronomers can capture pictures of very faint objects that would not otherwise be visible.

Putting Telescopes in Space

Today we even have large telescopes in orbit around Earth. The Hubble Space Telescope is positioned beyond our planet's atmosphere, so it does not have to deal with distortions caused by looking through the air. It can see more clearly and see objects that are fainter and farther away than telescopes on the ground can see. Space telescopes can even see in wavelengths of light that aren't visible from Earth's surface.

Imagine what you might discover if you could use the Hubble telescope to see seven times farther into space than humans have ever seen before! ■

Meteorite
Messengers

Pretend that you're a giant. Build yourself a huge snowball, about 5 km (3 mi) wide. Stuff some dirt and rocks in with the snow. Let the whole thing freeze rock-hard. Then send it hurtling through space at about 250,000 km/h (155,000 mph).

Aim your snowball so that it will swing in toward the Sun, go completely around it, and then head back out into the most remote regions of the solar system before it returns. The snowball's path should look like a long, thin oval.

Congratulations! You have now created your own **comet** and launched it into an elliptical (e lip'ti kəl) orbit around the Sun.

Snowballs That Melt in the Sun

A comet can look like a ball of fire. Yet real comets begin just as your imaginary one did, as giant chunks of ice. At the core, comets are mostly frozen water, ammonia, and methane, mixed with enough dust and debris to create what you might call a "dirty snowball."

Each comet spends most of its lifetime drifting through the cold outer reaches of the solar system. But when its orbit brings it in closer to the Sun, that's when the show begins!

Because the main body of a comet is made of frozen material, it is doomed to slow destruction by the Sun's heat. Yet the "fire" you see is really not fire at all. Instead, as the comet approaches the Sun, its body begins to melt, releasing its frozen gases into space. These gases spread out to form a huge misty head around the comet's front end.

A comet's tail is made of gases and grains of dust—the "dirt" streaming off the dirty snowball. A stream of charged particles given off by the Sun, called the

◀ Halley's comet—shown at the top of this page as a telescope on Earth would see it—follows an orbit similar to this one.

solar wind, causes a comet's tail to point away from the Sun, no matter in which direction the comet is moving.

Some comets with very long orbits have only appeared once during recorded history. Others have reappeared regularly many times. The most famous one, Halley's comet, revolves around the Sun once every 76 years.

Comets: The Meteor Makers

Throughout history, millions of tiny chunks of comets have broken off and been captured by Earth's gravity. These dust particles then speed into our atmosphere and burn up there as "shooting stars," or **meteors**.

Most meteors don't survive to reach the ground. Only rarely does one land

▲ **A close-up of the head of Halley's comet, photographed by a passing space probe**

that's large enough to do any damage. If a meteor does fall to Earth, the remaining material is called a **meteorite** (mē′tē ər īt). Not all meteors come from comets, but comets do appear to cause many large meteor showers.

SCIENCE IN LITERATURE

The Illustrated World of
SPACE
IAIN NICOLSON

THE ILLUSTRATED WORLD OF SPACE
by Iain Nicolson
Simon & Schuster Books for Young Readers, 1991

How will the Big Dipper look 100,000 years from now? What does it mean when a star winks? How bright would the Sun appear if you could see it from Pluto? You can look up the answers to these space questions, and more of your own, in *The Illustrated World of Space* by Iain Nicolson.

To find out more about how meteorites and comets are related to the beginning of our solar system, read pages 28–29 in *The Illustrated World of Space*. What role might ancient "dirty snowballs" have played in forming the planets?

▲ **Barringer meteor crater in Arizona**

Collisions between comets and planets are rare—but when they do occur, the results can be spectacular! You may have seen pictures of such an event that took place in 1994, when a comet called Shoemaker–Levy 9 struck the planet Jupiter.

Some scientists hypothesize that Earth's dinosaurs became extinct because a comet struck our planet in prehistoric times. But the chances of something like that happening today are very, very small. Most brushes with comets have good results. They help scientists get their hands on material from space in the form of meteorites.

Meteorites can be made of either metal or rock. The tiniest ones—like those in the activity on page B20— are so light that they often remain sus-pended in the atmosphere until a rain shower brings them to Earth.

Astronomers think that material from comets may date back more than 4 billion years, to the time of Earth's beginnings. By studying meteorites, scientists can learn about both comets and the origins of the solar system. ■

▲ **One of the impact sites of Comet Shoemaker–Levy 9 on the planet Jupiter**

INVESTIGATION 2

1. Describe how a comet can produce material that scientists collect and study on Earth.

2. Suppose you could build a telescope anywhere on Earth. Where would you build it, and what kind of telescope would it be? Explain the reasons for your choices.

REFLECT & EVALUATE

WORD POWER

axis
comet
constellation
meteorite
meteor
planet
reflecting telescope
refracting telescope
revolution
rotation
star

 On Your Own
Write a definition for each term in the list.

With a Partner
Mix up the letters of each term in the list. Provide a clue for each term and challenge your partner to unscramble the terms.

BUILD YOUR PORTFOLIO

Make a poster that shows what your favorite constellation looks like. Beside your drawing, write a short story that explains how the constellation got its name.

Analyze Information

Copy this drawing of the Little Dipper as it appears at 7:00 P.M. in the February sky. Then redraw the picture to show how it will appear at 1:00 A.M. the same night. Label Polaris in each drawing and add an arrow to show the direction in which the constellation appears to be moving. Explain why the constellation appears to move.

Assess Performance

Make a model to show Earth's rotation and revolution. Use two balls of different sizes and any other materials you wish. Use your model to show how Earth's motions make the stars appear to move during the night and throughout the year.

Problem Solving

1. Use what you have learned about the apparent motion of the stars to explain how stars might be used as a navigational tool.

2. You see an object in the night sky. To your unaided eye, it looks like a bright point of light. How would you go about identifying this object?

3. Suppose you want to learn all you can about a particular comet. Describe the different tools and methods you might use to study this object.

CHAPTER 2

THE SOLAR SYSTEM

Venus is called both the morning star and the evening star. It's the brightest of all the planets, and it's the closest planet to Earth. But Venus is shrouded in clouds, and its surface was a mystery until recently.

Visiting Our Next-door Neighbor

The Magellan spacecraft was launched from the space shuttle *Atlantis* in May 1989. Sixteen months later it reached Venus and began using radar to create pictures of the planet's surface and send them back to Earth. An international group of scientists gathered at NASA's Jet Propulsion Laboratory to process the billions of pieces of electronic data received from Magellan. The result was a startlingly clear picture of the planet's surface.

Hundreds of scientists and engineers worked on the Magellan project for 20 years. They gave us the first good look at our "sister" planet. Since Venus is similar to Earth in size and density, we increase our knowledge of Earth's development by visiting this unusual neighbor. How else do we learn about our solar system?

Coming Up

Magellan scientists use special glasses to view three-dimensional pictures of Venus's surface.

WHAT IS THE SOLAR SYSTEM MADE OF?

Our solar system's diameter is about 11.6 billion km. You can't picture that? Start walking at a rate of 5 km/h. Don't stop! You will walk a distance equal to the solar system's diameter in about 275,000 years. Now learn about the objects that make up our solar system and how they came to be.

Activity

When to Go Planet Watching

You've learned that the planets in our solar system seem to move across a narrow band in the sky. In this activity you'll discover how the planet Mars really moves in space—and how that motion affects how Mars looks in Earth's night sky.

Step 1

Procedure

1. Make a drawing in your *Science Notebook* like the one on this page. Your drawing should show the Sun, Earth's orbit around the Sun, and the larger orbit of the planet Mars around the Sun.

2. Choose two different small objects to represent the planets Earth and Mars. Place each object on top of your drawing at any location along its planet's orbit.

3. Use another color pencil or pen to draw a circle underneath each object and show its position in your drawing. Label the two circles *Earth* and *Mars*.

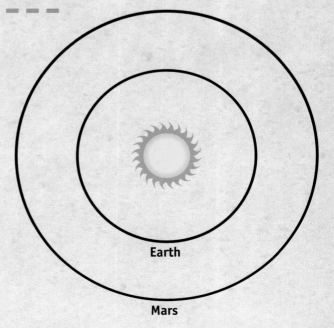

Earth

Mars

4. With a ruler, **measure** how far apart the two planets are in your drawing. **Record** that measurement.

5. Move both planet models along their orbits until you have them as close together as you can. **Draw** these positions, using a third color. Then **measure** and **record** the new distance between the two objects.

6. Move both planet models along their orbits until you have them as far apart as you can. **Draw** these positions, using a fourth color. **Measure** and **record** the distance between the objects.

Analyze and Conclude

1. Look at the locations of the Sun, Earth, and Mars when Mars is as close to Earth as it can be. **Predict** what time of day you'd look for Mars in Earth's sky when the real planets are positioned this way. Would Mars be visible from the daytime or nighttime side of Earth?

2. Look at the locations of the Sun, Earth, and Mars when Mars is as far from Earth as it can be. **Predict** what time of day you'd have to look for Mars when the real planets are positioned this way. Would the daytime or nighttime side of Earth be facing Mars? Where would Mars appear to be in Earth's sky in relation to the Sun? Would you be able to see Mars from Earth at this time?

3. Look at the first positions you chose for the Earth and Mars objects. **Predict** whether you'd be able to see Mars from Earth if the planets were positioned in this way.

INVESTIGATE FURTHER!

RESEARCH

For planets such as Mars that are farther from the Sun than Earth is, the point of closest approach to Earth is called opposition. At this time the planet is at its brightest. Call a planetarium to find out when each planet is at opposition. Plan one or more outdoor sessions to observe the planets in the nighttime sky.

Step 4

Activity
Comparing Planetary Distances

How far from Earth and from the Sun are the other eight planets? How can you better understand such large distances in the solar system? Here's one way to do it.

MATERIALS
- 400-sheet roll of toilet paper
- *Science Notebook*

Procedure

1. To create a model of planetary distances, go with nine other students to a long hallway, a gym, or an outdoor playground on a dry, still day. Choose one student to represent the Sun and have each of the others represent one of the nine planets.

2. Have the Sun student sit on the ground with one hand holding down the end of a roll of toilet paper.

3. Have the planet students unroll the toilet paper and count the tissue sheets, until each student comes to the sheet number that's listed on the table for his or her planet. At that point the student should sit beside the line of unrolled paper with a hand on the sheet representing his or her planet's average distance from the Sun.

Step 3

Planet	Sheet Number
Mercury	3
Venus	between 5 and 6
Earth	between 7 and 8
Mars	between 11 and 12
Jupiter	40
Saturn	74
Uranus	149
Neptune	233
Pluto	305

Step 4

4. Back in the classroom, **calculate** the shortest distance between each two neighboring planets in terms of toilet paper sheets. To get the distance between Mercury and Venus, subtract Mercury's sheet number from Venus's sheet number. (When the table says Venus is between sheets 5 and 6, count that as sheet $5\frac{1}{2}$.) Do the same calculations for the distance between Venus and Earth, between Earth and Mars, and so on. **Record** the answers in your *Science Notebook*.

5. **Calculate** and **record** the distance in sheets between each planet and Earth, at the time when each planet is closest to Earth.

Analyze and Conclude

1. **Compare** the distances between neighboring planets. Which two are closest together? Which two are farthest apart? As a group, which set of planets is closest together—those nearest the Sun or those farther out?

2. With other students, **hypothesize** about the effects of a planet's distance from the Sun. Which planets would be hottest? Which would be coldest? What would the Sun look like from each one? How long would a year be on each planet? **Compare** your ideas with those of your classmates.

3. Suppose you want to send a radio signal from Earth to each of the other planets, at the time when each planet is closest to Earth. Which planet would receive a signal fastest? Which would take the longest to get a signal? Use the results of step 5 to make a list of the planets according to their distance from Earth.

UNIT PROJECT LINK

Future trips to other planets may begin from an Earth-orbiting space station. Create a docking port for your simulated space station. Begin to collect information so that you can decorate the docking port area with travel posters of different planets and moons. Which ones would you and your classmates like to visit most?

Earth's Neighborhood:
The Solar System

Do you remember how the resource on star patterns on pages B10 and B11 compared each constellation to the state in an address? If you continued this comparison, you might call a solar system a neighborhood.

A **solar system** consists of a star and the objects that revolve around it. A model of our own solar system—the only one we've been able to detect so far—is shown here. In addition to the Sun itself, our solar system includes nine known planets, the moons that orbit those planets, and many smaller objects such as comets and the small rocky bodies known as asteroids. The four inner planets and five outer planets are separated by a belt of asteroids that orbit the Sun.

When you did the activity on pages B32 and B33, you learned how large the distances are between planets. The planets themselves are tiny compared to those distances. The objects in this model are shown much larger than they should be, compared to the size of their orbits, so that they can be seen better. ■

comet

Mercury

Earth

Venus

Mars

Saturn

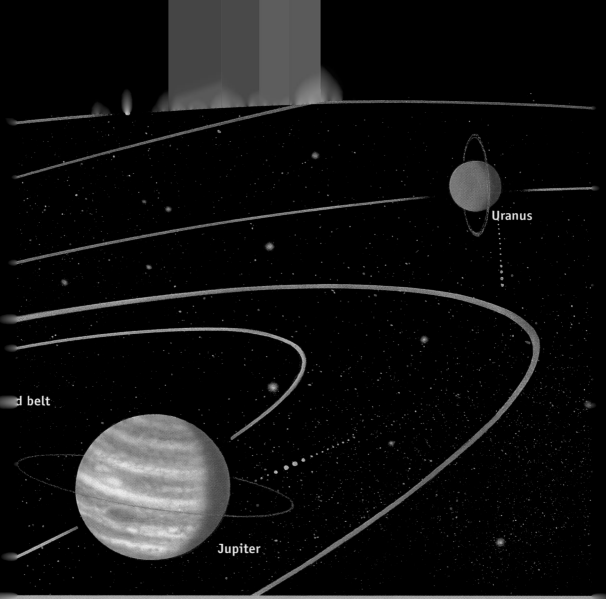

Uranus

d belt

Jupiter

Planet	Average Distance From the Sun (in millions of km)	Period of Revolution (in Earth years)	Number of Known Moons
Mercury	58	0.24	0
Venus	108	0.62	0
Earth	150	1.00	1
Mars	228	1.88	2
Jupiter	778	11.86	16
Saturn	1,429	29.46	18
Uranus	2,875	84.01	15
Neptune	4,504	164.79	8
Pluto	5,900	248.60	1

Ptolemy
Was Right–and Wrong!

"Pygmies placed on the shoulders of giants see more than the giants themselves." It may seem to you that this saying has little to do with science. But consider how it applies to two giants in the world of astronomy. One of these men was totally wrong about a major principle, yet his work prepared the way for later astronomers to arrive at a better understanding of the universe.

That man's name was Ptolemy, and he lived in Egypt in the second century A.D. Ptolemy tried to understand why the planets seem to wander across the sky. After charting their movements, he worked out a model that seemed to explain what he was seeing.

The Maya in Central America use astronomical observations to create the most accurate calendar in the world.
300

Greek philosopher Aristarchus proposes that Earth and the other planets are spheres that revolve around the Sun.
260 B.C.

145 A.D.
Ptolemy, an astronomer studying in Egypt, popularizes the theory that the Sun, Moon, and planets all revolve around a motionless Earth.

3000 B.C.
The Chinese begin recording and predicting the apparent movements of the Sun, Moon, and planets.

Sun

Earth

▲ **Ptolemy's model of the solar system**

Copernicus's model of the solar system ▼

Earth

Sun

Polish scholar Nicolaus Copernicus concludes that Aristarchus was right: Earth and the other planets orbit the Sun.
1543

Mathematician Aryabhata I of India proposes that Earth rotates on its axis.
497

900
Al-Battani, an Arabian astronomer, makes more precise measurements of celestial movements and recognizes that Ptolemy's model doesn't fit all his observations.

400
Hypatia, an Egyptian mathematician, helps develop instruments to measure an object's apparent position in the sky.

Ptolemy's model was an Earth-centered or **geocentric** (jē ō sen′trik) **model**. To him that seemed perfectly logical, since Earth appeared to Ptolemy to be steady and unmoving. To explain the motions of the Sun, Moon, and planets, he reasoned that they all must revolve around Earth.

Ptolemy's model was used for more than a thousand years. But in 1543 a Polish clergyman named Nicolaus Copernicus put forth a different idea. Copernicus positioned the Sun at the center of the universe and suggested that all the planets, including Earth, revolve around it.

Ptolemy himself had thought about such a Sun-centered or **heliocentric** (hē lē ō sen′trik) **model**, but he had rejected the idea. We really can't blame him for doing that. Ptolemy's model explained the solar system based on the best data available to him at the time. It's a basic principle in science that you can't get the right answer if you don't have all the necessary information. But you can't always wait for everything to be discovered before you try to use what you know, either.

That's where "standing on the shoulders of giants" comes in. When Copernicus came along, he had a head start because he was able to build on Ptolemy's work. By adding his own observations to Ptolemy's, Copernicus could create a more accurate hypothesis that would form the basis for all of modern astronomy. ■

Birth of the Solar System

▲ **The Big Bang Theory**

Where did the solar system come from? This is one of the biggest questions that human beings have ever asked. The answer may never be completely discovered or proved to everyone's satisfaction. But based on all the evidence people have uncovered over the centuries, here is what most scientists consider the best explanation so far.

The Big Bang

All the matter and all the energy that have *ever* existed or will *ever* exist in the universe were once concentrated in an incredibly tiny, extremely hot, unbelievably dense ball. In this case, the word *dense* means very closely packed.

Then all at once, at least 10 billion years ago, this churning ball of matter and energy exploded. The explosion sent a vast cloud of matter swirling out in all directions into space.

Time passed—*lots* of time. As it did, little by little, concentrations of matter began to form within the massive, expanding cloud. Each separate concentration was huge beyond anything we can imagine. Together they must have been millions of times bigger than Earth and all the planets combined, to have contained enough material to condense into all the objects that now exist.

But condense they did, thanks to the force of gravity. Very slowly, each individual clump of material began to contract. Different clumps joined together, forming bigger clumps. And as these clumps contracted, they began to spin. At the same time, each clump continued to move outward, away from all other clumps.

These huge spinning concentrations of matter would eventually become galaxies—the giant clusters of stars that you'll learn more about in Chapter 3.

The Sun and Planets Form

More time went by—more billions of years. Then, within one of the galaxies, one particular collection of matter began to condense. This was an event of special importance to us, for this material would eventually form our solar system!

As this cloud of matter rotated and flattened, most of the material collected in the center, where it would become our Sun. At the same time, in the swirling clouds surrounding this future Sun, separate eddies or "whirlpools" also began condensing to form the different planets, including Earth. By about 4.6 billion years ago, the major objects in our solar system were finally in place.

What was happening in our own neighborhood was just one tiny chapter in a much larger story. For throughout the billions of kilometers of emptiness that make up outer space, other concentrations of matter were also condensing to form other galaxies, other stars, and even—scientists think—other planets around those stars.

How Do We Know It's All True?

The story you've just read is commonly known as the **Big Bang Theory** of the origin of the universe. How do scientists know it all happened this way? Well, they don't, not for certain. But the evidence continues to mount as we gather more and more data about the universe. Piecing together the cosmic puzzle of our origins is the biggest job ever—and maybe, someday, you can help solve the puzzle! ■

▲ **Three stages in the formation of the solar system**

INVESTIGATE FURTHER!

RESEARCH

Find out about different theories regarding the origins of particular objects in the solar system. Go to the library and look up some of these subjects in a recent encyclopedia or astronomy book: the Moon, the satellites of Mars, the asteroid belt, Saturn's rings, Pluto, comets.

Trajectory to the Planets

Distances between the planets are *huge!* Remember that figure at the beginning of this investigation—the one that said the solar system is more than 11 billion km (7 billion mi) wide? Well, it would take more than a decade for even our fastest space probe to travel that far.

Furthermore, a spacecraft doesn't travel in a straight line from Earth to another planet. It begins by traveling along with planet Earth in orbit around the Sun. As the space probe passes planets, their gravity causes its path to curve. This curved course is called a trajectory (trə jek'tə rē).

Remember, both Earth and the spacecraft's target planet are constantly moving. To calculate a craft's trajectory, its builders must use powerful computers that take into account the different bodies' movements, their gravity, and all the other factors that might influence the spacecraft's course. The probe must be aimed at the point in space where its moving target will be *when the probe gets there.*

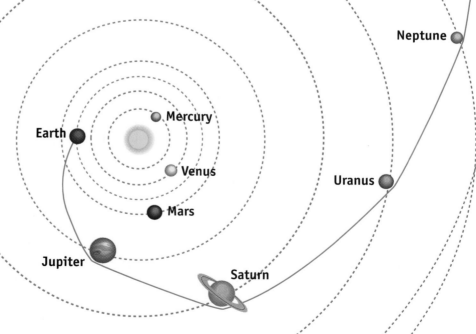

▲ The Voyager 2 space probe's trajectory

A spacecraft carries fuel that can be used to make small changes in its course. But major changes in direction use up a lot of fuel. Often, mission planners use a technique called a gravity assist. In such a maneuver, a probe uses the gravitational pull of a planet to change its direction and even its speed. Instead of using up its own fuel, when the spacecraft passes near a planet, it lets the gravity of that body fling it in a new direction. By coming up "behind" a moving planet and letting the planet's gravity pull it along, a probe can wind up leaving the planet's neighborhood with more speed than it had coming in.

Perhaps the best example of a spacecraft using this "slingshot" technique was a probe that was launched by the United States in 1977, Voyager 2. As it left Earth, Voyager 2 was traveling at about 40,000 km/h (25,000 mph). Because its targets, the four giant outer planets, happened to be lined up in just the right way, Voyager 2 was able to visit Jupiter, Saturn, Uranus, and Neptune in turn. At each planet the spacecraft was tar-

▲ **Voyager 2 at Jupiter**

geted to receive a gravity assist that would send it on to the next planet.

By the time Voyager 2 completed its "grand tour" in 1989, it had attained a speed of about 97,000 km/h (60,000 mph)—making it the fastest object ever built by human beings to date! ■

INVESTIGATION 1

1. Name five kinds of objects that exist in our solar system. Explain where each kind may be found in relation to one of the other kinds.

2. Explain why we never see the planet Venus in the sky at midnight.

INVESTIGATION 2

HOW DO THE PLANETS DIFFER?

My Very Elegant Mother Just Served Us Nine Pickles.
This sentence is a tool that will help you remember the names of the planets in order of their distance from the Sun. Each word's first letter is the first letter of a planet. Now learn what distance from the Sun has to do with the characteristics of each planet.

Activity

Measuring Planet Sizes

Which planets are the biggest? Which are the smallest? How large is the difference between them? Find out!

MATERIALS
- sheet of paper
- *Science Notebook*

Step 2

Procedure

1. Make an Earth ruler like the one pictured on the facing page. Place the edge of a sheet of paper just below the picture. **Draw** lines on the paper's edge at exactly the same places as the lines in the picture. Number the spaces on your ruler as shown.

Pluto

Neptune

Uranus

Saturn

2. Place your Earth ruler over the picture of each planet on these two pages. Use the ruler to **measure** the distance across the middle of each planet in terms of Earth diameters. **Record** each measurement in your *Science Notebook*.

3. Make a list of the planets that ranks them from smallest to largest.

4. **Make a bar graph** showing the diameters of the nine planets. List the planets' names on one side of the graph and the number of Earth diameters on the other.

Analyze and Conclude

1. With a group of classmates, **hypothesize** about the differences between the larger planets and the smaller ones. For example, how strong might each planet's gravity be compared to Earth's gravity? Do you think each planet could hold onto an atmosphere? **Discuss** and **compare** your ideas.

2. Imagine that you lived on a moon around each planet in turn. Assume that each moon is about the same distance from its planet as Earth's Moon is from Earth. **Predict** how big each planet would look in the sky from its moon. About how much of the sky would each of the planets fill up?

3. **Compare** the pictures of large planets with those of small planets. Besides size, what differences do you observe? Make a list of those differences.

INVESTIGATE FURTHER!
....
RESEARCH

Look at the order of the planets. Are the biggest planets close to the Sun or far away? Can you hypothesize why those giant planets are located where they are? Look in an astronomy book that tells about the origins of the solar system to find out scientists' theories about this.

EARTH RULER

(Earth diameters)

| 1 | 2 | 3 | 4 | 5 | 6 | 7 | 8 | 9 | 10 | 11 | 12 | 13 | 14 | 15 | 16 | 17 | 18 | 19 | 20 |

Jupiter Mars Earth Venus Mercury Sun

The Inner Planets

The inner planets are Mercury, Venus, Earth, and Mars. These four have something else in common besides being close to the Sun. They all resemble Earth in size, in density, and in their mainly rocky composition. Because of this, they are known as **terrestrial** (tə res′trē əl) **planets**, meaning those that are Earth-like.

Two of the inner planets and all of the outer ones have satellites. Astronomers use the terms **moon** and **satellite** interchangeably when they refer to natural objects that revolve around a planet. (The word *satellite* can also mean an orbiting object built by humans.) Now let's look at each of the inner planets. ■

☿ MERCURY

MERCURY is the closest planet to the Sun and the second smallest of the nine planets. It looks a lot like Earth's Moon, with a rocky surface covered by craters. Mercury has almost no atmosphere, just faint traces of helium and one or two other gases that it probably "captured" from the Sun. Surface temperatures on Mercury get hot enough to melt lead. This speedy planet takes just three months (measured in Earth time) to revolve around the Sun.

♀ VENUS

VENUS is the second planet from the Sun. Although it's named after the Roman goddess of beauty, it's not a very pleasant place. The Venusian (vi noo′-shən) atmosphere consists mainly of carbon dioxide with sulfuric acid clouds. It's so dense that the atmospheric pressure on the planet's surface is tremendous. Temperatures there reach about 500°C (900°F).

Venus's clouds appear featureless in normal light, but certain cameras reveal swirling patterns (above right). Radar provided this computer-generated view of the surface (right). ▶

⊕ EARTH

EARTH is the only planet in the solar system on which life is known to exist. It's the third planet from the Sun and the largest of the four inner planets. Earth has a vast core of molten metal and rock, with a thin crust of solid rock. Our planet's atmosphere is about 78 percent nitrogen and 21 percent oxygen, plus traces of other gases. As seen from space, Earth is one of the most beautiful planets, with bright blues indicating the abundant water and swirling whites, its scattered clouds.

▲ **The Moon** is Earth's only natural satellite. A rocky, cratered body with no atmosphere, it's one of the largest satellites in the solar system.

♂ MARS

▲ **The features on Venus** range from smooth plains to volcanic mountain ranges. A computer created this false-color ground view from radar data.

▲ **Venus's surface** was photographed by a Russian probe that landed on the planet but survived only a few minutes in its harsh conditions.

MARS, the fourth planet from the Sun, resembles Earth more than any other planet. Mars is smaller and less dense than Earth, which gives it less gravity and a thinner atmosphere. But the Martian day is only 41 minutes longer than the Earth day, and the planet has four seasons similar to those on Earth. Surface temperatures on Mars dip down to −90°C (−200°F) and seldom rise above 0°C (32°F). Iron oxide gives Martian soil the reddish color of rust. There are also white polar caps that grow and shrink with the seasons, and dark patches that were once mistaken for canals or vegetation. We now know that these dark areas come and go as dust storms cover and uncover darker rock.

MARS continued

◀ **Olympus Mons** (ō lim′pəs mänz) is a huge extinct volcano on Mars, nearly three times the height of the tallest mountain on Earth.

◀ **Phobos** (fō′bəs) is a Martian satellite just 27 km (17 mi) long. Its companion moon Deimos (dī′məs) is even smaller. Many scientists think these rough-shaped objects are asteroids that were captured by Mars's gravity.

◀ **The Martian surface** was photographed by a U.S. lander that scooped up and analyzed soil samples.

SCIENCE IN LITERATURE

THE ILLUSTRATED WORLD OF SPACE
by Iain Nicolson
Simon & Schuster Books for Young Readers, 1991

Reference books like *The Illustrated World of Space* are fun to read because you can pick them up and start reading on any page. They are also the perfect place to find the answers to specific questions.

Use the index in *The Illustrated World of Space* to look up each of the planets in our solar system. Read about the planets and examine the illustrations that show the layers of each planet. Then make a chart to summarize what you find out about the compositions of the planets. In your chart, include columns for the planets' cores, mantles, crusts, and atmospheres. Share your chart with your classmates.

The Outer Planets

Four of the five planets farthest from the Sun are very much alike. They're quite large in comparison to the inner planets, they have ring systems, and they're made up mostly of substances that would be gases on Earth. Jupiter, Saturn, Uranus, and Neptune are therefore often referred to as the **gas giants**. The outermost known planet, Pluto, seems to be more like the inner terrestrial planets in size and composition. Let's take a closer look at this planet and its neighbors. ■

♃ JUPITER

JUPITER is the fifth planet from the Sun and the largest planet in our solar system. When the solar system was forming, Jupiter almost became a star. It couldn't sustain the nuclear reactions that keep the Sun burning, however, so Jupiter cooled and became a planet instead. It's composed mainly of gaseous and liquid hydrogen and helium, probably surrounding a small rocky core. The planet's upper atmosphere features swirling cloud bands and the Great Red Spot, a huge circular storm that's lasted for centuries. Jupiter has a set of rings, but they're so thin and dark that they're practically invisible in natural light.

Io (ī′ō), a satellite of Jupiter, is the most volcanically active object we know of in the solar system. This rocky moon's volcanoes regularly recoat the satellite's surface with lava. ▶

Io's volcanoes send up towering plumes of gas, like this one seen in a false-color view. ▶

♄ SATURN

SATURN is the sixth planet from the Sun and the last planet you can easily see with your unaided eye from Earth. It's almost as big as Jupiter, with a very similar composition and banded atmosphere. Strong winds sweep across Saturn almost constantly, reaching speeds of 1,800 km/h (1,100 mph). The planet's spectacular rings are its most distinctive feature.

▲ **Saturn and some of its moons** are shown in this composite photo. Saturn has the most known satellites of any planet. Some have rocky surfaces and others are ice-covered.

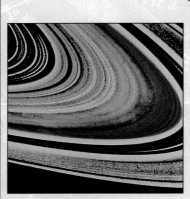

▲ **Saturn's rings** are shown in a false-color view that brings out their details. A planet's ring system is made up of countless ice and rock fragments. These fragments orbit so closely together that the rings look solid from a distance.

▲ **Titan**, the largest of Saturn's satellites, is the only moon in the solar system with a dense atmosphere. Its haze is shown clearly in this false-color photo. Titan's atmosphere may resemble that of early Earth.

♅ URANUS

URANUS (yoor'ə nəs), blue-green in color, is the seventh planet from the Sun. It has thin, dark rings like those of Jupiter that are too faint to be easily photographed. Since this planet can't readily be seen from Earth without a telescope, its existence was recognized only in the 1700s. Because of its distance from the Sun, Uranus is very cold, with temperatures near −150°C (−300°F) in the cloud tops.

▲ **The tilt of Uranus's axis** is the most unique feature of this planet. Compared to Uranus's orbit, the axis is tilted way over on its side, so that the poles take turns pointing toward the Sun.

◄ **Uranus and its moon Miranda** (mə ran'də) are seen in this computer-generated photo. The picture shows what Uranus's faint rings might look like from nearby. Miranda has been called the most bizarre object in the solar system. Scientists think the patchwork appearance of this satellite's surface resulted when the moon was torn apart by collisions and then reassembled by its own gravity.

♆ NEPTUNE

NEPTUNE was discovered in the 1800s. It's a planet very similar to Uranus, but it doesn't share the feature of a severely tilted axis. Neptune's rings, like those of Uranus, are too faint to be seen from a distance. While Uranus's cloud tops present a pretty bland face, Neptune's atmosphere has swirling blue and white features.

Triton is a rocky, ice-covered moon of Neptune that seems to be active despite being very cold. It has geyserlike features that send up plumes of material into Triton's thin atmosphere. ▼

CHAPTER 3

STARS AND GALAXIES

The main entrance to an ancient ceremonial hall in New Mexico faces the North Star. The ceilings of some caves in Arizona are covered with drawings of stars. Native Americans identified and located stars and planets thousands of years ago. Why did they do it? How accurate were they?

Ancient Astronomers

Two thousand years ago in Mexico, a large city was laid out according to knowledge of the Sun, Moon, planets, and stars. A pyramid was built facing the point in the sky where the Pleiades star cluster set. A hall was built so that it would align a distant point with the Sun on the first day of spring.

Carved rocks found throughout the Americas were used to mark the rising and setting of stars. From their knowledge of the positions of stars, early Native Americans designed a 365-day calendar. They determined the four compass directions and decided when to plant crops. As you study stars and galaxies, you'll learn more about these objects that the ancient astronomers observed so carefully.

Coming Up

◀ An ancient Native American rock carving of stars, from New Mexico

WHAT ARE STARS AND HOW DO THEY DIFFER?

When you look at the stars at night, do they all look the same? The next chance you get, look carefully at the night sky. You might be surprised at some of the differences you can observe among the stars.

Activity

Capturing Colors

Stars come in many colors. Find out how astronomers observe the colors in starlight.

MATERIALS

- lamp with a clear-glass bulb
- red and green filters
- spectroscope
- colored pencils
- *Science Notebook*

SAFETY

Do not touch the bulb.

Procedure

In a dark room, view a glowing light bulb. Describe what you see in your *Science Notebook*. Observe the bulb through a red filter, then through a green filter. Describe what you see through each. Observe the bulb through a spectroscope. Draw a color picture of the band of light, or spectrum, that you see. Place the red filter over the opening of the spectroscope, view the bulb, and draw a color picture of what you see. Do the same with the green filter.

Analyze and Conclude

1. How did the filters and the spectroscope affect the appearance of the bulb? Based on your observations, what can you infer about white light?

2. Brainstorm how astronomers might use filters and spectroscopes to help them obtain information about the stars.

Activity

How Big Is Betelgeuse?

Stars come in many sizes. Betelgeuse (bet'l jōōz) *is a giant red star. Our Sun is a medium-sized yellow star. What would our solar system be like if Betelgeuse were our star? Find out!*

- -

Procedure

1. On a large sheet of paper, draw a model of the solar system out to Jupiter. First, place a dot in the center of the paper. This dot represents the Sun in your model.

2. Next, use a string as shown in the picture to draw the orbits of the planets. The information in the table tells you how large to make the orbits. Label each one.

Step 2

3. Finally, draw a circle 12 cm in diameter around the Sun in your model. Shade everything inside this circle red. This circle represents Betelgeuse.

Analyze and Conclude

1. What does your model indicate about the relative sizes of the Sun and Betelgeuse?

2. In your *Science Notebook*, hypothesize what would happen to Earth if our Sun were to grow to the size of Betelgeuse. Use your model to support your hypothesis.

Planet	Distance From the Sun
Mercury	1.2 cm
Venus	2.2 cm
Earth	3.0 cm
Mars	4.6 cm
Jupiter	15.6 cm

How Stars Differ
From One Another

When Galileo first looked through his telescope at the night sky, he began to notice differences among the stars. Some were so dazzling they took his breath away, but others seemed dim and plain. Scientists now know that stars differ from one another in a great many ways. Four of the most obvious differences have to do with brightness, size, temperature, and color.

The Characteristics of Stars

You don't need a telescope to know that some stars are brighter than others. Stars also range in size from dwarfs to supergiants. The largest body in our solar system, the Sun, is an average-sized star with a diameter of about 1.4 million km (865,000 mi). A supergiant can have a diameter up to 1,000 times that of the Sun. Some dwarf stars have diameters less than half that of Earth.

The temperature and color of a star are closely linked. In fact, temperature determines a star's color, as it sometimes does with materials here on Earth. A furnace that glows with a white light, for example, is hotter than one that glows with an orange light.

Stars exhibit a wide range of colors, indicating a variety of temperatures. Astronomers use spectroscopes to study the light given off by stars, just as you used a spectroscope to study light in the activity on page B54.

The surface temperature of the hottest stars may be as high as 50,000°C (90,000°F). These stars shine with a bluish light, while the coolest stars shine with a red light.

Star Color	Surface Temperature	Examples
Blue	11,000°–50,000°C	Regulus, Rigel
Blue-white	7,500°–11,000°C	Deneb, Sirius
White	6,000°–7,500°C	Canopus, Procyon
Yellow	5,000°–6,000°C	The Sun, Alpha Centauri
Orange-red	3,500°–5,000°C	Aldebaran, Arcturus
Red	2,000°–3,500°C	Betelgeuse, Proxima Centauri

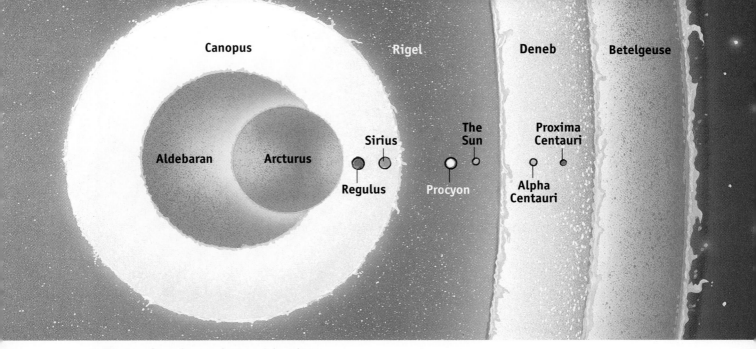

▲ Stars of various sizes and colors

The table on the left shows the relationship between star color and temperature.

The picture above shows the relative sizes of the stars in the table. Find the red star Betelgeuse, which you drew in the activity on page B55. Now find the red star called Proxima Centauri. These two stars are the same color and so have similar surface temperatures. But stars of the same color can vary greatly in size.

How a Star Gets Its Energy

Although stars have different visible features, they all have one thing in common: the way they produce energy. A star is a gigantic ball of hot gases—so hot that the gases at the star's surface glow. Energy is generated by nuclear reactions that convert hydrogen into helium in the center of the star. It's as if millions of hydrogen bombs were detonating there every second.

Unlike a hydrogen bomb, a star doesn't explode and fly apart. It has so much mass that it's held together by its own gravity. So the energy released by the nuclear reactions moves throughout the star, generating heat and light. ■

━━━━━ INVESTIGATION 1 ━━━━━

1. Identify four ways in which stars may differ from one another.

2. A red star and a blue star appear from Earth to be equally bright. What other inferences could you make about these two stars?

B57

INVESTIGATION 2

HOW FAR AWAY ARE THE STARS?

If you traveled beyond our solar system at the speed of light, you could reach the closest one of these objects in about four years. What are these objects? They are stars.

Activity

Making a Paraffin Photometer

Can you tell how far away a star is by looking at it? Do all stars shine with the same brightness? In this activity you'll make a photometer to help you measure brightness and relate it to star distances.

Procedure

1. **Measure** and cut out a 12 × 12 cm piece of aluminum foil.

2. Fold the foil in half, shiny side out, to form a 12 × 6 cm rectangle.

3. Make a "sandwich" by placing the aluminum foil between two blocks of paraffin. Use rubber bands to hold the sandwich together. You have now made a simple photometer (fō täm′ət ər).

Step 3

B58

4. Stand your photometer on a flat surface and darken the room. Have another group member shine a flashlight beam on one side of the photometer. Observe how the lighted side of the photometer compares with the side away from the light. Record your observations in your *Science Notebook*.

Step 4

5. Predict how the lighted side of the photometer will change when the light is moved closer to it and farther from it. Have the group member with the light move it and check your predictions. Record your observations.

6. Have a third group member shine another flashlight on the other side of the photometer. One of the two flashlights should be held still. The other flashlight should be moved toward or away from the photometer until both paraffin blocks shine with the same brightness. Then measure and record the distance between the photometer and each flashlight.

Analyze and Conclude

1. Describe how the distance between a flashlight and the photometer affects the brightness of the paraffin.

2. In step 6, what did you observe about the distances between each flashlight and the photometer? From this information, what can you infer about the brightness of the light given off by each flashlight?

3. Brainstorm how techniques like those used in this activity might be used to study light from different stars.

4. Besides measuring a star's *apparent* brightness, infer what else astronomers need to know about that star to determine its *actual* brightness.

INVESTIGATE FURTHER!

EXPERIMENT

Light bulbs are rated by wattage. The higher the wattage, the brighter the light that is produced. Use your photometer to compare the brightness of bulbs of different wattages.

Measuring
Distances in Space

Incredibly large distances separate stars from Earth. Scientists can't run a tape measure across space to measure these distances. Instead, they measure something called parallax (par'ə laks).

To understand parallax, try this exercise. Close one eye. Hold up one finger at arm's length. Line up your finger with a reference point, such as a mark on a chalkboard. Keeping your finger and head still, open your closed eye and close the eye that was open. Observe how your finger *appears* to move in relation to your reference point.

In this exercise, nothing actually moved. But your finger appeared to shift position because you were viewing it from a slightly different location when you changed eyes. Such an apparent shift in position is called parallax.

Astronomers use parallax to figure out distances to nearby stars. As shown below, they view a star from two different places in Earth's orbit. Then they measure how far the star appeared to move in relation to other, more distant stars. They use this information to calculate the distance to the star.

Distance and Brightness

The measure of a star's brightness is called magnitude (mag'nə tōōd). Astronomers use photometers—devices similar to the one in the activity on pages

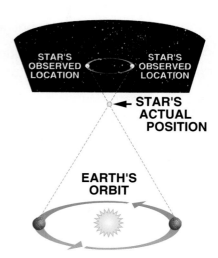

▲ **A student's finger appears to shift due to parallax, just as a star's position against more distant stars appears to shift.**

B58 and B59—to measure how bright a star *appears* to be. That is the star's **apparent magnitude**, and it depends on two things: (1) how far away the star is, and (2) the star's absolute magnitude. **Absolute magnitude** is the amount of light a star actually gives off.

Imagine looking at a bonfire and a match. If these two sources of light are the same distance from you, the bonfire will seem brighter. However, if the bonfire is a kilometer away and the match is at arm's length, the match will appear brighter. The "absolute magnitudes" of the two light sources won't have changed—but their apparent magnitudes will vary with distance.

Astronomers can determine the absolute magnitude of a star if they know the star's apparent magnitude (which can be measured) and its distance from Earth (from the parallax method). They can also use magnitude to estimate the distance to faraway stars, where parallax cannot be used.

Because distances between stars are so great, astronomers measure these distances using units called light-years. A **light-year** is the distance that light travels in one year. Since the speed of light is about 300,000 km (186,000 mi) per second, a light-year is about 9.5 trillion km (5.9 trillion mi). Imagine having to write out numbers such as these! ■

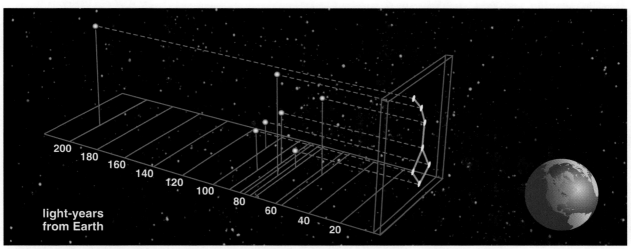

▲ **The stars in the Big Dipper lie at different distances from Earth.**

INVESTIGATION 2

1. Why is the light-year a useful unit for measuring distances to stars?

2. The star Sirius (sir′ē əs) appears to be about ten times brighter than the star Deneb. Yet scientists have found that Deneb gives off much more light than Sirius does. How can you explain this puzzling situation?

INVESTIGATION 3

WHAT IS THE LIFE CYCLE OF A STAR?

The stars that you see today are the same ones that ancient astronomers viewed thousands of years ago. But stars do change over very long periods of time. In this investigation you'll discover the different stages a star can go through.

Activity

Studying Nebulas

A nebula (neb′yə lə) *is a cloud of gases and dust in space. In this activity you'll learn about the role nebulas play in the life cycles of stars.*

▲ **A nebula in Vela**

▲ **The Orion Nebula**

▲ **The Horsehead Nebula**

Procedure

1. Each of the six photographs below includes a nebula. Study the photos carefully and **describe** each one in your *Science Notebook*.

2. Astronomers think that stars form from the gases and dust that make up nebulas. **Identify** the photo or photos that show evidence that stars may have recently formed or may be forming now. **Describe the evidence** you see.

3. It is thought that the gases and dust in nebulas come from old stars that have exploded. **Identify** the photo or photos that support this hypothesis. **Describe the evidence** you see in those photographs.

4. Evidence indicates that, under certain conditions, stars may form in groups or clusters. **Identify** the photo or photos that provide such evidence. **Explain the evidence** you see.

Analyze and Conclude

1. **Compare** the nebulas in the photographs. What characteristics do they have in common? How are they different?

2. Many of the photographs show some dark areas. What can you **infer** about the nature of such dark areas?

3. Explain why you think astronomers study nebulas to learn about the life cycles of stars.

INVESTIGATE FURTHER!

RESEARCH

On a star chart in an astronomy book, locate the types of objects you studied in this activity. Find out which objects, if any, might be visible in the sky over where you live. Go outside and see if you can spot any of these objects. If binoculars are available, they will make your task easier.

▲ **The Helix Nebula**

▲ **The Lagoon Nebula**

▲ **The Pleiades**

The Life Cycle of a Star

Although a star is not a living thing, it has a "life cycle." Like a living thing, a star passes through several stages as it ages. These stages include "birth," growth and development, middle age, old age, and "death."

The life cycle of a star covers a huge span of time. For example, our Sun is a middle-aged yellow star of average size and temperature. It has been shining just as it does today for more than 4.5 billion years. It should continue to shine for another 4.5 billion years before it begins to change very much.

The Birth of a Star

Huge clouds of gases and dust, called **nebulas**, are scattered through many regions of space. Nebulas provide the raw materials from which stars form. Under certain conditions, portions of a nebula begin to contract, forming clumps of spinning gases. Over millions of years, gravity causes these clumps to shrink, or condense, into dense pockets of matter within the nebula. These pockets of matter form the beginnings of stars and are called **protostars** (prō′tō stärz).

Stages in the life cycles of stars. Each star's fate depends on its mass. ▼

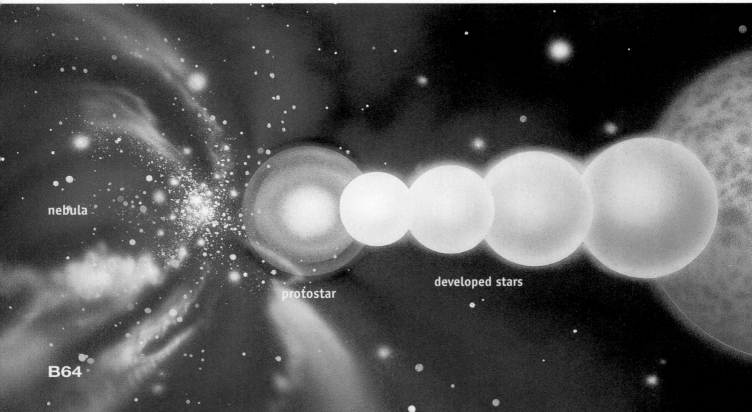

nebula

protostar

developed stars

As a protostar continues to condense, its particles are squeezed closer and closer together, creating enormous pressure at the center. This pressure causes the core of the protostar to become very hot. When the core's temperature reaches about 15,000,000°C, nuclear reactions begin, releasing tremendous amounts of energy. At this point, the protostar stops shrinking and begins to shine. It is now a full-fledged star.

The Life of an Average Star

How long does a star "live"? The main factor that determines a star's life span—and the kind of death it will have—is the star's mass. A star of medium mass, like our Sun, shines for billions of years by converting its hydrogen into helium.

Eventually, though, the star's hydrogen fuel begins to run out. The star's core, now made up mostly of helium, shrinks and releases energy as it collapses. This energy, when added to the energy of the remaining nuclear reactions, causes the outer layers of the star to expand far out into space, swelling the star to many times its original size.

As the outer layers expand, they move farther from the star's central furnace. The outer layers then cool, the light they give off reddens, and the star becomes a **red giant**. This is what will happen to our Sun, though not for billions of years.

After a long period as a red giant, the last traces of fuel will run out, and the Sun will collapse one final time. It will become a **white dwarf** star, not much larger than Earth is now. At this stage, the Sun will still be shining, but only dimly. Its atoms will be packed tightly together at a density a million times greater than that of water. Finally

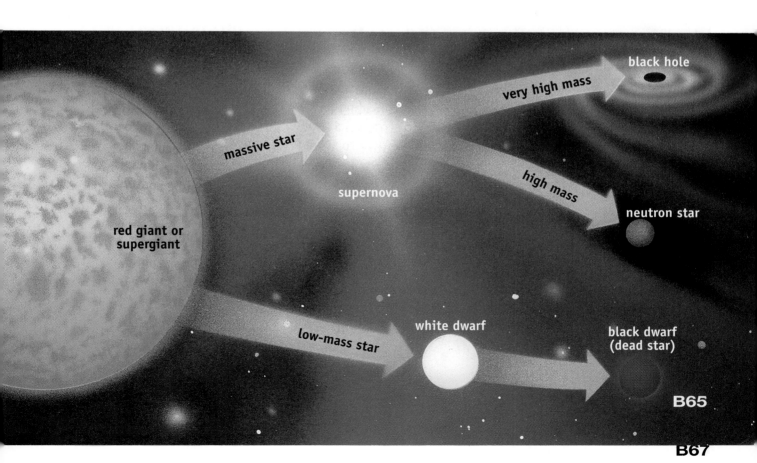

red giant or supergiant

massive star

supernova

very high mass

black hole

high mass

neutron star

low-mass star

white dwarf

black dwarf (dead star)

B65

The Milky Way
and Other Galaxies

If a visitor from outer space asked you your address, what would you say? You'd probably mention a house or apartment number, a street, a city or town, and a state. You could then add a country and even a planet—Earth. But how could you tell the visitor the location of your planet?

Earth and eight other planets are members of a solar system, all revolving around a star we call the Sun. The solar system belongs to a gigantic cluster of stars known as the **Milky Way Galaxy**.

Our Sun is just one of more than 100 billion stars that make up the Milky Way.

Is there anything bigger than a galaxy? Yes! You, your planet, your solar system, and your galaxy are all part of the **universe**, which includes absolutely everything that exists.

"Building Blocks" of the Universe

A **galaxy** is a huge collection of stars. A typical galaxy may contain hundreds of billions of stars, all revolving

The Milky Way Galaxy as seen in Earth's sky (*right*) and as it might look from outside (*below*)

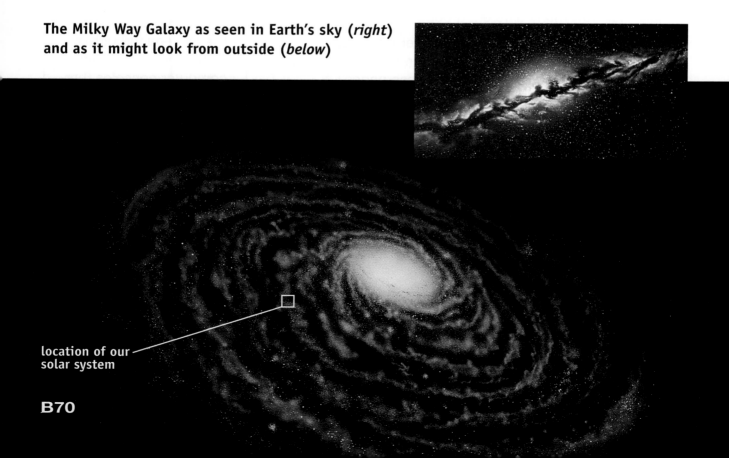

location of our solar system

▲ An elliptical galaxy   ▲ A spiral galaxy   ▲ An irregular galaxy

around a central core. Why can galaxies be thought of as building blocks of the universe? The reason is that they're the largest single structures that astronomers have identified so far. There may be as many as 100 billion galaxies in the universe.

Edwin Hubble (1889–1953)—the man for whom the Hubble Space Telescope is named—was a well-known American astronomer who spent many years studying galaxies. He found that they can be classified into three basic groups, based on their shapes. You tried classifying galaxies yourself in the activity on pages B68 and B69.

The most common type of galaxy is elliptical in shape—that is, it's shaped like a slightly flattened sphere, with no clear features. The second most common type is a spiral galaxy, with arms that make it resemble a pinwheel spinning in space. The third type of galaxy is irregular, having no definite shape.

The Milky Way Galaxy

The Milky Way is not a "special" galaxy in any way—except, of course, that you and everyone you know live inside it! The Milky Way is a spiral galaxy with at least two arms that

extend out from a central bulge. This bulge is some 20,000 light-years in diameter and 10,000 light-years thick. A trip from one side of our galaxy to the other, traveling at the speed of light, would take about 100,000 years.

From our vantage point in one of the galaxy's arms, the Milky Way appears as a broad band of light stretching across Earth's night sky. You can see this band for yourself if you're out in the country, away from bright city

INVESTIGATE FURTHER!

RESEARCH

Learn more about how Edwin Hubble discovered that all galaxies are moving away from each other. Look up the term *Doppler effect* in an astronomy or physics book. Find out how the Doppler effect operates in everyday life—for example, when you hear a sound produced by a moving object, such as a train blowing its whistle. Then learn how Hubble applied this principle when he studied the colors of light produced by distant galaxies.

CHAPTER 4

LIVING IN SPACE

"Houston? This is *Freedom*. We have just received a signal that may have been sent by extraterrestrials! Request advice."
Will space station *Freedom* send this kind of message some day?
What should we be doing to prepare for such an event?

Space Kids

Every week, the U.S. Space Camp in Huntsville, Alabama, welcomes a new bunch of campers. They will experience a hands-on course in space technology. The campers participate in a simulated two-hour flight of the space shuttle *Endeavour*, complete with authentic ground control. Launch, Earth orbit, and landing are realistically simulated. Student astronauts perform various tasks in space, solve in-flight emergencies, and experience simulated weightlessness.

During the five days at camp, participants study the Apollo 16 spacecraft that flew to the Moon. They build model rockets and tour the camp's missile park and model space station. As you study living in space, you'll have many experiences that could help you design your own space camp program.

Coming Up

◀ A camper at U.S. Space Camp

HOW DO HUMANS SURVIVE IN SPACE?

What would you pack for a trip to another planet? You'd need more than just a change of clothing! What would you eat and drink? What would you breathe? What would you use for shelter? In this investigation you'll think about what humans need to survive and then explore some answers to these questions.

Activity

Requirements for a Space Mission

How much food, oxygen, and water would you need to survive in space? You may be surprised to find out.

Procedure

1. Imagine you're planning a space mission. Calculate how much food you'll need to eat each day, using the following table as a guide. How many total grams of food will you require daily? How much energy will you get from that food? Record your calculations in your *Science Notebook*.

Type of Food	Mass Requirement	Energy Requirement
Carbohydrates	416.7 g/person/day	1,682 Calories/person/day
Proteins	124.7 g/person/day	505 Calories/person/day
Fats	90.7 g/person/day	834 Calories/person/day

2. Using the second table, **calculate** and **record** how much oxygen you will need each day. Plan on taking one daily extravehicular (eks trə vē hik'yōō lər) activity, or EVA—a trip outside the spacecraft. You must use the air lock once when you leave the spacecraft and once when you return.

Oxygen Use	Requirement
Breathing	0.8 kg/person/day
EVA	0.6 kg/person/8-hour EVA
Leakage	1.0 kg/day
Air lock losses	7.0 kg/air lock use

3. Using the third table, **calculate** and **record** how much water you will need each day.

Water Use	Requirement
Drinking	1.9 kg/person/day
Food preparation	1.2 kg/person/day
Washing clothes	12.5 kg/person/day
Washing hands	1.8 kg/person/day
Showering	3.6 kg/person/day
Flushing toilet	0.5 kg/person/day
EVA	4.4 kg/person/8-hour EVA

Analyze and Conclude

1. Suppose you're part of a crew of eight astronauts going to Mars. Your round trip to Mars will take two years. **Calculate** how much food, oxygen, and water your crew will need if nothing can be recycled. (Don't include EVAs.)

2. **Identify** the items on your list that could be recycled. **Describe** how you might recycle these things.

3. **Identify** the items that could be produced on board your ship. **Describe** how they could be produced.

Throughout this unit you've learned about the solar system and objects beyond the solar system. How will you use what you've learned and share that information with others? Here are some ideas.

Hold a Big Event
to Share Your Unit Project

Invite parents, friends, and other classes to view your completed space-station simulator. Plan and conduct a simulation that will show your visitors what each part of the space station does and what life is like in space. Have different students play different roles, such as chief engineer, medical officer, and astronomer. Include an exciting event in your simulation that might really happen in space.

Experiment

Extend one of the activities in this unit by using different materials or adding new elements. You might expand on your film-canister viewer to make a miniature planetarium. You might develop an improved telescopic camera or use the old one in new ways. You might create new experiments to investigate free fall or to observe light through a spectroscope. Set up a plan for your experiment and show it to your teacher before you begin.

Research

Find out more about a particular object or group of objects in space. You might choose a constellation, a planet or moon, a star or galaxy, or any other object in this unit. Use reference materials to learn as much as you can about your subject. Make a scrapbook highlighting what you discover. If the object can be seen in the sky where you live, locate it and observe it. Use binoculars or a telescope if you can. Describe and sketch what you see and add this to your scrapbook.

UNIT C

ENERGY, WORK, AND MACHINES

Theme: Systems

GET READY TO

OBSERVE & QUESTION

What are work and friction?

Are the people in this picture working, or playing? It might surprise you to learn that work is being done as the toboggan races down the hill. But who or what is doing the work? How would this picture be different if it was summer instead of winter?

EXPERIMENT & HYPOTHESIZE

How can energy be changed to other forms?

Studying the behavior of a bouncing ball will help you learn about different kinds of energy and about how energy changes from one kind to another. This activity can also help you learn how energy is stored in different kinds of matter.

INVESTIGATE!

RESEARCH & ANALYZE

As you investigate, find out more from these books.

- ***Racing the Iditarod Trail*** by Ruth Crisman (Dillon Press, 1993). This book traces the history of a famous sled dog race. It also describes a sport in which a great deal of energy is used to do work.

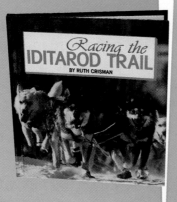

- ***The Winter Room*** by Gary Paulsen (Dell, 1991). What kinds of tools were used on a Minnesota farm years ago? How are these tools related to simple machines that we use every day? Read this book to find out.

WORK TOGETHER & SHARE IDEAS

How can you model the building of an Egyptian pyramid using simple machines?

Working together, you'll have a chance to apply what you've learned to an ancient project—the building of the pyramids in Egypt. Find out if your group can use energy, work, and machines to overcome some of the obstacles faced by the Egyptians as they were constructing the Great Pyramid at Giza.

1

ENERGY AND WORK

You're climbing ever so slowly upward. As you look skyward, your heart pounds, and you tightly clutch the safety bar over your lap. You finally reach the top, pause for one agonizing moment, and then hurtle downward with terrifying speed! You're on a roller coaster, a ride that zooms with energy.

Designing for Speed

Ron Toomer is a mechanical engineer who designs roller coasters. President of Arrow Dynamics, Inc., of Clearfield, Utah, Toomer has designed some of the highest roller coasters in the world.

When Ron Toomer begins to design a roller coaster, he builds a model to help him visualize the ride. Then, using a computer, he determines how to construct an exciting, but safe, roller coaster whose cars will have enough energy to speed over the entire track. What gives a roller coaster energy? Find out through the Investigations in this chapter.

◀ One of Ron Toomer's roller coasters

C5

WHAT ARE SOME DIFFERENT FORMS OF ENERGY?

Make a list of all the things in your classroom that contain energy. In this investigation you'll discover what forms of energy these things contain, how energy changes, and how it travels.

Activity

It's a Stretch

Do you know how to store energy? In this activity you'll see how to store and release energy—just by working with a balloon and a rubber band.

Procedure

1. Blow up a balloon and tie its neck so that no air escapes.

2. Hold the balloon firmly out in front of you with your fingertips while your partner pushes the eraser end of a pencil into the balloon. Release the balloon. In your *Science Notebook*, **describe** what happens to the balloon.

Step 2

3. Place the balloon on a flat surface. Make a fist with your thumb pointed up and place a rubber band over the tip of your thumb.

4. Stretch the rubber band back and aim it at the balloon as shown. **Predict** what will happen if you release the rubber band. Release it and **describe** what happens.

Step 4

5. Blow up a second balloon. Hold the neck tightly, but don't tie it off. **Predict** what will happen if you release the balloon. Release it and **describe** what happens.

Analyze and Conclude

1. How did you store energy in the balloon in step 2? in the rubber band in step 3?

2. Releasing stored energy often causes something to move. In this activity, **tell what evidence** you used to determine that stored energy was released.

3. Moving objects have energy. **Tell what evidence** you observed that indicated that stored energy can be changed to energy of motion.

INVESTIGATE FURTHER!

EXPERIMENT

Create your own experiment with a rubber band and a balloon. Be sure to wear your goggles. Describe the energy forms you observe.

Sound energy can shatter glass (*left*) and damage eardrums (*right*).

jumped into the air.

Energy can also cause temperature to change. If you could have taken the athlete's temperature, you would have found that it went up while she was running and leaping. Energy released in her body made this happen.

Kinds of Energy

There are many kinds of energy, and each kind can cause things to change. The athlete used mechanical energy to make things change. Mechanical energy includes everything having to do with an object's motion.

If you watched the track event on television, you used electricity, another form of energy. In most power plants, coal or oil is burned to produce heat energy, which is used to make electricity. The burning of fuel releases energy that has been stored in the fuel's chemicals for millions of years. This kind of stored energy is called chemical energy.

You have already seen chemical energy being used. In the activity on page C8, the electricity in the wires came from chemical energy that was stored in the battery.

It doesn't have to take millions of years to store energy in something. In fact, you can store energy in this book just by lifting it up and holding it steady. "Come on," you might say, "there's nothing in this book but pages." OK, then let go of the book. What happens? The book moves toward the floor. All of a sudden, it has energy of motion. Where did the book get that energy? You put it there when you picked up the book. And the energy of motion in the falling book is about equal to the energy you used to lift it.

Let's return one last time to the track star. The energy she used in running and jumping came from chemical energy stored in food she had eaten earlier. Now it's time for the woman to "recharge her batteries." With a little rest and a balanced meal or two, she'll be ready to take another shot at the long-jump record. ■

Energy Transfer

A farmer shades his eyes from the blinding light of a summer day. Waves of heat rise up from the fields around him. Sweat trickles down his tanned neck as he glances at a nearby thermometer. The thermometer reads a sizzling 35°C (95°F).

High in the sky over the farmer's head—150,000,000 km away—is the source of his discomfort. It's the Sun, a blazing star. Deep within the Sun, tremendous amounts of energy are produced continuously. This energy leaves the Sun and travels outward through space in the form of waves. Such energy is called electromagnetic (ē lek'trō-mag net'ik) energy.

Energy Travels in Different Ways

Light is electromagnetic energy you can see. There are other kinds of electromagnetic energy you can't see, such as X-rays, ultraviolet radiation, and infrared radiation.

Electromagnetic energy can travel through empty space. You know this, because energy from the Sun reaches Earth. And there is little between Earth and the Sun except empty space. As stated earlier, electromagnetic energy travels as waves. The transfer of energy by waves is called **radiation**.

If you hold your hand near a hot object—a radiator, for example—you can feel the heat without touching the

Energy from the sun can make you squint and make your skin feel hot. ▼

How does heat travel from the radiator to your hands? ▼

HOW CAN ENERGY BE CHANGED TO OTHER FORMS?

Where does your body's energy come from? On a sheet of paper, make a drawing of a person. Around the person, draw pictures that show where the person gets energy. Add to your diagram to show where the energy in these sources comes from. Use arrows to show where you think energy changes form.

Activity

To Bounce or Not to Bounce

A flashlight has energy stored in its chemicals. How can an object placed on a high shelf also have stored energy? How can that energy change?

MATERIALS
- small rubber ball
- clay
- meterstick
- *Science Notebook*

SAFETY //////
Be careful not to lose your balance when standing on a chair.

Procedure

1. Hold a ball in front of you at a height of 1 m. Release the ball and have another student **measure** how high the ball bounces. **Record** the height of the bounce in your *Science Notebook*.

2. Stand on a chair and hold the ball at a height of 2 m, as shown. **Predict** how high the ball will bounce after it hits the floor. Release the ball and have a group member **measure** and **record** the height of its bounce.

3. Shape the clay into a ball about the size of the rubber ball. Drop the clay ball from a height of 1 m. **Describe** how the clay looks after hitting the floor.

Step 2

4. Reshape the clay into a ball and drop it from a height of 2 m. **Describe** how the clay looks after it hits the floor.

Analyze and Conclude

1. **Tell what evidence** you observed that the rubber ball and the clay ball at a height of 1 m had stored energy.

2. What happened to the amount of energy stored in the balls as you raised them from a height of 1 m to a height of 2 m? How do you know?

3. What happened to the energy stored in the balls when you released them? How do you know?

4. Some materials can store energy as they change shape when striking a surface. Which material, rubber or clay, stores more energy this way? How do you know?

Steps 3 and 4

INVESTIGATE FURTHER!

EXPERIMENT

In this activity you discovered that a rubber ball bounces differently than does a clay ball. Now get together with your group members and design an experiment to find out how balls made of other materials respond to being dropped from different heights. You might also design an experiment to find out if the mass of a ball affects how high it will bounce. After you have designed your experiment and described it in writing, show it to your teacher. If your teacher approves, carry out your experiment and record your results.

Energy Changes

▲ **All of these objects contain stored energy.**

Look at the pictures on this page. What do the sugar, the dynamite, and the skier at the top of a steep hill have in common? They all have energy stored in them.

Sugar is a source of quick energy that can help you do something like dash around a basketball court. Dynamite can blow rocks out of a mountainside. And when a skier moves onto the slope of a hill, he or she has enough energy to speed swiftly to the bottom of the hill.

So the sugar, the dynamite, and the poised skier contain enough energy to cause something to change position, or to move from one place to another. However, the energy in these things isn't being used. It's just sitting there, waiting for something to set it loose. This energy-in-waiting is called potential energy. **Potential energy** is stored energy.

Chemical Storehouses

Energy is stored in different ways. Consider a packet of sugar and a stick of dynamite. Although one of these materials is harmless and the other can be very destructive, both materials store energy in the same way.

The energy in sugar and dynamite is stored in the chemical bonds that link their atoms. A bond can be compared to the rope in a tug of war. The atoms are like people pulling on opposite ends of the rope. The energy the people exert is stored in the rope. The rope holds the people together. But if the rope breaks, the people go flying in opposite directions. When this happens, the energy that was stored in the rope is released.

When you eat sugar, the chemical bonds that

C18

store energy in the sugar are broken down by chemicals in your body. This action releases energy for you to use. With dynamite, the bonds are broken down by a spark or a jolt of electricity. When these bonds break, a great deal of energy is released very quickly. Because the energy in sugar and dynamite is stored in chemical bonds, it is called chemical potential energy.

How Much Energy?

How much energy is stored in that packet of sugar you read about earlier? If you read the label on a packet, you'll find that the sugar contains 16 Calories. But what does that tell you about the amount of stored energy in the sugar?

A Calorie is a measure of energy. One Calorie is the amount of heat energy needed to raise the temperature of 1 kg of water 1°C. So if changed to heat energy, the stored energy in a packet of sugar could raise the temperature of 1 kg of water 16°C.

The Calorie is a useful unit for finding the stored energy in different foods. But scientists deal with many different forms of energy, and they need a unit of measure that can be applied to all of

▲ **Food is burned in a calorimeter (kal ə rim′ət ər) to find out how many Calories the food contains.**

them. The **joule** (jo͞ol) is the basic unit of energy used by scientists.

The joule is named after an English scientist who studied the relationship between heat and other forms of energy. One joule is the amount of energy that is needed to raise the temperature of 1 g of water 4.18°C.

Transfer of Energy

Look at the photograph on page C20. A couple of seconds before the picture was taken, the two acrobats on the end of the seesaw were standing up on the platform to their right. The acrobat flying through the air was standing on the other end of the seesaw.

Energy stored in the rope is released when the rope breaks. ▼

WORK AND MACHINES

Some words just go together: *salt* and *pepper, day* and *night, hot* and *cold, on* and *off*. What words seem to go with *knife, hammer*, and *tennis racket*? You might answer *fork, nails*, and *tennis ball*. However, in this chapter you'll find *one* word that goes with *knife, hammer*, and *tennis racket*. That word is *machine*.

What a Racket

During a two-week period that begins in late August, the U.S. Open Tennis Championships are held at the National Tennis Center in New York City. This tournament features the top tennis players in the world. Among them is Zina Garrison Jackson, a professional American tennis player who is among the very best. To play tennis at Zina's level, an athlete must have stamina, quickness, and the ability to hit a tennis ball with great accuracy. Of course, one other item is essential: A TENNIS RACKET!

Through countless hours of practice, Zina Garrison Jackson has developed techniques for hitting winning shots with power and precision. She has mastered the machine of tennis. That's right—a tennis racket is a type of simple machine known as a lever. In this chapter, you'll learn how levers and other machines help you do work.

◀ Zina Garrison Jackson, tennis professional

HOW DO RAMPS HELP US DO WORK?

Imagine that you are planning to hike to the top of a mountain, and you have the choice of two trails. One trail winds around the mountain at a gentle slope to the top; the other follows a straight path up the side of the mountain. Both trails start at the same point and end at the same place. Yet one trail is much easier to climb. Why? Which trail would you take?

Activity
Ramps and Rocks

The mountain trails are types of ramps. Suppose that, after returning from your hike, you had to move a heavy rock from the ground onto the back of a truck. Would it be easier to lift the rock straight up or slide it up a ramp?

MATERIALS
- goggles
- string
- small rock
- paper clip
- thin rubber band
- metric ruler
- smooth board
- 3 books
- *Science Notebook*

SAFETY
Wear goggles during this activity

Procedure

1. Tie a piece of string around a small rock. Bend a paper clip into a double hook. Connect it to the rock, as shown.

2. Measure the length of an un-stretched rubber band and record the length in your *Science Notebook*. Hook the rubber band to the paper clip and rock. Use the rubber band to lift the rock. Have a group member measure and record the length of the stretched rubber band.

Step 1

3. Make a ramp by placing one end of a smooth board on a pile of books. Place the rock at the bottom of the ramp.

4. **Predict** how much the rubber band will stretch when you pull the rock up the ramp. Slowly pull on the rubber band until the rock starts to move up the ramp. Continue to pull at a slow, steady rate so that the rubber band remains stretched at a constant length. Have a group member **measure** and **record** how far the rubber band stretches as you pull on it.

Analyze and Conclude

1. What force does the stretching of the rubber band measure?

2. How do you know that you are doing work in step 1 and in step 4?

3. Did you have to exert more force to lift the rock or to pull it up the ramp? Explain your answer.

4. How does using a ramp make the job of raising a heavy object easier?

INVESTIGATE FURTHER!

RESEARCH

Look for a construction project underway around your school or neighborhood. See if a ramp is in use there. Prepare a report explaining how the ramp is being used.

Step 4

INVESTIGATION 2

WHAT ARE LEVERS AND PULLEYS?

Imagine that you are rowing across a lake. You pull on the oars in one direction, and the rowboat moves in the opposite direction. An oar is a type of simple machine called a lever. You might be surprised at the number of levers you use every day.

Activity

The Ups and Downs of a Seesaw

A seesaw is a type of lever. To make your end of the seesaw go up, you need someone to push down on the other end. How much force does that person have to use? Where should he or she sit? Let's find the answers to these questions.

MATERIALS
- tape
- 3 round pencils
- 2 small paper cups
- metric ruler
- modeling clay
- paper clips
- *Science Notebook*

Procedure

1. Tape three pencils together to make a triangle, as shown. Tape a paper cup to each end of a metric ruler.

2. Place the ruler on the pencils so that the middle of the ruler (the 15-cm mark) rests on the top of the triangle. You have made a lever. The point where the ruler touches the pencils is called the **fulcrum**.

3. Place a piece of clay the size of a large marble in the cup attached to the zero end of the ruler.

4. Add paper clips, one at a time, to the cup at the other end until the zero end of the ruler is lifted.

Step 1

5. In your *Science Notebook*, **make a chart** with two columns. In the first column, **record** the distance between the cup of paper clips and the fulcrum; in the second column, **record** the number of paper clips needed to lift the clay.

6. Take the paper clips out of the cup. Move the ruler so that the fulcrum is at the 10-cm mark of the ruler. Repeat step 4 and **record** the data.

7. Take the paper clips out of the cup and move the fulcrum to the 5-cm mark. **Predict** how many paper clips it will take to lift the cup containing the clay. **Record** your prediction; then repeat step 4 and **record** the data.

Analyze and Conclude

1. **Describe** the relationship between the distance of the clay from the fulcrum and the number of paper clips needed to lift the clay.

2. **Talk** with members of your group and **predict** how many paper clips you would need if the fulcrum were at the 8-cm mark. Then check your prediction.

3. **Predict** how many paper clips you would need if the fulcrum were at the 20-cm mark. Try the experiment and check your prediction.

4. What can you **infer** about how a lever makes the job of lifting the clay ball easier?

INVESTIGATE FURTHER!

EXPERIMENT

Suppose you and a friend are going to ride on a seesaw. Predict how you would adjust your position on the seesaw if you were using it with a friend who weighs less than you do. How about if your friend weighs more than you do? The next time you're on the playground, check your predictions.

Step 3

C47

Levers

If you've ever pried a rock from the ground with a crowbar, moved dirt with a wheelbarrow, or swung a baseball bat, you've used a lever. A **lever** is a simple machine made up of a bar that turns, or pivots, around a fixed point.

What All Levers Have in Common

Basically all levers are bars, although they don't all look like bars. The fixed point around which the bar is free to move is called the **fulcrum**.

You apply a force called the effort force on one part of a lever. The effort force causes the lever to pivot, or turn, around the fulcrum. At some other point on the lever is a force called the resistance force. This force must be overcome if work is to be done.

The resistance force might be the weight of an object to be moved, or it might be friction to be overcome, as when a nail is removed from a board.

How Levers Differ

Study the pictures showing the three classes of levers on these pages. Notice that a first-class lever has the fulcrum between the effort force (E) and the resistance force (R).

Suppose that you want to use a lever to move a heavy rock. A first-class lever will reduce the force you exert and make it easier to move the rock. A first-

1ST CLASS LEVER

When the fulcrum of a first-class lever is close to the resistance, a small effort on one end of the lever will move a large resistance at the other end.

E

R

fulcrum

class lever also changes the direction of the force. However, the effort force must be exerted through a large distance to move the resistance a small distance.

In a second-class lever, the resistance force is between the fulcrum and the effort force. A second-class lever can reduce the force you have to exert, but it can't change the direction of that force. Notice that the nail shown will move in the same direction as the effort force.

In a third-class lever, the effort is exerted between the resistance and the fulcrum. A third-class lever does not reduce the force you exert or change its direction.

2ND CLASS LEVER

A hammer that is used to pull a nail from a board is an example of a second-class lever. As shown in the picture, the effort force is exerted at the end of the handle. The fulcrum is located where the hammerhead turns against the board. The resistance is offered by the nail. What causes this resistance force?

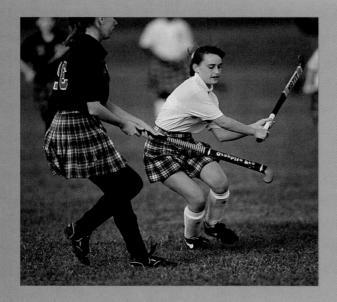

3RD CLASS LEVER

When the player pushes the hockey stick, she exerts the effort through a short distance. The curved end of the stick moves a greater distance. This means that the resistance force moves farther and faster than the effort force. This advantage can be used to make an object, such as a field hockey ball, move away from the stick at great speed.

▲ **Bottle opener**

▲ **Wheelbarrow**

▲ **Oars**

Look at the picture of the field hockey player on page C51. When the player pushes on the stick, she exerts a strong effort force that doesn't move very far. The curved end of the stick exerts a force on the ball. This resistance force is not as strong as the effort force, but it moves much farther and faster than the effort force moves.

You use different kinds of levers every day, often without thinking about it. The pictures above show a variety of ways that people use levers to make their work easier to do. Study the pictures and identify the class of lever shown in each. ■

SCIENCE IN LITERATURE

THE WINTER ROOM
by Gary Paulsen
A Yearling Book, Dell Publishing, 1991

In spring his brother uses a chisel and hammer to carve his name in a tree trunk. In summer his father takes the plow to be sharpened. In fall they use a pulley and rope to pull a slaughtered steer up to the ceiling. In winter his Uncle David told amazing stories. One was about a woodcutter. "It was said that no man could use an ax like him. The wood of the handle seemed to grow out of his hands, and there was nothing he could not do."

The winter room is where the farm families of long ago spent their waking time on long dark evenings. Through the eyes of a Minnesota farm boy, observe the change of seasons and their relationships to simple machines when you enjoy *The Winter Room* by Gary Paulsen.

Pulleys

How can you move a bag of cement from the ground to a roof 10 m above your head without moving your feet? Sounds impossible, doesn't it? But there is a simple machine that can make what seems like an impossible task possible. The simple machine is a pulley.

A **pulley** is a wheel around which a rope or chain is passed. If you attach an object to one end of the rope or chain and pull down on the other end, you can lift the object. And you can do this without moving your feet.

A Single Fixed Pulley

The drawing below shows a single fixed pulley similar to the one you set up in the activity on pages C48 and C49. The word *fixed* means that the pulley can't change position. It is attached to one place. In the drawing, the bag of cement is the resistance. A person is supplying the effort by pulling down on the rope.

A single fixed pulley is similar to a first-class lever with its fulcrum halfway between the effort and the resistance. In a pulley, the wheel is the fulcrum, and the rope supports the resistance that is to be moved.

A single fixed pulley doesn't change the effort force. It changes the direction of the force. When you pull down on the rope, the bag of cement goes up. This is certainly easier than carrying the bag of cement up a staircase.

A Single Movable Pulley

Do you recall the other single pulley you set up in the activity on pages C48 and 49? As shown in the drawing below, the arrangement of this pulley is different from that of the single fixed pulley just discussed. The pulley below is free to move. It is a single movable pulley. One end of the rope is fixed, and the other end is loose. If a person pulls on the loose end of the rope, the

A single fixed pulley ▼

A single movable pulley ▼

▲ **You'd be surprised how much work can be done with the right pulley combination.**

pulley and the bag of cement will move in the same direction as the effort force. In this case, the person pulls up, and the pulley and the cement both rise toward the roof.

What advantage is there to using such a pulley? It cuts the effort force exerted in half. This force is halved because the cement is supported by two lengths of rope instead of one.

What price do you pay for cutting the effort force in half? You have to exert that force through twice the distance that the resistance moves. In this case, for every meter that you raise the cement, you have to pull 2 m of rope through the pulley.

Pulley Combinations

The drawings at the bottom of the page show pulley systems that reduce effort three times, four times, and seven times. You can tell how much a pulley system will reduce effort by counting the lengths of rope that support the resistance. However, you don't always count the "effort" rope—the length of rope you're pulling on.

You only count the effort rope when the effort is exerted in the same direction that the resistance is moved. So if you pull down on a length of rope to lift a resistance, you don't count that length of rope.

Look at the pulley system below that reduces the effort three times. This system has two fixed pulleys and one movable pulley. The resistance moves in the opposite direction to the effort force. So you count the three ropes supporting the resistance, but not the effort rope.

To reduce the effort force by four, you would need a system that has four lengths of rope supporting the resistance.

Pulley combinations ▼

MA = 3

MA = 4

MA = 7

C54

The pulley system shown in the middle is such a system.

Distance Makes the Difference

As the picture at the right shows, machines make it possible to do certain tasks that would be very difficult to accomplish otherwise. Because machines make work easier, it often seems as if they reduce the amount of work that is done.

If you ever find yourself thinking that a machine reduces work, recall this formula: $W = F \times D$. If you discount friction, W doesn't change when using a machine. For example, the work done in raising the piano from the ground to the window is always the same, no matter how you get it up there.

Most machines reduce the amount of force you have to exert to do work. To get this reduction, you sacrifice distance. So, if the F in the formula gets smaller, the D gets bigger, and W stays the same. For every meter that the workers raise the piano, they have to pull 4 m of rope through the pulley system.

Sometimes it takes longer to get work done using a machine. But distance and time are small prices to pay to get a job done. After all, how else are

▲ **Lifting a heavy object is no problem with a combination of pulleys.**

you going to get that big, heavy piano from the sidewalk up to the second floor of that apartment building? ■

INVESTIGATION 2

1. How is a single fixed pulley like a first-class lever? How are the two machines different?

2. You use a wheelbarrow to remove a pile of rocks from a vacant lot. What class of lever is the wheelbarrow? How do you know?

WHAT IS A WHEEL AND AXLE?

Suppose someone removed the handlebars from your bicycle. Could you turn the front wheel by gripping the small shaft your handlebars were attached to? How do the handlebars help you do work on the front wheel?

Activity

Wheel and Axle

In this activity you'll find out how a wheel and axle work together to make a machine.

- -

Procedure

1. **Draw a circle** with a diameter of 6 cm on a piece of posterboard. Cut it out and use the scissors to make a small hole in the center of the circle.

2. Insert a pencil through the hole in the center of the circle. The pencil is now the axle of your wheel and axle. Mark one point on the edge of the wheel.

Step 2

MATERIALS
- goggles
- drawing compass
- ruler
- posterboard
- scissors
- round pencil
- screwdriver
- screw in a board
- *Science Notebook*

SAFETY //////
Wear goggles. Use caution when working with scissors, screwdriver, and compass.

3. Roll the wheel along the table top. Notice that the pencil turns once when the wheel turns once.

4. In your *Science Notebook*, **measure** and **record** the distance that the wheel travels in making one complete turn along the table top.

5. Remove the pencil from the wheel and roll the pencil on the table. **Measure** and **record** how far it travels in one complete turn.

6. Now grip a screwdriver by its metal shaft. Try to remove a screw from a board while gripping the screwdriver in this way.

Step 6

Step 7

7. Repeat step 6 while gripping the screwdriver by its handle, as shown.

Analyze and Conclude

1. How does the circumference of the posterboard wheel **compare** with that of the pencil "axle"? [Hint: You determined the circumference of each in steps 4 and 5.]

2. Suppose you were to grip the pencil axle and use it to turn the posterboard wheel. Through what distance would the axle have to turn to make a half-turn of the wheel? How does this type of machine help do work?

3. **Compare** the diameter of the screwdriver handle with the diameter of the shaft. Which is the wheel and which is the axle? Was it easier to turn the screw when you gripped the screwdriver by its shaft or by its handle?

4. How does a wheel and axle make work easier when force is applied to the wheel?

UNIT PROJECT LINK

The ancient Egyptians used some simple machines to help them move the pyramid blocks. Use wood blocks as model pyramid blocks. Design and build some simple machines to help you move the blocks across a flat surface and to raise them some distance above the surface.

Throughout this unit you've investigated questions related to energy, work, and machines. How will you use what you've learned and share that information with others? Here are some ideas.

Hold a Big Event
to Share Your Unit Project

After you have designed machines to help you move large wooden blocks, use them to build a pyramid. Better yet, work with a group to design your own building or structure. Draw up plans and show them to your teacher for approval. Then use your machines to build it. Invite your parents and friends to visit your classroom to view the machines your group has made and to learn about how ancient Egyptians might have used similar devices in building the Great Pyramid at Giza.

Experiment

Plan a long-term project based on an activity in this unit. You might want to build a scale model of a real roller coaster or a compound machine that combines all the different simple machines. Set up a plan for your experiment and show it to your teacher before you begin.

Research

Read one of the books mentioned in this unit. You might want to learn about what life was like on a farm years ago and compare the machines used then with the types of machinery used on a modern farm.

Take Action

Did you design a new, breathtaking roller coaster ride? Did you figure out how a simple machine can make some task at school or home a little easier? Choose one of these ideas or develop one of your own and take action. Share your information with others.

UNIT D

POPULATIONS AND ECOSYSTEMS

Theme: Systems

GET READY TO

OBSERVE & QUESTION

What is biodiversity and how is it changing?

Think this brown tree snake is at home in any old rain forest? Think again! Each place on Earth has organisms and conditions that make it special. In this unit you'll find out about these places and learn what makes them unique.

EXPERIMENT & HYPOTHESIZE

How are living things in an ecosystem related?

What can an organism's lunch tell you about where and how it lives? Why is it important to learn? Activities in this unit will show you!

INVESTIGATE!

RESEARCH & ANALYZE

As you investigate, find out more from these books.

- *The City Kid's Field Guide* by Ethan Herberman (Simon & Schuster, 1989). There are ecosystems everywhere! Whether you live in or visit a city, you'll want to take this book with you to learn what life is like for organisms in cities around the world.

- *Bears* by Joni Phelps Hunt (Silver Burdett Press, 1995). There are only eight species of bears in the world and all of them are in danger of becoming extinct. Find out what the future may hold for them, and for the ecosystems they inhabit.

WORK TOGETHER & SHARE IDEAS

How would you show how your ecosystem has changed over the years?

Working together, you'll have a chance to create an exhibit like those displayed at a science museum. The exhibit will portray your local ecosystem as it existed in the past and exists today. Look for the Unit Project Links for ideas on how you can build this science exhibit that will teach people about how ecosystems change.

CHAPTER 2

ENERGY AND MATTER IN ECOSYSTEMS

An ecosystem is like a bustling city. Producers are busy capturing energy. Consumers are always "shopping" for energy. And decomposers keep the city clean. The citizens of this "city" are plants, animals, and other living things.

● ●

Visiting an Ecosystem

Would you like to visit a real "energy city," where there is always something exciting going on? The kids at Byram Intermediate School in New Jersey have discovered such a place. For them, it is a neighborhood river called Lubbers Run. The Run is a sleepy old waterway that crawls, not runs, past their school. With their teacher, Wayne McGarva, the Byram students have discovered the fascinating watery world of beavers, turtles, and long-legged wading birds.

They have also discovered something else. They have found out that the recent growth of their little town has affected the Run. Now, with Byram's Environmental Commission, the students are measuring and studying those effects.

Somewhere near you is an ecosystem teeming with life. Perhaps it is a salt marsh, a wooded park, or a creek that appears only in rainy seasons. Whether it is large or small, it's worth exploring. Use this chapter as your tour guide!

◀ Wayne McGarva and his students at the Byram Intermediate School

HOW DOES ENERGY FLOW IN AN ECOSYSTEM?

Energy moves through an ecosystem by being transferred from one organism to another. How does this happen? Find out in Investigation 1!

Activity

Energy in a Pond

A food chain shows the path that energy takes from the Sun through producers and consumers. You can trace some of the paths energy takes in a pond.

MATERIALS
- strip of paper (100-cm long)
- metric ruler
- scissors
- *Science Notebook*

Procedure

1. The table to the right lists pond organisms and their sources of food or energy. Use the information in the table to **identify** which organisms are producers and which are consumers. **Draw** a pond food chain. **Record** the data and the drawing in your *Science Notebook*.

2. You will work with three other students. Each person will play the role of one of the organisms in the food chain. One of you will be a producer, another will be the first-order consumer, a third will be the second-order consumer, and a fourth will be the third-order consumer. As you do this activity, remember that the organism you choose represents an entire population of these organisms.

Organisms	Food or Energy Source
Pondweeds	sunlight
Algae	sunlight
Snails	pondweeds
Waterfleas	algae
Dragonflies	waterfleas
Minnows	snails, waterfleas
Perches	snails, minnows

3. The energy captured by a producer is stored in the food made by the producer. A 100-cm strip of paper represents this captured energy. If you are the producer, measure and cut 90 cm of the paper strip. This represents the amount of captured energy you use for growth and other activities.

4. If you are the consumer eating the producer (the first-order consumer), take the 10 cm left from the 100-cm strip. This is the amount of captured energy available to you. Measure and cut 9 cm from the 10-cm strip. This represents the energy you use.

5. If you are the consumer eating the first-order consumer (the second-order consumer), take the 1-cm strip from the first-order consumer. Measure and cut 9 mm from the 1-cm strip. This represents the energy you use. Pass the 1-mm strip on to the third-order consumer. This is the amount of captured energy left to pass on to that consumer.

Analyze and Conclude

1. Identify the producer and the consumers in your food chain.

2. About what percentage of the energy captured by producers is available to first-order consumers?

3. About what percentage of the energy obtained by first-order consumers is available to second-order consumers? by second-order consumers to third-order consumers?

4. Do you think this food chain could support a fourth-order consumer? Explain.

5. There are usually more producers than consumers in an ecosystem. Suggest a hypothesis to explain why this is so.

INVESTIGATE FURTHER!

RESEARCH

Visit a pond or a nature study center in your area and collect some organisms for study. Using tools, such as a hand lens and a garden trowel, look for organisms that live in the pond water and in the mud. Observe the actions and interactions of these organisms. Are producers or consumers more in evidence? Return samples to the environment when you are finished.

The Carbon Dioxide–Oxygen Cycle

1 During cell respiration, living things use oxygen that plants give off to break down food and obtain energy. When organisms carry out this process, carbon dioxide is given off into the air and the water.

▲ **How carbon dioxide and oxygen are cycled in ecosystems**

Take a deep breath. As you inhale, you take in oxygen, as well as nitrogen, carbon dioxide, and water vapor. When you exhale, you breathe out mostly carbon dioxide—*more* than you took in! Each time you breathe, you take part in the worldwide **carbon dioxide–oxygen cycle**. Follow the steps in this cycle in the drawing.

Into the Soil

Did you know that soil is a major part of the carbon dioxide–oxygen cycle? Plant roots deep in the soil take in water. The water is combined with carbon dioxide to make sugar, a carbon compound rich in energy. Fallen leaves and other plant matter contain these carbon compounds. Carbon is released as carbon dioxide when decomposers break down plant and animal matter. The use of oxygen to break down carbon compounds and release energy is called **cell respiration** (res pə rā′shən). You saw evidence of this process in the activity "Every Breath You Take."

Into the Ocean

Carbon dioxide and oxygen cycle through ocean ecosystems, too. For

2 During photosynthesis, plants use carbon dioxide, water, and energy from the Sun to make food in the form of sugar. They give off oxygen as a waste product.

4 As plants decay, they add carbon compounds to the air and soil.

3 A plant breaks down some food for energy and stores the rest. This stored energy is passed from one organism to another in the food chain.

▲ **Shells are storehouses of carbon and oxygen on the ocean bottom.**

instance, in ocean food chains, algae are producers. Algae are plantlike organisms that carry out photosynthesis. The oxygen released may be used by other sea creatures to break down carbon-containing compounds to obtain energy. So carbon dioxide is released into the water.

The ocean acts as a storage site for carbon dioxide and oxygen. Some ocean organisms use carbon and oxygen along with calcium to make their shells. When these organisms die, their shells settle on the ocean floor, trapping carbon.

The carbon dioxide–oxygen cycle is important to organisms in ecosystems on land as well as in water. Without the delicate balance of both carbon dioxide and oxygen, organisms could not survive. ■

The Water Cycle

2 As water vapor rises, it cools and changes back into a liquid. forming clouds. Eventually the clouds release this water as precipitation.

1 An evaporating puddle is only a very small part of the world-wide cycling of water. The Sun's energy causes liquid water to evaporate from all over Earth's surface.

▲ **How water is cycled in ecosystems**

Like carbon dioxide and oxygen, water moves in a continuous cycle among Earth's land and seas, the air, and living things. This constant movement of water is called the **water cycle.** The Sun is the main engine driving the water cycle.

Have you ever watched a puddle disappear after the Sun came out? Where does the water go? Some of it seeps into the ground. Much returns to the air as water vapor. The process by which liquid water changes to water vapor is **evaporation** (ē vap ə rā'shən).

Much of the water that evaporates from Earth's surface—about 84 percent—comes from the ocean. When water vapor reaches the cool air above Earth, it changes back into a liquid. The process by which water vapor is changed to liquid water is called **condensation** (kän dən sā'shən). After water has condensed in the clouds, it falls back to Earth in the form of precipitation (prē sip ə tā'shən).

Living things form an important link in the water cycle. All living things need water to survive. Water carries

3 Much precipitation falls into the ocean, lakes, and streams. Some water runs along the ground and ends up in bodies of water. Water also seeps into the ground.

4 Organisms take in water for their daily activities. Through transpiration, plants return some water back to the atmosphere. Both plants and animals also release water as a result of respiration.

▲ **Condensation or precipitation?**

nutrients, flushes away wastes, and is needed for life processes. Animals drink water or take in water in the food they eat. Some of this water is released back to the environment as waste products of digestion and cell respiration.

Plants also cycle water through ecosystems. Precipitation that seeps into soil may be taken in by plants through their roots. Recall that plants use some of this water, along with carbon dioxide and sunlight, to carry out photosynthesis and

produce sugars. When the plants break down the sugars through cell respiration, water is formed as a waste product. Water is released through leaves in a process called transpiration (tran spə rā'shən).

In places with a great many plants, such as tropical rain forests, as much as 90 percent of the rainfall is cycled back to the air by the plants. You saw this process for yourself in the activity on page D32. What happens to the water once it is again in the air? ■

Recycling Waste Water

Water—we drink it, cook with it, and bathe in it. We flush our toilets with it. We wash our clothes, dishes, and cars with it, and sprinkle our lawns with it. Farms and factories also use large quantities of water. An average of 2,000 L (500 gal) of water per person every day is used for all of these activities. How can we get along without water?

The answer is we can't. The human body is about two-thirds water. In this regard, we are similar to most organisms. As you know from the activity on page D32, plants also need water. In fact, all living things contain and need water.

In addition to being essential to life, water is useful in many ways. And there's a lot of it around. In fact, about three fourths of Earth's surface is covered by water.

HOW THE WORLD USES WATER

Did You Know?

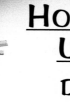

- Sugar cane plants need 681 L (180 gal) of water to produce 1 kg (2.2 lb) of sugar.

- It takes 1,242 L (328 gal) of water to produce 2.2 kg (1 lb) of rice.

- A hen must drink 769 mL (26 oz) of water to produce 1 egg.

- A cow must drink 3.78 L (1 gal) of water to produce .94 L (1 qt) of milk.

- An automobile manufacturing plant uses 3,785 L (1,000 gal) of water to make 1 car.

With all of the water on Earth, you might think that people never need to worry about having enough water. But this is not the case. Not all of Earth's water is usable. Much of it is salt water. Some water is frozen in polar ice caps or locked up in soil. Also, when we use water, we get it dirty with soaps and detergents. When water combines with food wastes and wastes from our bodies, this used water becomes sewage.

When people dump sewage into rivers and lakes, these bodies of water get dirty. Soon there's less clean water for all organisms to use. That's why towns and cities now have sewage treatment plants—places that clean up waste water.

Sewage treatment plants can't cure all sewage problems. For one thing, it may not be possible to remove all types of wastes that get added to water as it is used. Some microscopic organisms present in sewage may not be removed during the sewage treatment process. Also, sewage treatment plants are expensive to build and maintain. They can break down and spill untreated sewage back into Earth's waterways. Some towns are running out of money to treat their sewage.

Many people are trying to find new ways to solve sewage treatment problems. They have found that they can use natural processes of plants and microscopic organisms called bacteria to do so.

SCIENCE IN LITERATURE

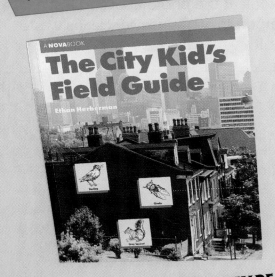

THE CITY KID'S FIELD GUIDE
by Ethan Herberman
Simon & Schuster, 1989

Would you like to see up close how important water is to an ecosystem? Just get permission to explore a vacant city lot. On pages 38–41 of *The City Kid's Field Guide* by Ethan Herberman, you'll find helpful hints about how to observe and record the flow of energy in any vacant lot.

So get a notebook and pencil and bring some caution and patience. As you examine the plants and the creatures that live among them, you'll begin to see how they relate to one another. Draw some food chains and even a food web of your vacant lot.

▲ **Marshes are used in sewage treatment in Arcata, California.**

One Town's Solution

The town of Arcata, California, has found a solution to its sewage treatment problems. Instead of using a huge sewage treatment plant, Arcata uses marshes that teem with wildlife to clean its water.

Arcata's sewage flows first into a holding tank. Next, it moves into a huge concrete tub, where solid materials settle to the bottom. The waste water is then drained from the tub into a large pond with no vegetation. Here, bacteria begin to break down the harmful compounds in the water. When the water leaves the pond, it is treated with chlorine to kill disease-causing organisms. (The chlorine does not stay in the water long, because it soon evaporates.)

Next the water enters a series of marshes. These marshes are filled with many kinds of aquatic plants, including duckweed, cattails, and bulrushes. Bacteria and other small organisms cling to the underwater stems of these aquatic plants. These bacteria filter and clean the waste water. By the time the water flows into a nearby bay, it is cleaner than the bay water itself.

The people of Arcata have a sewage treatment facility that doesn't smell bad and doesn't break down. It's also not expensive to maintain. It's a recreation area and wildlife preserve, attracting wildlife, joggers, and birdwatchers. (Look at the photo above.) Most importantly, the facility cleans waste water very well. ■

UNIT PROJECT LINK

How have populations of living and nonliving things changed in your neighborhood over the past 200 years? Do research to learn about how people lived, learned, and had fun. Consider how these activities affected both living and nonliving things in the neighborhood. Also consider how the cycles of energy and matter may have changed over the years. Then create a display that highlights what you discovered.

The Nitrogen Cycle

You know that living things need energy, oxygen, and water. Living things also need proteins. **Proteins** are compounds that act as the building blocks of living things. Some proteins control chemical processes that take place in the human body. Other proteins make up body structures such as hair, cells, and nails.

Nitrogen is needed to make proteins. Earth's atmosphere is about 78 percent nitrogen gas. With all this nitrogen, you might think that your body could use the nitrogen that you inhale. But that isn't so. Nitrogen gas can't be used directly by most organisms. Before nitrogen can be used, it must be "fixed," or changed into nitrogen compounds.

You can see from the illustration on the next page that dead organisms and the wastes that organisms produce are sources of nitrogen. Decomposers feed on dead organisms and waste products. The nitrogen they release from the wastes is in the form of ammonia, which plants can use. Ammonia is changed into other compounds that may be used by plants. Unused compounds are broken down by bacteria that release nitrogen gas back to the air.

Inhaled and exhaled air have the same percentage of nitrogen, showing that nitrogen in air is not used directly to form protein. ▼

nitrogen

78 percent

78 percent

oxygen

21 percent

17 percent

argon

.03 percent

carbon dioxide

4 percent

other gases

Air breathed in

Air breathed out

1 In the **nitrogen cycle**, nitrogen gas is converted to a usable form and eventually returned to the atmosphere as nitrogen gas.

2 Lightning changes some nitrogen gas into nitrogen compounds. These compounds are washed to Earth in rain. Some of the nitrogen compounds enter the soil with rainwater.

5 When organisms die, the proteins in their bodies are broken down by decomposers to ammonia, nitrites, and nitrates. These compounds are used by plants or break down into nitrogen gas, which passes into the air.

3 Nitrogen is made usable by bacteria that grow on the roots of plants such as beans and peas. These bacteria turn nitrogen into ammonia. Other bacteria change ammonia into nitrates that can also be used by plants.

4 Plants use ammonia and nitrates to make proteins. Animals get nitrogen by eating plants or other animals.

▲ **How nitrogen is cycled in ecosystems**

INVESTIGATION 2

1. Modern farming practices speed up the decomposition of matter in soil. How might this affect the nitrogen cycle?

2. A compost pile is made from grass clippings, leaves, and food wastes that can be broken down for use as fertilizer. What organisms must be part of a compost pile?

REFLECT & EVALUATE

WORD POWER

carnivores food web
condensation herbivores
evaporation omnivores
food chain proteins
carbon dioxide–oxygen cycle
cell respiration
nitrogen cycle
water cycle

 On Your Own
Write a definition for each term in the list.

 With a Partner
Make up a quiz, using all the terms in the list. Challenge your partner to complete the quiz.

BUILD YOUR PORTFOLIO

Obtain pictures of at least ten different kinds of plants and animals that live in your community. Use the pictures to create a bulletin-board display or poster showing a possible food web for the organisms.

Analyze Information

Study the drawing. Then explain each organism's role in food chains and food webs.

Assess Performance

Add a small amount of food coloring to water. The food coloring represents a poison in sewage. Using only water and a plastic jar, show how a small amount of material in sewage can pollute water.

Problem Solving

1. Imagine that Earth stopped receiving light from the Sun. What effect would the lack of sunlight have on food chains and food webs? What effect would it have on the carbon dioxide–oxygen cycle? the water cycle? the nitrogen cycle?

2. Suppose you work on a farm. Identify three ways that you could improve the nitrogen content of the soil. What are the advantages and disadvantages of each of your proposed improvements?

CHAPTER 3

DIFFERENT KINDS OF ECOSYSTEMS

Do you live in the American Southwest? If so, you may see cactuses outside your window. Perhaps you live somewhere else. You may see the Northeast's maple trees or the Southeast's palms. Wherever you live, you are part of one of the large ecosystems on this planet. If your ecosystem changes, your life and the life of every other organism will change, too.

A Daring Rescue

If you had visited Kenya in 1977, you would have seen a land stripped of trees. Ninety percent of Kenya's forests had been cut down. As the forests disappeared, so did Kenya's streams and wildlife. Wood for fuel had nearly vanished. Without fuel, it was difficult to cook healthful foods. As a result, children were not eating well. The natural ecosystem was being destroyed. Every organism in the ecosystem suffered.

That same year a Kenyan biologist named Wangari Maathai began to save the ecosystem. She started a tree-planting project called the Green Belt Movement, in which young trees are given to women farmers to plant. Maathai's idea has been a great success. In just the first ten years of the project, the Green Belt planted 5 million trees!

As you read this chapter, think about how a movement like Maathai's might save other ecosystems.

INVESTIGATION 1

HOW DO EARTH'S MAJOR ECOSYSTEMS DIFFER?

INVESTIGATION 2

WHAT IS BIODIVERSITY AND HOW IS IT CHANGING?

▲ Wangari Maathai's Green Belt Movement helped restore Kenya's ecosystem.

HOW DO EARTH'S MAJOR ECOSYSTEMS DIFFER?

Some ecosystems, like the plot you studied near your school, are very small. Others, such as deserts or oceans, cover vast areas of Earth's surface. Find out the characteristics that make each of Earth's major ecosystems unique in this investigation.

Activity

Make a Mini-Biome!

Ecosystems that cover large areas of Earth's land surface are called biomes. In this activity you can make a model of the biome of your choice and see how abiotic factors affect it.

Procedure

1. From the table on the next page, choose the kind of plant you wish to grow. Your teacher will give you several of these plants.

2. Cover the bottom of a jar with a layer of activated charcoal 0.5 cm thick. Use the table to find the kind of soil your plants need—potting soil, sand, or a potting soil/sand mixture. Place a layer of this soil, 3 cm thick, on top of the charcoal.

MATERIALS
- newspaper
- gardening gloves
- plants (several of the same kind)
- large plastic jar
- activated charcoal
- metric ruler
- potting soil
- sand
- grass seed
- water in a spray bottle
- *Science Notebook*

SAFETY
Use gardening gloves to handle plants that have needles or spines.

Step 2

aquarium filter carbon

D46

PLANTS FROM DIFFERENT BIOMES

Kind of Plant	Soil Type	How Often to Water
Broad-leaved	potting	every 2–3 days
Cactus	sand	lightly, every 2 weeks. Let soil dry completely between waterings.
Grass	potting	every other day
Needle-leaved	potting/sand mixture	weekly

3. Carefully lift the plants out of their pots, making sure that most of the soil clings to the roots. Place the plant roots in the soil. Be sure the roots are completely covered so that the plant is well anchored. If you choose to grow grass, scatter the seeds on the soil and cover them with a thin layer of soil.

4. Place your mini-biome in a sunny spot. Use a spray bottle to moisten the soil. Use the table as a guide to watering the plants.

5. **Observe** your mini-biome daily. **Record** your observations in your *Science Notebook*.

6. **Observe** the mini-biomes of the other students. **Compare** the various biomes represented in your class.

Analyze and Conclude

1. The biomes varied as to the kind of plants, type of soil, and amount of watering. What abiotic factors were the same for all the biomes represented?

2. Which two biomes had the most similar growing conditions? Which two had the least similar conditions? What would happen if you switched the plants growing under the least similar conditions?

3. What is the relationship between abiotic factors in a biome and the kind of plant life found there?

Step 3

Land Ecosystems—
Earth's Biomes

The abiotic characteristics of an area include things such as climate and soil type. Along with the biotic factors, such as plants and animals, abiotic characteristics determine an area's ecosystem. Ecosystems that cover large areas of land are called **biomes**.

The major biomes on Earth are the deciduous forest, the desert, the grassland, the taiga, the tropical rain forest, and the tundra. This map shows you where these biomes are found. Humans live in all biomes, but some biomes support human populations better than others do.

UNIT PROJECT LINK

Which biome do you live in? How can biomes change? Work with others to create a model of your biome as it might have looked before any people inhabited it. Include any extinct plants and animals that once lived there.

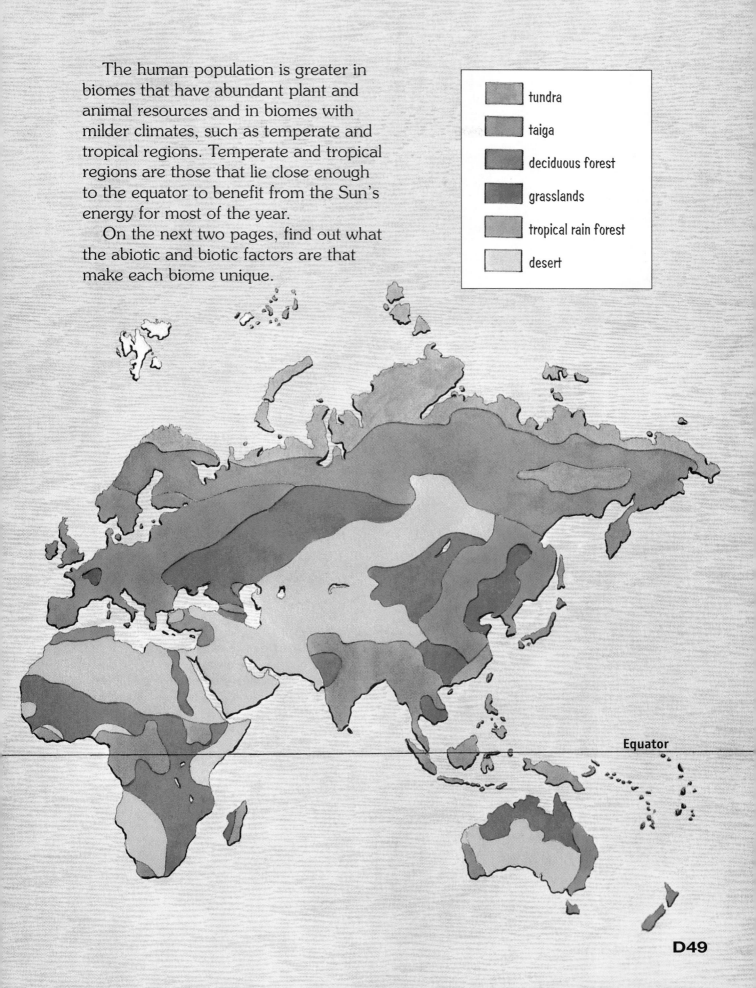

The human population is greater in biomes that have abundant plant and animal resources and in biomes with milder climates, such as temperate and tropical regions. Temperate and tropical regions are those that lie close enough to the equator to benefit from the Sun's energy for most of the year.

On the next two pages, find out what the abiotic and biotic factors are that make each biome unique.

tundra

taiga

deciduous forest

grasslands

tropical rain forest

desert

Equator

D49

Toucan

Earth's Land Biomes

◄ **TROPICAL RAIN FOREST**
Tropical rain forests are lush and green year-round. Heavy rainfall and a warm climate create an environment in which an amazing variety of plants and animals thrive. These plants and animals live in "layers" of the forest, from the ground to the tops of trees. Tree branches form one layer known as the canopy.

GRASSLAND **Grasslands** are ► wide-open fields of grass that once covered vast expanses of every continent except Antarctica. The amount of rainfall affects the particular grasses that will thrive in a grassland. Wetter areas have taller grasses; drier areas have shorter grasses. Grasslands attract grazing animals and rodents, as well as their predators.

Field mouse

◄ **DESERT** **Deserts** can be either hot or cold, but they are always very dry. So desert plants and animals have to survive without much water. As a result, few types of plants grow in desert ecosystems. Animal populations also are not diverse.

Horned lizard

D50

▲ **DECIDUOUS FOREST** Deciduous (dē sij′oo əs) **forests** grow where winters are cold and summers are warm and wet. The large leaves of deciduous trees—maple, oak, and birch, for example—carry out photosynthesis. Their leaves are lost in autumn. There is plenty of food for insects, birds, rodents, and other animals.

Beetle

TAIGA The **taiga** (tī′gə) contains coniferous forests—evergreens such as spruce, pine, and fir trees. These trees grow in areas where the winters are long and cold. On the forest floor are low-growing mosses and lichens. Many birds and mammals prey on needle-eating insects and seed-eating rodents. ▶

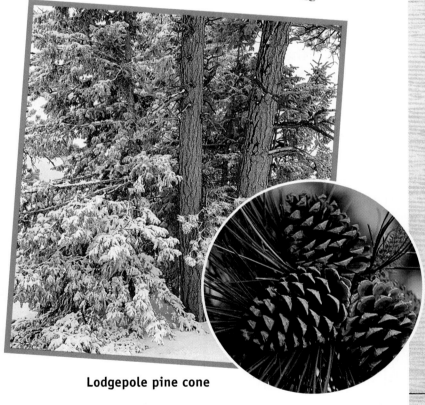

Lodgepole pine cone

◀ **TUNDRA** The **tundra** is the Arctic grassland north of the taiga where the subsoil is frozen year-round. The tundra has long, cold winters and cool summers. There is little precipitation. A thin layer of snow and ice covers the ground most of the year. The few plants and animals that live in the tundra survive a growing season that is only two to three months long.

Saxifrage

Saltwater Ecosystems

ghost crab

gray seal

SHORELINE The shoreline is where the ocean meets the land. It may be only a narrow strip of land, but it circles every bit of land on Earth! Tides and waves affect the organisms that live along the shoreline, as does the type of shore—rocky, sandy, or pebbly.

sponges

jellyfish

COASTAL OCEAN The coastal ocean is home to kelp, jellyfish, and many kinds of fish—as well as whales. The coastal ocean is shallow enough that sunlight can shine all the way down to the coastal floor. Plankton—the organisms that form the basis of the food chain in coastal ocean ecosystems—abound.

corals

Saltwater Ecosystems

Ninety-seven percent of Earth's water is salty ocean water. If you look at a globe, you'll see that the oceans actually are one continuous body of water. The forms of life this ecosystem supports vary from tiny one-celled organisms to mammals as large as any animals that ever lived. In general, different organisms are found at different depths.

Ocean water generally contains about 3.5 percent salt, but this amount can vary. This variation is important. The amount of salt in water can either support or kill organisms. Other factors such as water pressure, temperature, and light affect the types of organisms that live in salt water. So there are really several different saltwater ecosystems.

So the next time someone talks about the ocean as if it were one big ecosystem, you can tell him or her that saltwater ecosystems are not as simple as they seem. They require a lot of close-up study and observation. ■

sailfish

Atlantic mackerel

hammerhead shark

gray whale

sunfish

white shark

OPEN OCEAN   The **open ocean** is the vast expanse you see over most of the globe. In fact, the open ocean forms the largest ecosystem on Earth. In the upper layers of open ocean water, plankton and the organisms that feed on it are plentiful. Many species of fish swim in the open ocean, as do whales and squid. Organisms that live on the ocean floor survive by manufacturing their own light or live without light.

squid

anglerfish

viperfish

lantern fish

manta ray

INVESTIGATION 1

THINK IT WRITE IT

1. Deciduous forests and grasslands have been able to support a large human population. Why do you think this is so? Have humans really adapted to these biomes, or have humans forced the biomes to adapt to them?

2. What abiotic factors determine the type of water ecosystem found in an area?

WHAT IS BIODIVERSITY AND HOW IS IT CHANGING?

Earth's ecosystems are home to millions of species of living things. Each species in an ecosystem plays a role. In this investigation you'll find out how diverse ecosystems are in the species they support, and how changes in this diversity affect an ecosystem.

Activity
Vanishing Species

When ecosystems change, many species are displaced or may even die out. See if you can determine one factor that has led to the decline of a rain forest in Ecuador by doing this activity.

MATERIALS
- globe
- graph paper
- metric ruler
- *Science Notebook*

Procedure

1. Locate the country of Ecuador on a globe.

2. Look at the maps to the right, which show how the area covered by forests in Ecuador has changed since 1938. Forested areas are green on the map. In your *Science Notebook*, **describe** what has happened between 1938 and 1988.

3. Refer to the table on the next page. **Draw a bar graph** that shows the change in Ecuador's forested area based on data from the years 1961, 1971, and 1991 (the years for which precise figures are available). Use the figures provided for the square kilometers of forest and woodland.

FORESTS OF ECUADOR 1938-1988

Forest Cover 1938

Forest Cover 1958

Forest Cover 1988

4. During those 30 years, the human population in Ecuador had grown. **Draw a bar graph** that shows the change in Ecuador's population based on data from the years 1961, 1971, and 1991 (the years for which census figures are available). Use the figures provided.

ECUADOR			
	1961	**1971**	**1991**
Forest & Woodland	173,000 km^2	153,000 km^2	112,000 km^2
Population	5,162,000	7,035,000	10,782,000

Analyze and Conclude

1. **Compare** the graphs you drew. What relationship has there been between the change in the human population and the change in the amount of forested land in Ecuador? What reasons are there for this relationship?

2. There are no census or forestation figures for 1981. Based on your bar graphs, **infer** what happened to Ecuador's population and forested area between 1971 and 1991.

3. Based on your knowledge of food webs, what do you think happens to a rain forest community when the primary producers—trees—are cut down?

SCIENCE IN LITERATURE

BEARS
by Joni Phelps Hunt
Silver Burdett Press, 1995

"Polar, Panda, Brown, Black, Sloth, Moon. All may soon be gone . . . ." The world's eight species of bears are in danger of becoming extinct. You'll begin to see that for yourself at the beginning of *Bears* by Joni Phelps Hunt. A map shows where brown bears used to live and the smaller area that they now inhabit.

In *Bears* you'll find spectacular close-up photos of these intelligent mammals. You'll also read about how bears live, what they eat, and how they raise their young. Find out what animals are predators of bears and what threats humans pose to bears' survival.

Variety in Ecosystems

Try to imagine 1,000 beetles, each a different species. Tough, isn't it? But if you go to the forests of Central and South America, you can find more than 1,000 different beetles on a *single* tree. Now try to imagine *300,000* different species of beetles. Impossible! Can there really be that many? Yes, there can. There probably are at least that many. But scientists think they have actually identified only a tiny fraction of all the species of beetles in the world.

Scientists believe our planet may be home to as many as 100 million different species of organisms. Only about 1.4 million of them have been identified!

The great abundance of different life forms is called **biodiversity** (bī ō də-vʉr′sə tē). *Biodiversity* is a combination of the words *biological* and *diversity*. The term refers to the millions of species that can live in Earth's many ecosystems. Biodiversity refers not only to the variety of species on Earth but also to diversity within a single species. Think about all the earthworms you might find in a plot of soil. They are not all exactly the same length, the

same color, or the same diameter. In fact, each one is a little different, just as you are different from your mother, brother, neighbor, and classmates. Yet, just as humans are all members of the same species, *Homo sapiens*, earthworms are all members of the same species, *Lumbricus terrestris*. Yet each earthworm is slightly different from every other earthworm.

Diversity—A Lot or a Little?

The amount of biodiversity varies among ecosystems. One ecosystem may contain thousands of different species; another, fewer than 50. What makes the difference? The biodiversity of an ecosystem depends on three major factors: its size, its terrain, and its latitude, or distance from the equator.

Large ecosystems support a greater number of species than smaller ecosystems. Over a larger area, abiotic factors are more variable. For example, suppose a 1,000-km^2 island covered with forests is home to 50 different species of butterflies. Another island, also forested, but covering 10,000 km^2, may contain 100 kinds of butterflies. Why? Perhaps a tall mountain rises on the larger island. Mountains can cause the amount of rainfall and the temperature to vary across the island. The result? The larger island has many more different ecosystems than the smaller one. And different ecosystems have different populations of organisms. Thus, the larger island, with more variable abiotic factors and more ecosystems, also supports more species of butterflies.

Latitude also affects abiotic factors. Away from the equator, temperatures are not consistently high, sunlight is intense only part of the year, and precipitation is not as steady. These conditions become more extreme the farther an ecosystem is from the equator.

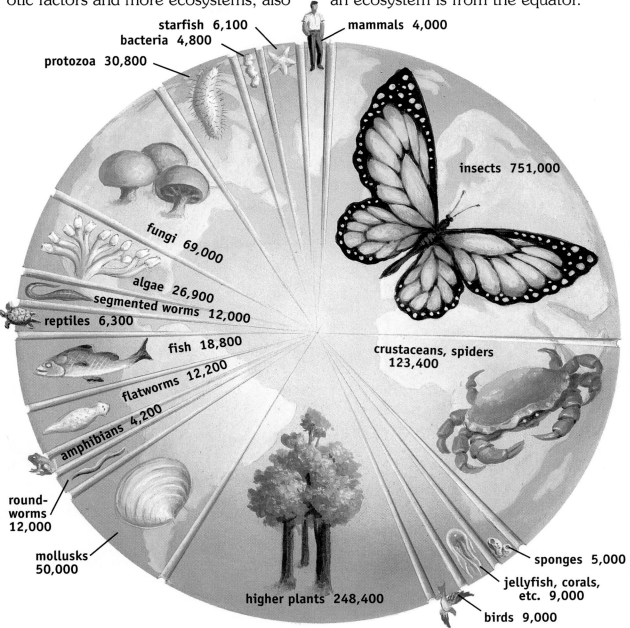

starfish 6,100
bacteria 4,800
protozoa 30,800
mammals 4,000
insects 751,000
fungi 69,000
algae 26,900
segmented worms 12,000
reptiles 6,300
fish 18,800
flatworms 12,200
amphibians 4,200
crustaceans, spiders 123,400
round-worms 12,000
mollusks 50,000
higher plants 248,400
sponges 5,000
jellyfish, corals, etc. 9,000
birds 9,000

▲ **VARIETY ON EARTH**   This is a "species-scape." The number of known species of each major group of organisms is listed. The sizes give a rough approximation of the abundance of each group.

Close to the equator, temperatures are high, sunlight is intense, and rain is plentiful. Plants can grow all year. As a result, producers in tropical ecosystems are abundant and varied. They also can support more consumers, of a greater variety, than the producers in a colder or drier climate. Most rain forests are in tropical locations. Thus, rain forests have the highest biodiversity of any ecosystem. Remember the activity on pages D56 and D57? In the forests of Ecuador, Colombia, and Peru—just 2 percent of the world's land surface—there are more than 40,000 species of plants!

The stable climate of the tropics has led to interesting relationships among organisms, which also increases biodiversity. As you know, a single tree rooted in the ground is part of a forest. The tree also supports another whole ecosystem in its canopy layer. The canopy is laden with plant life—mosses, ferns, orchids, and even small trees. In turn, this miniature forest is home to a great many consumers, from one-celled organisms to snakes, tree-dwelling frogs, mammals, and beetles, of course!

Tinkering With Biodiversity

Do you think the dandelions in your back yard, the tumbleweed that rolls across the prairie, and the Norway maple are "all-American"? Like most of us, you'd probably think so. But you'd be wrong! Dandelions, tumbleweed,

▲ **The brown tree snake**

and Norway maples are three of the more than 3,000 species of plants that were introduced to the United States by accident or on purpose. Animal species have been introduced from other places, too. For example, the fierce brown tree snake was introduced to Hawaii from Guam in 1991. Scientists believe the snake survived a plane flight wrapped around the aircraft's wheels.

Native species can be driven out of their habitats by introduced species. Ecologists are trying to restore some ecosystems to their native biodiversity. ∎

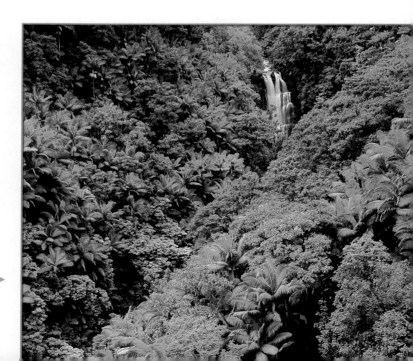

The rain forest canopy ▶

The Challenge of Biodiversity

Have you ever seen a dinosaur? Did you ever hear of a dusky seaside sparrow? Have you ever used the expression "dead as a dodo"?

Neither you—nor anyone else—has ever seen a live dinosaur, and none of you ever will. You may have heard of a dusky seaside sparrow, but you will never see one alive. Both dinosaurs—all kinds—and dusky seaside sparrows are as dead as dodos. These species are **extinct**. None remains alive. They are gone forever.

Some species, such as the giant panda, are not *yet* extinct. However, many species are **endangered** or threatened. Endangered species are those in danger of becoming extinct. Threatened species are in danger of becoming endangered. Eleven percent of the world's bird species are endangered.

The greatest threat to biodiversity is habitat destruction. For centuries, habitats have been destroyed in many ways, for many reasons. Early farmers cut down Europe's forests many centuries ago, destroying their native ecosystems.

Settlers plowed under the prairies of the midwestern United States and planted crops. Developers fill in the wetlands to build suburban housing developments. Habitats can also be harmed without being destroyed. Pollution can poison a healthy habitat. The introduction of species can drive out native organisms.

But why do we have to care about biodiversity? Why should we care what happens to plants and animals, as long as we're all right? Why should we stop destroying habitats, as long as our homes are safe?

Will the highly endangered panda (*right*), meet the same fate as the the passenger pigeon (*top right*)?

▲ The dodo is extinct. Are all the species in the rain forests headed in the same direction?

Humans cannot live alone on Earth. As you know, plants and animals provide us with food, raw materials for clothing, and building materials. More than 40 percent of all medicines come from living organisms. The complex web of plant life on Earth provides us with oxygen for life processes. Decomposers keep the soil fertile for growing crops. Bacteria and other microscopic organisms break down wastes and purify water. The diversity of life on Earth is inspiring and awesome.

Aside from all these reasons, many people feel that human beings have a responsibility to preserve Earth. We have the power to destroy ecosystems and drive species to extinction. We also have the power—and the knowledge—to save ecosystems and encourage species' survival. We know the consequences of doing both. What will we do? ■

━━━━━━━ INVESTIGATION 2 ━━━━━━━

1. Identify a favorite species you have read about that you fear is in danger of becoming extinct. Why is it endangered? Can we do anything to save it?

2. What is biodiversity and why does it vary among ecosystems?

REFLECT & EVALUATE

WORD POWER

biodiversity
biomes
deserts
endangered
extinct
grasslands
coastal ocean
deciduous forest
open ocean
tropical rain forest

lake
river
shoreline
taiga
tundra
wetland

On Your Own
Review the terms in the list. Then use at least five terms in a paragraph about Earth's biomes.

With a Partner
Write each term in the list on one side of an index card and the definition on the other. Use the cards to quiz your partner.

BUILD YOUR PORTFOLIO

Imagine you are building a zoo. Make a drawing of a biome to include in your zoo. Obtain pictures of plants and animals for your biome. List the abiotic factors needed.

Analyze Information

Study the table below. Based on the data, which two biomes are farthest north? Which biome shows the greatest temperature range? Which shows the smallest temperature range?

Biomes	Average Temperature Range (yearly)
Tundra	-26°C to 4°C
Taiga	-10°C to 14°C
Deciduous forest	6°C to 28°C
Tropical rain forest	25°C to 27°C
Grassland	0°C to 25°C
Desert	24°C to 32°C

Assess Performance

Build a simple ecosystem, either land or water. Choose some organisms to include in the ecosystem. Identify the biotic and abiotic factors in the ecosystem. Vary one of the factors and note any effects on the ecosystem.

Problem Solving

1. Many scientists hypothesize that dinosaurs became extinct after an asteroid struck Earth. Earth's atmosphere was filled with dust that blocked out the Sun's rays. Discuss this theory in terms of concepts from this chapter.

2. Compare the variety of ecosystems in the ocean and on land. Suggest reasons why there is greater variety on land than in the ocean.

3. How has Earth's biodiversity been affected by the development of civilization?

Throughout this unit you've investigated questions related to populations and ecosystems. How will you use what you've learned and share that information with others? Here are some ideas.

Hold a Big Event
to Share Your Unit Project

Turn your classroom into a museum exhibit about the history of your ecosystem. Divide your classroom into two sections. Using your knowledge of what organisms currently live in your ecosystem and what organisms used to live in your ecosystem, develop posters, dioramas, and videotapes showing how organisms, energy, and matter have interacted in your ecosystem over time. Group the displays on the history of your ecosystem in one section of the classroom; in the other section set up your showcase of what your ecosystem looks like now. Invite others to view your display. Have on hand a brochure or tape to guide them through the ecological history of the community.

Experiment

What kind of water ecosystem is found near you—shoreline, river, ocean, lake, or wetland? Choose one of these areas and then conduct some field tests, as environmental engineers do. Some examples:
• Use a pH strip to find out if the water is acidic, basic, or neutral.
• Evaporate a little bit of water to see what materials are in it.
• Note the organisms living in and around the ecosystem.
• Catalog any signs of pollution or other problems.
• Talk to people who have lived in the area for many years to find out how the ecosystem has changed.

Take Action

Your class can "adopt" an acre of rain forest. To find out how, write or call a rain forest protection agency such as: The Nature Conservancy Adopt An Acre Program, 1815 North Lynn Street, Arlington, VA 22209, 1-800-628-6860

THE SOLID EARTH

Theme: Constancy and Change

GET READY TO

OBSERVE & QUESTION

How do rocks bend?

Rocks are used by people to make buildings and monuments. In nature, rocks may also build hills and mountains. How do forces both inside Earth and on its surface create structures such as the one shown?

EXPERIMENT & HYPOTHESIZE

How can fossils help tell us how old a rock is?

Make your own series of rock layers—with fossils in the layers. The order of the layers along with the fossils they contain are clues to the ages of the rocks.

INVESTIGATE!

RESEARCH & ANALYZE

As you investigate, learn more from these books.

- ***Rocks, Minerals, and Fossils*** by Keith Lye (Silver Burdett Press, 1991.) Ever wonder how you can tell the difference between jewelry made of glass and that made of real diamonds? This book will tell you how to find out.

- ***My Side of the Mountain*** by Jean Craighead George (Puffin Books, 1991). What would it be like to live in the mountains? Read this book for one person's story.

Our World
ROCKS, MINERALS AND FOSSILS
Keith Lye

WORK TOGETHER & SHARE IDEAS

How can you build an organized mineral collection?

Working together, you'll begin a collection of rocks, fossils, and minerals. Then you will share your new knowledge with others by creating a museum-type display of your collection and by publishing a guide to local rocks, fossils, and minerals.

CHAPTER 1

MINERALS

Have you ever visited a jewelry store or a museum and admired jewelry containing gemstones such as rubies or diamonds? Have you ever seen bracelets or necklaces made of shiny metals such as silver or gold? Both gemstones and metals have something in common. They are *minerals*.

Prospecting for Gold

The Alaska gold rush of 1898 brought a flood of hopeful prospectors to the North. Alaska still boasts of some hardy individuals who search for gold in rugged, remote areas. Three such people are Paul and Grace Byrd and their daughter, Blyss. During the summer, the family prospects for gold in Bonanza Creek, a stream in southeastern Alaska's Wrangell-St. Elias National Park. The Byrds use a portable suction machine to suck up stones and sand from the creek bottom. The reward for their hard work is finding about 28 g (1 oz) of gold per day.

Gold is just one of a group of substances called minerals. Minerals vary greatly in appearance and texture. Sparkling diamonds, gleaming gold, and graphite are all minerals. What properties make something a mineral? Through the investigations in this chapter, you'll find out.

Coming Up

◀ The Byrd family
prospecting for
gold in Alaska

HOW CAN YOU IDENTIFY MINERALS?

A mineral is a solid element or compound from Earth's crust that has a definite chemical composition and crystal shape. Now see if you can name this mineral. It is most often black or brown. It's used in tools for drilling. It's highly prized when it is colorless or blue-white. If you said diamond, you are right!

Activity

The Way Minerals Look

Think about it—you identify most things just by looking at them. Minerals aren't any different. When you get to know them, you'll be able to look at them and name them. The key is getting to know them.

MATERIALS
- cardboard egg carton
- mineral set
- marker
- white unglazed ceramic tile
- *Science Notebook*

Procedure

1. Use your egg carton to store your mineral specimens. Open the carton and use the marker to number the pockets from 1 through 12.

2. **Observe** each mineral specimen. Does each look like it is made up of all the same kind of material? Is there any evidence of crystal structure in the minerals? **Record** your observations in your *Science Notebook*.

Step 1

3. Make a chart like the one shown, with 8 columns and 12 rows. Any columns you don't fill in during this activity will be filled in during later activities.

MINERAL PROPERTIES CHART							
Mineral Number	Luster	Color	Streak	Hardness	Cleavage	Special	Name

4. The way a mineral reflects light is called **luster** (lus'tər). Some minerals reflect light well—they appear shiny. They have a *metallic* luster. Those that don't have a metallic luster have a *nonmetallic* luster. Separate your mineral specimens into two sets, one set that looks shiny like metal (such as brass, gold, or iron) and the other that doesn't look like metal.

Step 5

5. Put each mineral in your egg carton. As you do it, write on your chart *metallic* or *nonmetallic* under *Luster* and opposite the number of the pocket.

6. Inspect each mineral specimen and write its color in the next column of your chart. If needed, use more than one word, such as *yellow-brown* or *brass yellow*.

7. When a mineral is ground to a powder, its color is called its **streak**. **Predict** each mineral's streak. With each mineral, try to make a mark (like a pencil mark) on the tile. The color of the mark is the color of the streak. **Record** each mineral's streak in your chart.

Analyze and Conclude

1. **Compare** the color and streak of each mineral in your collection. What conclusions can you draw about the color and streak of a mineral?

2. How are the properties of streak and luster useful in getting to know minerals?

INVESTIGATE FURTHER!

RESEARCH

You use two minerals every day in your classroom. In fact, you use them for their streak. Find out what they are.

Activity

Scratching Minerals

You may have noticed that some minerals are harder than others. Hardness is an important property in identifying minerals. Geologists test a mineral's hardness by seeing what objects will scratch or be scratched by the mineral. Try this scratch test yourself.

MATERIALS
- goggles
- mineral set in egg carton from previous activity
- Mineral Properties Chart
- pane of glass, 8-cm square
- steel nail
- copper wire, 10 cm in length
- *Science Notebook*

Procedure

1. Try scratching one mineral with another; do just a little scratch. Don't scrub the minerals together or you'll damage them. Can you find the hardest mineral in your set? How about the softest? **Record** your findings in your *Science Notebook*. Remember to return each mineral to its numbered pocket.

2. Geologists often use a set of tools to judge the hardness of a mineral. The tools include a piece of glass, a fingernail, a steel nail, and a piece of copper. **Predict** which of these items will be the hardest. Then scratch each tool with the others to rank the tools from softest to hardest.

3. Try to scratch each mineral with the edge of your fingernail. Always rub your finger over a mark to make certain it's a scratch and not a streak. A streak will rub off, but a scratch won't. If your fingernail scratches the mineral, write *H < F* ("hardness is less than a fingernail") for that mineral in your chart.

SAFETY

Put on goggles. When using the glass, keep it flat on the desk. Press the mineral specimen onto the glass and pull it across the glass. DO NOT HOLD THE GLASS IN YOUR HAND.

Step 3

Step 4

4. Find out if the copper wire will scratch the minerals that your fingernail did not scratch. For those that the copper scratches, write *F* < *H* < *C* ("hardness is greater than a fingernail but less than copper").

5. Now try the steel nail on those minerals that the copper didn't scratch. If the nail scratches the mineral, write this in the chart, using an *S* for "steel": *C* < *H* < *S*.

6. Finally, try scratching the glass plate with any mineral that was not scratched by the steel. **Record** those that scratch the glass as *H* > *G* ("hardness is greater than glass").

Analyze and Conclude

1. What was the order of hardness for your hardness tools?

2. Did your predictions match your results? Which mineral did you find to be the hardest? Which was the softest? **Compare** your results with those of your classmates. Did your classmates get the same results? If not, repeat the test and compare.

INVESTIGATE FURTHER!

RESEARCH

One of the important properties of gemstones is that they are hard. After all, you wouldn't want to wear a gem if it scratched easily. Look up the hardness of diamonds, rubies, sapphires, emeralds, topaz, and garnets. How do they compare? What scale is used to compare hardness?

Activity

Minerals That Break Funny

MATERIALS
- salt
- hand lens
- mineral set
- Mineral Properties Chart
- *Science Notebook*

If you have ever broken some glass, you were proba-bly more concerned with cleaning it up than with how the glass broke. However, the way something breaks can tell us something important. Find out how minerals break.

Procedure

1. **Observe** some salt with a hand lens. Can you see the flat sides? They are called **cleavage** (klēv′ij) planes. The salt crystals always break along their cleavage planes. Pick out a large crystal and try to crush it with your pencil. How are the pieces like the original crystal? **Record** your observations in your *Science Notebook*.

Step 1

2. **Observe** some large salt crystals with a hand lens. Can you see cleavage planes inside the crystals? They often look like cracks. The cracks look as though the crystal might break along them. Sometimes you can see cleavage planes inside a crystal when you can't find them on the outside.

3. **Observe** your mineral samples. Can you find any that have flat surfaces where the mineral has broken? The surfaces are probably cleavage planes. Can you see cleavage planes inside the mineral? If you find one or more cleavage planes on a miner-al, write *yes* under *Cleavage* in your chart.

Analyze and Conclude

1. **List** the minerals that have cleavage planes.

2. **Compare** your mineral observations with those of your class-mates. Do you agree on which minerals show cleavage? **Hypothesize** why you did or did not get the same results.

Activity
Name That Mineral

MATERIALS
- mineral set
- Mineral Properties Chart
- *Science Notebook*

Now that you can recognize mineral properties, you can find out the name for each of the minerals in your mineral set.

- - - - - - - - - - - - - - - - - - -

Procedure

1. Take mineral number 1 from its pocket in the egg carton. Use your chart to review the properties of the mineral.

2. Refer to the "Properties of Minerals" table on page E19. Look at the left column. Notice that it divides the table into two sections, minerals with metallic luster and minerals with non-metallic luster. In which section of the table does your mineral belong? **Record** your observations in your *Science Notebook*.

3. Now move to the second column in the table. It is for hardness. How hard is your mineral? Find the part of the column that describes the hardness of your mineral. Remember to stay in the section for the luster of your mineral when finding the hardness.

4. Move from left to right through the columns of the table. Information about streak and cleavage is sometimes in the column labeled *Special*. You should find the name of the mineral in the right-hand column. Write its name in the last column of your chart.

5. Repeat steps 1–4 for all the other minerals in your set.

PROPERTIES OF MINERALS

Luster	Hardness	Color	Streak	Special	Name
Metallic	Harder than glass	Black	Black	magnetic	MAGNETITE
Metallic	Harder than glass	Brassy yellow	Black	"fools gold"	PYRITE
Metallic	Softer than glass	Steel gray	Red or reddish brown	may have reddish patches	HEMATITE
Metallic	Softer than steel	Brassy to gold yellow	Black	often has blue, red & purple tarnish	CHALCO-PYRITE
Metallic	Harder than a fingernail	Silver gray	Gray to black	heavy, shows cleavage	GALENA

Luster	Hardness	Color	Special	Name
Non-metallic	Harder than glass	white, pink, gray	hardness is very close	FELDSPAR
Non-metallic	Harder than glass	yes ( )		AMPHIBOLE
Non-metallic	Harder than glass	yes (2)		PYROXENE
Non-metallic	Harder than glass	no		
Non-metallic	Softer than steel	yes (6)		
Non-metallic	Softer than steel	yes (4)	purple, yellow	
Non-metallic	Softer than copper	yes (3)	white, pink	crystal faces are usually curved
Non-metallic	Softer than copper	yes (3)	colorless, white, yellow	cleavage planes make parallelograms	CALC...
Non-metallic	Softer than a fingernail	yes (3)	colorless, white	tastes salty, breaks in cubes	HALITE
Non-metallic	Softer than a fingernail	yes (1)	colorless, white	sometimes transparent	GYPSUM
Non-metallic	Softer than a fingernail	yes (1)	colorless, silvery, black	peels in thin sheets, can be green	MICA
Non-metallic	Softer than a fingernail	yes (1)	light green to white	usually flakey	TALC
Non-metallic	Softer than a fingernail	no	yellow to brown	looks like rust	LIMONITE
Non-metallic	Softer than a fingernail	no	red	earthy	HEMATITE

Analyze and Conclude

1. Were you able to find the name of each of your minerals? **Hypothesize** why you were or were not able to find all of the minerals' names.

2. How are properties useful in identifying minerals?

Mineral Properties

Did you know that the "brain" of a computer, called a computer chip, is made from a mineral found in beach sand? A **mineral** is a solid element or compound from Earth's crust that has a definite chemical composition and crystal shape. Minerals can look very different from one another—colorless like quartz, silver or red like hematite, or shiny like gold and silver—but we find ways to use them all.

Look around and you'll see minerals being used. People may be wearing jewelry made of a gemstone like a ruby, an emerald, or an opal. The walls in your home are probably made of wallboard, which is gypsum sandwiched between layers of paper. The windows in your classroom are made from quartz. The body powder you use may be made from the mineral talc. When you talk to a friend on the telephone, copper wires transmit your voice. Your lunch may be wrapped in aluminum foil, made from the mineral bauxite. Perhaps you can think of other minerals you use every day. How many are there?

Why are minerals used in so many ways? They have different properties that make them right for many different uses. These same properties help scientists tell minerals apart, just as they helped you in the activities. What are some of the properties of minerals you examined in the activities?

baby powder

USED IN HOSPITALS

WT 9 OZ (255g)

▲ The mineral gypsum is used to make wallboard, or drywall.

▲ Talc is a mineral that you may sprinkle on your skin after a shower.

▲ A mineral's luster is a clue to its identity. Silver, at left, has a metallic luster. Fluorite, right, has a nonmetallic luster.

Luster

Luster is one property that can be used to classify minerals. **Luster** refers to the way light reflects from the surface of a mineral. Look at the graphite in your pencil or at a piece of silver or gold jewelry. The shiny appearance of these minerals is called metallic luster. Any mineral that reflects light like polished metal has a metallic luster. All other minerals have nonmetallic luster. Minerals that have nonmetallic luster vary in the way they look. For example, the luster of a nonmetallic mineral may be dull like cinnabar, pearly like mica, or glassy and brilliant like diamond.

Hardness

A mineral's **hardness** is a measure of how easily it can be scratched. Talc is the softest mineral. It can be scratched by all other minerals. Diamond is the hardest mineral. It can scratch the surface of any other mineral, but no other mineral can scratch a diamond.

You can estimate a mineral's hardness by using Mohs' scale, shown in the table below. This scale lists the hardness of

MOHS' SCALE OF MINERAL HARDNESS		
Mineral	**Hardness**	**Simple Test**
Talc	1	easily scratched by fingernail
Gypsum	2	scratched by fingernail
Calcite	3	barely scratched by copper
Fluorite	4	easily scratched by steel knife
Apatite	5	scratched by steel knife
Orthoclase feldspar	6	scratches glass with difficulty
Quartz	7	scratches glass and steel
Topaz	8	scratches quartz
Corundum	9	no simple test
Diamond	10	no simple test

ten common minerals. To test a mineral for hardness, find out which mineral on the scale is the hardest one that your mineral scratches. For example, a mineral that can scratch calcite but can't scratch fluorite has a hardness between 3 and 4. Also, just as you did in the activity on page E8, you can use your fingernail, copper, steel, glass, and the simple scratching tests listed in Mohs' scale to estimate hardness. What would be the hardness of a mineral that can be scratched by copper but not a fingernail?

Hardness is caused by the arrangement of matter in a mineral. For example, both diamond and graphite consist only of carbon. One arrangement produces the hardest natural mineral (diamond), and the other arrangement produces one of the softest minerals (graphite).

Color

Another mineral property is color. The elements making up a mineral determine its color. For example, chromium gives ruby its unusual red color. Although color is the easiest mineral property to observe, it's not the most reliable for identifying minerals. Many different minerals have similar colors. Some minerals vary in color due to the presence of tiny quantities of other substances. Pure quartz is colorless, but traces of other substances can make it become white, pink, or purple.

Streak

Most minerals aren't as hard as a ceramic tile. When you scratch a mineral against a tile called a streak plate,

SCIENCE IN LITERATURE

ROCKS, MINERALS AND FOSSILS
by Keith Lye
Silver Burdett Press, 1991

Read about fool's gold and true gold on page 25 of *Rocks, Minerals and Fossils* by Keith Lye. Make a table to summarize all the tests that can be done to tell these two minerals apart. Make sure you include the expected results of each test.

When you're done, browse through this colorful reference book. You'll find it's easy to locate information that interests you by looking at the pictures, reading the large titles, or using the index. For example, if you're not sure what makes a mineral different from a rock, look on page 13. There's a photo of a rock, called granite, and the four kinds of minerals that make it up.

some minerals crumble off as a powder. The color of this powder is the mineral property called **streak**.

The streak of most minerals is either colorless or the same color as the mineral. However, for a few minerals, the color of the mineral and the color of the streak aren't the same. For example, if you scratch silver-colored hematite on a streak plate, you find its streak is red! Apatite is a dark mineral with a white streak. Pyrite is brassy yellow and leaves a greenish-black streak. Which of the minerals that you tested had a colored streak?

▲ **A mineral's streak may be different from its color.**

Cleavage

Some minerals split easily along flat surfaces, a property called **cleavage**. If you have ever handled mica, you know how easily it splits apart. Mica breaks along cleavage surfaces that are all in the same direction. Some minerals have cleavage surfaces in more than one direction. The salt you observed in the activity on page E10 is the mineral halite. Its cube shape occurs because halite splits along cleavage surfaces in three directions.

You may think that gemstones break naturally along several cleavage surfaces. But most gemstones do not break along cleavage surfaces. Therefore, gem cut-

▲ Calcite can be cleaved in three directions, or planes.

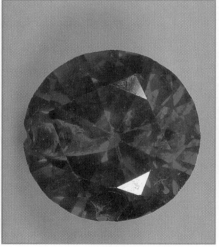

▲ Rubies, like many other gemstones, have no cleavage.

▲ Mica cleaves along one plane, and peels in thin sections.

ters must grind the gems to create the flat, shiny faces, called facets, that give gems their different shapes.

Using Mineral Properties

How are mineral properties useful? If you were a gold miner, using the properties you just learned about might make you a fortune! You would need mineral properties to tell gold from other minerals you find.

Compare the samples of gold and pyrite shown. At first glance they may seem alike. Notice that they both have a brassy yellow color. They both also have a metallic luster, and neither mineral has cleavage.

Pyrite is known as fool's gold. Based on color, luster, and cleavage alone, you might easily mistake pyrite for gold. A smart gold miner would also compare the minerals' hardness and streak. Pyrite has a hardness of about 6 and gold has a hardness of about 3. Pyrite leaves a greenish-black streak; gold's streak is golden-yellow. Gold has a greater value than pyrite, so it pays to be able to tell them apart. ■

▲ Pyrite, shown here, has some properties similar to those of gold.

▲ Gold, shown here, is softer than pyrite and has a different streak.

UNIT PROJECT LINK

Start a collection of minerals. There are many ways to get mineral samples. You could join a mineral club. There may be some adults in your community who are collectors and would be happy to help you. You could write to students in schools in other parts of the country and trade minerals through the mail. Or you could go out and collect local mineral samples from road cuts and streambeds. To determine the name of any unknown minerals in your collection, see the activity on page E11.

Identifying Minerals

A key is an organizer designed to help you identify things. The table on page E19, "Properties of Minerals," is a key designed to help you identify minerals. To identify an unknown mineral, match the properties you observe in your sample with the properties listed in the table.

Let's try an example. Say you are given the unknown mineral shown below. What is it?

Using the Table: Nonmetallic Minerals

Step 1. Luster
Is it metallic or nonmetallic?

What kind of luster does your mineral have? It doesn't look like polished metal, so it's nonmetallic. Find in the table the column labeled *Luster*, and locate all the nonmetallic minerals.

Step 2. Hardness
What scratches it?

If you had your mineral sample in front of you, you would use the materials from the activity on page E8 to test for hardness. The sample can be scratched with a fingernail. Locate this under the column labeled *Hardness*. Notice that there are only six minerals in the table that are both nonmetallic and softer than a fingernail. Your sample must be one of those six.

Step 3. Cleavage
Is there any? In how many directions?

You can see that your sample does have cleavage in one direction. You can

STEP 1

STEP 2

STEP 3

E17

rule out any of the six minerals that don't have one direction of cleavage.

Step 4. Color
What is it?

Observe that your sample is colorless. Look under the column labeled *Color* and notice that two minerals fit the bill: mica and gypsum. Which is it?

Step 5. Special Properties
Are there any?

Find the *Special* column. Since your sample peels easily in thin sheets, as is listed for mica, it must be mica. How might the procedure vary for a metallic mineral? Let's try it for the sample shown.

Using the Table: Metallic Minerals
Step 1. Luster
Is it metallic or nonmetallic?

Notice that the sample looks like polished metal. You can rule out all nonmetallic minerals, so cover the part of the table that shows nonmetallic minerals.

Step 2. Hardness
What scratches it?

If you could test it, you'd find that your sample can scratch glass. Look in the table to see which metallic minerals are harder than glass. Notice that there are only two minerals with this property: magnetite and pyrite.

Step 3. Color
What is it?

Observe that your sample is black. Look under the column labeled *Color* and notice that pyrite is brassy yellow. Your mineral must be magnetite. But to make sure, check its other properties.

Step 4. Streak
What is it?

If you could scratch your sample along a streak plate, you would see that its streak is black. This agrees with the data in the table under the column labeled *Streak*.

Step 5. Special Properties:
Are there any?

If you had a magnet, you would see that your sample is attracted to it. You can use this property and others in the table to confirm that your unknown sample is indeed magnetite. ■

STEP 1

STEP 4

STEP 5

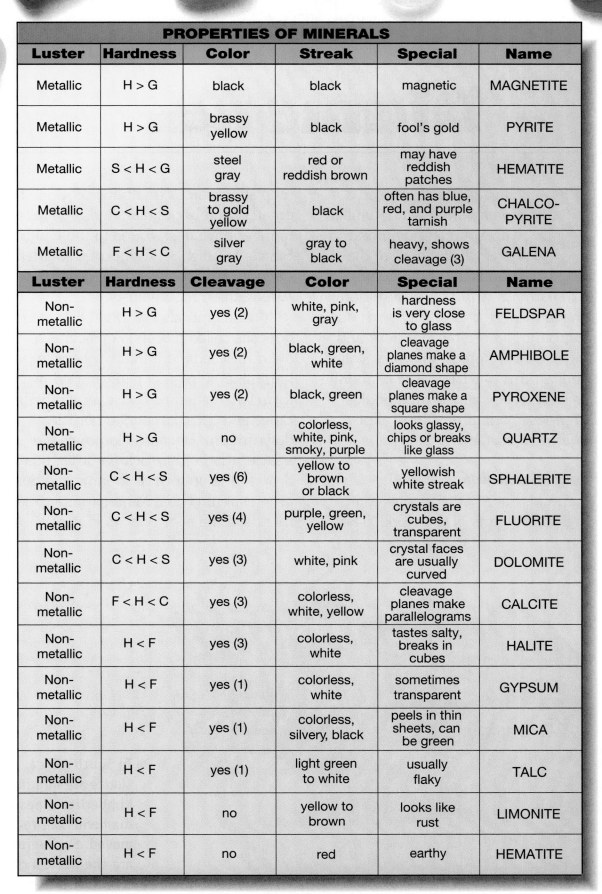

PROPERTIES OF MINERALS

Luster	Hardness	Color	Streak	Special	Name
Metallic	H > G	black	black	magnetic	MAGNETITE
Metallic	H > G	brassy yellow	black	fool's gold	PYRITE
Metallic	S < H < G	steel gray	red or reddish brown	may have reddish patches	HEMATITE
Metallic	C < H < S	brassy to gold yellow	black	often has blue, red, and purple tarnish	CHALCO-PYRITE
Metallic	F < H < C	silver gray	gray to black	heavy, shows cleavage (3)	GALENA

Luster	Hardness	Cleavage	Color	Special	Name
Non-metallic	H > G	yes (2)	white, pink, gray	hardness is very close to glass	FELDSPAR
Non-metallic	H > G	yes (2)	black, green, white	cleavage planes make a diamond shape	AMPHIBOLE
Non-metallic	H > G	yes (2)	black, green	cleavage planes make a square shape	PYROXENE
Non-metallic	H > G	no	colorless, white, pink, smoky, purple	looks glassy, chips or breaks like glass	QUARTZ
Non-metallic	C < H < S	yes (6)	yellow to brown or black	yellowish white streak	SPHALERITE
Non-metallic	C < H < S	yes (4)	purple, green, yellow	crystals are cubes, transparent	FLUORITE
Non-metallic	C < H < S	yes (3)	white, pink	crystal faces are usually curved	DOLOMITE
Non-metallic	F < H < C	yes (3)	colorless, white, yellow	cleavage planes make parallelograms	CALCITE
Non-metallic	H < F	yes (3)	colorless, white	tastes salty, breaks in cubes	HALITE
Non-metallic	H < F	yes (1)	colorless, white	sometimes transparent	GYPSUM
Non-metallic	H < F	yes (1)	colorless, silvery, black	peels in thin sheets, can be green	MICA
Non-metallic	H < F	yes (1)	light green to white	usually flaky	TALC
Non-metallic	H < F	no	yellow to brown	looks like rust	LIMONITE
Non-metallic	H < F	no	red	earthy	HEMATITE

*Numbers in parentheses give number of cleavage planes.

Key: H—hardness; G—glass; S—steel; C—copper; F—fingernail; <—less than; >—greater than.

Diamonds

Have you ever passed a jewelry store window filled with sparkling diamond rings? Just what are diamonds and how do we get them? Diamond is the hardest mineral. It is made of pure carbon. It forms deep underground, where temperature and pressure are very great, in a rock called kimberlite (kim'bər līt). Most kimberlite forms long, tube-shaped rock bodies called pipes. Sometimes these pipes reach Earth's surface.

Mining Diamonds

Diamonds have been discovered in many different parts of the world. The map shows areas that have provided the greatest number of diamonds. A limited number have been found in the United States, in northern California, southern Oregon, Arkansas, and the eastern Appalachian Mountains.

Most diamonds are found in stream deposits called placers. A placer is a deposit of sediment that contains important mineral fragments. Diamond placers form when streams flow over kimberlite pipes and carry kimberlite particles downstream. Because diamonds are heavier than other rock particles, they drop to the bottom of streams and build up on stream beds. Miners remove diamonds in the same way gold is panned.

◀ In South Africa, mine shafts are dug into kimberlite pipes and diamonds are removed. Such mines are the world's richest sources of diamonds.

Diamonds are also mined directly from kimberlite. This is done by digging either surface pits or deep underground mine shafts. Once removed from the ground, the kimberlite is crushed and the rock is washed away, leaving behind only the harder diamonds. Any remaining traces of kimberlite are separated and removed by machines.

After mining, diamonds are sorted according to quality. Only two out of every ten diamonds are of good enough quality to be made into jewels. The rest are cut up for other uses, like making abrasives, glass cutters, rock drill bits, and telecommunication products. The better-quality diamonds are then sorted, or graded, according to their color, size, and purity.

A Cut Above

After grading, diamonds are sent to a gem cutter. Gem-quality diamonds are cut because doing so shows off their brilliant nonmetallic luster. Next, the diamond is shaped. Finally, it is polished by holding it at an angle to a spinning disk coated with diamond dust. This step creates the sparkling facets, or faces, highly prized in gemstones. ■

▲ Raw diamonds are often found in kimberlite.

▲ Gem cutters cut and polish selected diamonds.

▲ Finished diamonds are sold around the world.

INVESTIGATION 1

1. Describe how you would use mineral properties to distinguish quartz from calcite.

2. When trying to identify an unknown mineral, list all the questions you would need to ask and answer about that mineral.

WHAT ARE MINERALS USED FOR?

Look around at your classmates. How many are wearing jewelry? You know that minerals are used to make much of that jewelry. Try to name as many minerals (think in terms of gems and metals) used in jewelry as you can. Can you think of other uses for minerals?

Activity

Growing Crystals

Mineral crystals are used in jewelry and in electronics. Some of these crystals are grown in laboratories. In this activity you can grow your own crystals!

Procedure

1. Fill a 500-mL jar with hot water from the tap. Dissolve as much alum as possible in the water (about 100 grams, or 3–4 oz). Cap the jar and let it stand overnight.

2. Pour a small amount of the solution from the jar into the bottom of a bowl and let it stand overnight. The next morning you should find some small crystals in the bowl. Use the spoon to remove one or two good crystals and pour the solution back into the jar.

3. Tie one of the crystals to the end of a piece of thread. Suspend the crystal in the baby-food jar.

4. Nearly fill the baby-food jar with solution from the large jar. Be careful not to pour any crystals into the baby-food jar. Tent a piece of paper over the jar to keep dust out. **Predict** about how much the crystal will grow each day.

MATERIALS

- goggles
- gloves
- glass jar, 500 mL, with cap
- hot tap water
- alum
- shallow bowl
- plastic spoon
- polyester thread
- large baby-food jar
- sheet of paper
- scissors
- metric ruler
- *Science Notebook*

SAFETY

Wear goggles and gloves at all times. Be sure to wash your hands after handling the alum.

5. Observe your crystal growing. It may take a few days. Each day, estimate the size of the crystal. If the level of solution in the jar goes down, add more. When the crystal stops growing, remove it from the solution and draw a picture of it in your *Science Notebook*.

Step 3

Analyze and Conclude

1. About how large was the crystal when you started?

2. How large was the crystal when you stopped growing it?

3. How many days did the crystal grow?

4. Did your crystal grow by the same amount each day? Describe your evidence.

5. Think of ways people use crystals. Infer why scientists might want to grow crystals in a laboratory.

INVESTIGATE FURTHER!

EXPERIMENT

You can grow crystals from other substances. Instead of alum, try sugar, Epsom salts, or rock salt. Compare the shape of the crystals and how easy they were to grow.

Quartz
A Versatile Mineral

If you've ever been to a beach or seen pictures of one, you know that beaches are made of sand. The words *sand* and *gravel* really refer to the size of a grain of mineral or rock, sand particles being smaller than gravel. Any rock or mineral can be broken into sand-sized or gravel-sized pieces.

The most common sand in the world is quartz sand. Quartz is also one of the most important minerals. It is made of only two elements, silicon and oxygen. The colors and names of common types of quartz include clear (rock crystal), pink (rose), white (milky), and gray (smoky). Some forms of quartz are semiprecious gemstones such as amethyst, tiger-eye, and citrine.

Native Americans used one form, flint, for tools such as arrowheads.

Building With Quartz

Quartz plays an important role in the building industry. Many building materials are made of rocks and minerals. **Concrete**, for example, is a rock material made of sand and gravel and a binder. The binder, called portland cement, is made by grinding limestone and shale, two kinds of rock, into a powder. This powder is baked at high temperature until it forms balls called clinker. Cooled clinker is crushed to a powder and mixed with gypsum, another mineral. This mixture is then mixed with quartz-rich sand, gravel, and water and allowed to harden to form concrete. How have you seen concrete used in your neighborhood?

From left to right: clear quartz, rose quartz, milky quartz, smoky quartz ▶

▲ Concrete, a building material, is made with quartz and other minerals.

▲ Without quartz, there would not be glass.

Seeing With Quartz

Quartz is also used to make glass. By ancient times, people in the Middle East had a good understanding of quartz and its properties. Glassmaking probably began about 4,000 years ago in Egypt or Mesopotamia. Today the art of glass-making is a worldwide industry.

Glass is easy to make if you have the proper tools. Powdered quartz is mixed with powdered limestone and soda (not the kind you drink, but a solid substance called sodium carbonate). The mixture is heated to about 1,600°C (2,912°F). At this temperature it melts. Then it is cooled quickly so that crystals cannot form. Crystals would make objects seen through the glass look wavy and deformed. Very old glass looks wavy because it has begun to crystallize. Look around you. How many ways can you see glass being used?

The Computer Mineral

Quartz can be separated into its two parts, silicon and oxygen. From the silicon, crystals can be grown (much as you did in the activity on pages E22 and 23) and later cut into thin pieces. These pieces of pure silicon are used in

◀ Quartz, a compound of silicon and oxygen, is one of the most abundant minerals in Earth's crust.

The brain of every desktop computer (*left*) is a silicon chip. Many chips, each the size of a fingernail, are obtained from silicon wafers (*center*). Each chip is etched with the electronic circuits (*right*) that carry out the calculations that make computers such time-savers.

the electronics industry, which is a major part of the world's economy. Computer chips, which are the brains of our computers, and solar cells, which power solar calculators, are made with silicon.

Perhaps the most amazing thing about quartz crystals is that they generate electricity. If the crystals are squeezed, they bend slightly and produce electricity. In addition, when a small electrical current is put through a crystal, it vibrates. The vibrations are very regular, making quartz crystals ideal for keeping time. Tiny quartz crystals are used to keep time in many types of watches.

Maybe you thought quartz was something you walked on as you viewed the ocean. But a world without window glass, portable electronic games, radios, CD players, computers, or concrete would be hard to imagine! ■

◀ You may be carrying a quartz crystal on your wrist. In watches with a quartz crystal, the crystal's vibrations keep time more accurately than those watches that use a spring to keep time.

How Iron Becomes Steel

In Arizona, there is a huge hole in the ground known as the Barringer Meteorite Crater. Scientists hypothesize the crater formed about 25,000 years ago when an 18-m (59-ft) wide chunk of iron from space collided with Earth. The chunk of iron from space shows that iron isn't found only on Earth. It's all over the universe! Maybe it should be called the universal metal!

Iron occurs in minerals. Magnetite and hematite are important iron-containing minerals. Minerals from which metals can be removed are called **ores**. An iron ore is made up of iron and other elements.

The most widespread source of iron is hematite, an ore made up of iron and oxygen. Over 2 billion years ago, hematite layers began to build up in the oceans. Over time the hematite was covered by layers of sediment. Later, parts of the ocean bottom were slowly lifted up to the surface, and the iron deposits eventually became exposed. That was the easy part! For us, the hard part is getting the iron ores out of the ground and the iron out of the ores.

Iron ore is mined all over the planet. In the United States, most of the iron we use comes from hematite mined in Canada and South America. Magnetite

Iron is used to make many different products such as the blades of skates (*left*), the rails of roller coasters (*center*), and the hulls of ships (*right*).

is not as easy to find as hematite, but it's a purer source of iron. The world's largest magnetite mine is in Sweden. Others are located in Wyoming, New York, Utah, South Africa, Austria, Italy, and Russia.

The process of removing metal from ore is called **smelting**. The first smelting of metal may have occurred about 9,000 years ago. Around 3,500 years ago, iron smelting became widespread. Iron was often used in making cooking tools and weapons. Because the intro-duction of iron affected cultures so greatly, that period of time was called the Iron Age. The diagram shows how pig iron is made.

1 To smelt iron, iron ore is mixed with a kind of coal called coke. Crushed limestone is added to the mixture.

2 The mixture is heated in a 10-story-high oven called a blast furnace. Coke burns very hot, so it provides the high temperatures needed to melt the ore. The limestone mixes with unwanted materials to form a waste product called slag.

3 The melted mixture works its way down through the blast furnace, getting hotter as it sinks.

4 Wastes that are less dense separate and float on the molten metal. This slag is drained off.

5 The remaining melted iron, called pig iron, is drained from the bottom of the blast furnace.

▲ **Pig iron is remelted and mixed with a small amount of iron, making steel.**

Because of impurities such as carbon present in pig iron, it is too brittle to be used for purposes requiring great strength. Instead it is remelted and poured into molds. Iron made in this way is called cast iron. Cast iron is used to make bells, wood stoves, bathtubs, railings, and other products.

Pig iron can also be remelted and converted into steel. In a furnace, melted pig iron is brought to a high temperature. Air is blown over the iron to increase the heat and remove excess carbon. When the metal is free of carbon, a measured amount of carbon is mixed in. It may seem strange that carbon is removed only to be added again, but an exact amount of carbon is needed to make useful steel. Too much carbon makes the steel brittle and too little makes it weak.

▲ **Steel can be produced in a variety of forms, including rolled sheets.**

Steel can be rolled into sheets or made into bars, blocks, and other shapes. It can be made as sharp as a razor or as blunt as a hammer. Other metals can be added to steel to make alloys, or mixtures of metals. For example, chromium is added to make steel resist rusting. Nickel is added to make steel stronger. Titanium makes steel more resistant to heat. Tungsten makes steel strong at high temperatures.

How did you get to school today? If you came by public transportation, car, or bike, steel helped you. What other uses for steel can you think of? ■

▲ **The liquid steel is poured into molds and allowed to cool.**

A World of Minerals

Mineral resources are in the ground all over the world. But they are not distributed evenly. As the map shows, some countries have more mineral resources than do others.

A country can mine its resources and use them to make products. The country can then sell some of its raw resources and products to other countries. The selling countries are called producers. Countries with few mineral resources must buy many resources or products. These buying countries are consumers. Consumers often buy raw resources to make products. If they sell these products to producers, the producers may actually be buying back their raw resources in a new form.

Worldwide Metal Resources

◆ TIN
○ BAUXITE
✖ LEAD & ZINC
◖ GOLD
△ SILVER
★ COPPER
■ IRON

Production (in millions of tons)

| 0 | 10 | 20 | 30 | 40 | 500 | 600 |

Copper 7.7

Aluminum 18

Zinc 6.2

Iron 600

Lead 3.8

▲ **Worldwide yearly production of selected metals**

For example, raw iron ore may be shipped from the United States to Japan. A Japanese company turns the ore into iron, the iron into steel, and the steel into bike frames. Some frames are sold in Japan and some are sold in other parts of the world, including the United States.

Minerals and mineral products are an important part of the world trading market. There are few places on Earth where iron or steel isn't used in some way. Aluminum is important to canning and cooking industries. Silver is valued for jewelry. What other ways are mineral resources used in the world?

Why Waste?

The uses of mineral resources are unlimited. The amount of mineral resources is not. Although most mineral resources are fairly abundant, finding new sources is getting more difficult. And mineral resources are being used up fast. Your old tricycle may be buried in the middle of a landfill right now. Cars sit rusting in junkyards and on roadsides. Aluminum cans float on ocean waves where they were thrown. Usable mercury gets thrown away inside dead dry-cell batteries. These items are not really gone from our environment. They're still here but they're scattered, making it almost impossible for them to be recovered and reused.

Recycling Mineral Resources

Many communities in the United States have laws stating that certain

▲ **Much of Earth's mineral wealth ends up in places like this.**

▲ The recycling of minerals helps keep their cost down.

items must be recycled. In addition to nonmineral products like paper and plastic, metals such as copper, steel, brass, and aluminum are being recycled. Recycling doesn't totally solve the problem of using up a mineral resource, but it does extend our use of such resources.

Many people on the planet still don't recycle, so we slowly but surely lose valuable mineral resources. As a resource becomes scarce, its price rises. Eventually a new resource must be used in its place. Could the same cycle be repeated with the new resource?

World Issues

The way that mineral resources are handled in one country can affect many other countries. Look at the map on page E30 and the bar graph on page E31 and discuss answers to the following questions with your classmates.

Which two metals are produced in the largest quantity? Do you think the U.S. has to import such resources? What happens when a nation doesn't have enough raw resources or money to trade evenly? What happens when countries are in competition for a product in limited supply? What happens if a country holds back on selling raw resources or products needed by other countries of the world? ■

INVESTIGATE FURTHER!

TAKE ACTION

Write to a local recycling center to find out which minerals can be recycled in your community. Then organize a recycling drive of those materials.

INVESTIGATION 2

1. Name six products made from minerals and at least one mineral used to make each product.

2. If you were building a house, list the materials made from minerals that you would use and explain why you would use them.

REFLECT & EVALUATE

On Your Own

Review the terms in the list. Then use as many terms as you can to write a brief summary of the chapter.

With a Partner

Make up a quiz using all the terms in the list. Challenge your partner to complete the quiz.

BUILD YOUR PORTFOLIO

Make an illustrated chart that shows minerals and products made from those minerals.

Analyze Information

Observe the properties of the mineral sample shown. This mineral's streak is gray to black. The mineral cannot be scratched with a finger-nail but can be scratched by glass. Use the "Properties of Minerals" table on page E19 to identify this mineral.

Assess Performance

Obtain one or more samples of minerals from your teacher. Perform the tests needed to iden-tify your samples. Refer to the "Properties of Minerals" table as you collect your data.

Problem Solving

1. You are about to take a mineral-collecting field trip. You plan to identify all the minerals you collect. List the materials you will need to take with you and explain what mineral property each material will be used to identify.

2. Compare the importance of quartz and iron to modern civilizations.

3. What might happen if, from now on, all min-eral resources found and used were recycled?

CHAPTER 2

ROCKS

Rocks are made of minerals, and you find rocks of all kinds and sizes everywhere! They range from the sandstone pebble in a city park to the gigantic granite face of a cliff. Most rocks appear sturdy and unchanging. Actually, however, natural processes are constantly changing rocks. People too can transform rocks.

On the Cutting Edge

Edward Torres of Seaside Heights, New Jersey, is a stonecutter. He skillfully turns sheets of white, black, beige, red, or green marble into custom-made items. He crafts such things as fireplace mantels and counter tops.

A typical job for Torres begins when his material is delivered. A 5-ft by 8-ft sheet of 3/4 in.-thick marble, weighing 600 lb, is gently deposited onto his worktable by a forklift! Torres then uses a circular, diamond-toothed, wet saw to precisely cut the hard stone to the proper measurements. (Water cools the saw blade.) The fully processed piece, completed and polished, is a beautiful and useful item.

What *natural* processes change some materials into marble, or into other kinds of rocks, in the first place? What properties distinguish one kind of rock from another? In this chapter you'll explore these and other questions.

Coming Up

◀ Edward Torres, Stonecutter

HOW ARE ROCKS CLASSIFIED?

Rocks are the "stuff" that makes up Earth. About 4 billion years ago, Earth was a molten ball of rock. Although some of Earth's rock is still molten, the rock in the outer layer is solid. You live on this rocky ball. In this investigation you'll find out how rocks are identified and classified.

Activity

Sort of Rocky

Rocks are made of minerals. Some rocks are made of only one mineral, but most rocks are made of more than one. In this activity you'll observe some properties of rocks and use those properties to classify the rocks.

MATERIALS
- paper punchouts
- marker
- white glue
- set of rocks
- hand lens
- egg carton
- *Science Notebook*

Procedure

1. Number paper punchouts from 1 to 12. With white glue, glue one punchout on each rock specimen.

2. Put all the rocks together on your desktop. Compare the rocks to one another and separate them into a dark-colored set and a light-colored set. In your *Science Notebook*, record the numbers for each set.

3. Mineral crystals in rocks are usually very small. They are shiny and have flat faces that look like tiny mirrors. Place all the rocks together, observe the rocks with a hand lens, and separate the rocks into a set with crystals and a set without crystals. **Record** the numbers for each set.

4. Use the hand lens to study the rocks again, separating the rocks into two new sets: one set in which the rocks appear to be made of more than one mineral and the other in which the rocks appear to contain only one mineral. **Record** the numbers for each set.

5. Separate the rocks with one mineral into two sets: rocks with crystals and rocks without crystals. Do the same for rocks with more than one mineral. **Record** your results.

6. Now **classify** each of the four sets from steps 4 and 5 into sets that contain dark-colored rocks and light-colored rocks. Then use the egg carton to store your rock specimens.

Analyze and Conclude

1. How many sets now contain only one rock?

2. List the properties that you used in this activity to classify rocks. **Infer** how these properties are used to classify rocks.

Activity
The Rock Key

A key is used in science to help identify something. The Rock Key will help you use the properties of rocks to find out their names.

MATERIALS

- goggles
- rock set
- square glass plate
- hand lens
- *Science Notebook*

SAFETY

Wear goggles during this activity. When using the glass plate, hold it firmly on the table. Press a point of the rock against the plate and pull the rock toward you. DO NOT HOLD THE GLASS PLATE IN YOUR HAND.

Procedure

1. Choose a rock specimen. Look at the descriptions at the left side of the Rock Key. Which description matches your rock? Does it have crystals? If it does, follow the line from "Rock has crystals" to the next level in the key. If it does not have crystals, follow the other line.

2. At most levels in the key, two choices are given. Match a choice to your rock and follow the line to your next observation and choice. Eventually, you will arrive at the name of your rock on the right side of the key. Be sure to follow the lines in the key; don't skip around.

3. If you need to find out whether the rock is hard or soft, test the hardness against glass, the same as you did with minerals. Hard rocks scratch glass; soft ones do not.

4. If you need to find out if a rock with crystals is coarse-grained, medium-grained, or fine-grained, look at the size of crystals. In a coarse-grained rock, most of the rock is made of crystals larger than a grain of rice. In a fine-grained rock, you need a hand lens to see crystals. In a medium-grained rock, you can see the crystals without a hand lens, but they are smaller than rice grains.

Steps 3 & 4

Analyze and Conclude

1. Use the Rock Key to identify each of your rocks. For each rock, **record** in your *Science Notebook* the rock's number, its properties, and its name.

2. Which rocks did you find hard to identify? **Make an inference** about what additional data would have helped you identify them more easily.

THE ROCK KEY

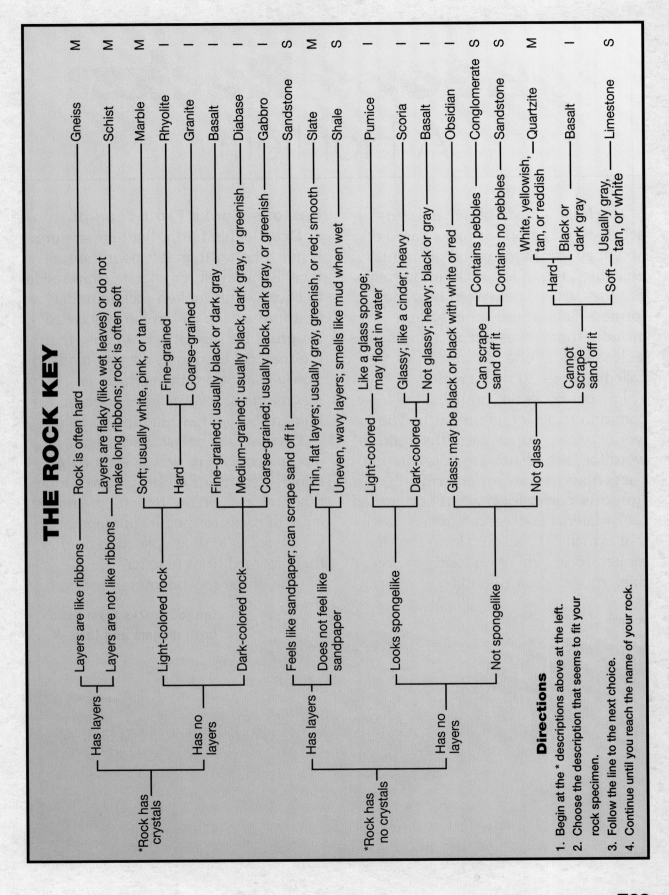

Rock has crystals
- Has layers
  - Layers are like ribbons — Rock is often hard — Gneiss — M
  - Layers are not like ribbons — Layers are flaky (like wet leaves) or do not make long ribbons; rock is often soft — Schist — M
- Has no layers
  - Light-colored rock
    - Soft; usually white, pink, or tan — Marble — M
    - Hard
      - Fine-grained — Rhyolite — I
      - Coarse-grained — Granite — I
  - Dark-colored rock
    - Fine-grained; usually black or dark gray — Basalt — I
    - Medium-grained; usually black, dark gray, or greenish — Diabase — I
    - Coarse-grained; usually black, dark gray, or greenish — Gabbro — I

Rock has no crystals
- Has layers
  - Feels like sandpaper; can scrape sand off it — Sandstone — S
  - Does not feel like sandpaper
    - Thin, flat layers; usually gray, greenish, or red; smooth — Slate — M
    - Uneven, wavy layers; smells like mud when wet — Shale — S
- Has no layers
  - Looks spongelike
    - Light-colored — Like a glass sponge; may float in water — Pumice — I
    - Dark-colored
      - Glassy; like a cinder; heavy — Scoria — I
      - Not glassy; heavy; black or gray — Basalt — I
  - Not spongelike
    - Glass; may be black or black with white or red — Obsidian — I
    - Not glass
      - Can scrape sand off it
        - Contains pebbles — Conglomerate — S
        - Contains no pebbles — Sandstone — S
      - Cannot scrape sand off it
        - Hard
          - White, yellowish, tan, or reddish — Quartzite — M
          - Black or dark gray — Basalt — I
        - Soft — Usually gray, tan, or white — Limestone — S

Directions

1. Begin at the * descriptions above at the left.
2. Choose the description that seems to fit your rock specimen.
3. Follow the line to the next choice.
4. Continue until you reach the name of your rock.

Igneous Rocks:
A Hot Item

Rocks are made of minerals. In the activities, you grouped rocks based on how they were similar and different. Scientists, too, place rocks into groups. But they group them as to how they formed. This classification system includes three types of rocks. Let's take a close look at one of those types, called igneous (ig'nē əs) rocks.

Igneous rocks are probably the most common rocks found on Earth. The word *igneous* comes from the Latin word for "fire." Knowing this, can you guess how igneous rocks form? **Igneous rocks** form when hot, melted rock material cools and hardens. Rock that is melted to a liquid form is called molten rock. Where on Earth do you think molten rock is found?

Igneous Rocks From Magma

Deep within Earth, the temperature is much hotter than it is near the surface. Rocks melt, or change from solids to liquids. This molten rock material that forms deep within Earth is called **magma**. Because it is less dense than the material around it, magma tends to slowly rise toward the surface. As magma rises, it sometimes cools and hardens before reaching the surface.

Because it is below the surface, magma cools very slowly. As it cools, mineral grains, or crystals, have a long time to form. So the mineral grains are large in rocks formed from magma. Which rocks in your collection do you think formed from magma?

One of the most common rocks

volcano

lava

magma

Igneous rocks form from both magma and lava. ▼

formed from magma is granite, which is shown below. Notice that it consists of different minerals. The pink-colored and gray-colored mineral is feldspar, the white mineral is quartz, and the black mineral is mica. Notice the size of the mineral grains that make up granite. Have you seen granite in use around your community? If so, how was this rock used?

Stone Mountain, which towers high above the surrounding land in the state of Georgia, is a mountain of granite. Where did this rock harden? How do you think this rock became exposed at Earth's surface?

Not all the igneous rocks that harden from magma are the same. They vary in the kinds of mineral grains that form. The kinds of minerals that form depend on the composition of the magma.

Gabbro is another kind of igneous rock. Like all rocks that cool from magma, it has large mineral grains. But notice that gabbro is mostly made of dark-colored minerals, in this case pyroxene (pī räks'ēn) and olivine. It has few light-colored minerals, such as quartz.

▲ **Stone Mountain in Georgia**

Igneous Rocks From Lava

You know that magma rises toward Earth's surface. What do you think might happen when it breaks through to the surface? Magma that reaches Earth's surface is called **lava**. Look back at the diagram showing lava and magma on page E40. An opening in Earth's surface through which lava flows is called a volcano. When lava cools and hardens at Earth's surface, it also forms igneous rock.

Three kinds of rocks that formed from lava are shown on page E42. Compare them with the photograph of granite. How do the sizes of the mineral grains compare? Use what you have learned about igneous rocks to explain why the grains differ in size.

▼ **Granite**

Gabbro ▶

▲ **Basalt**

▲ **Obsidian**

Rhyolite ▶

Basalt is an igneous rock that forms when lava rich in dark-colored minerals cools and hardens. Find *basalt* on the chart below and note that its composition is similar to that of gabbro. Because it flows out onto Earth's surface, lava cools faster than magma. So rocks cooled from lava, such as basalt, have smaller grains than rocks cooled from magma, such as gabbro. Large areas of the states of Washington and Oregon are covered by basalt, because of past volcanic activity.

Obsidian (əb sid'ē ən) is another igneous rock, often called natural glass. Lava that forms obsidian cools and hardens so quickly that mineral grains have very little time to grow. This rapid cooling gives the rock its glassy look.

Native Americans once used obsidian to make cutting tools such as blades, because obsidian forms sharp edges when broken.

Look at the photograph of the igneous rock rhyolite (rī'ə līt). Find it on the chart. How do you think rhyolite forms? ■

	Contains more light-colored minerals	**COMPOSITION**	Contains more dark-colored minerals
LARGE mineral grains: forms from MAGMA	**Granite**		**Gabbro**
SMALL mineral grains: forms from LAVA	**Rhyolite**		**Basalt**
NO mineral grains: forms from LAVA	**Obsidian**		

INVESTIGATE FURTHER!

EXPERIMENT

Work with a partner to make a model that shows how igneous rocks form. Make "magma" by dissolving as much salt or sugar as possible in very little hot water. Cool half the magma very slowly at room temperature. Cool the other half quickly in a refrigerator. Which magma produced larger "minerals"? Why?

Sedimentary Rocks:
Rocks From Pieces

Sedimentary (sed ə men'tər ē) **rocks** are rocks that form at Earth's surface when sediments harden into rock. **Sediments** include bits of existing rocks, minerals, and organic materials. (Remember that things that are called organic were once living.)

There are many different kinds of sedimentary rocks. In fact, you probably use one sedimentary rock every day in school. Can you guess which sedimentary rock is used by students and teachers in the classroom? You also may have used it to draw on the sidewalk. Chalk is a sedimentary rock.

Animal, Vegetable, or Mineral?

Just like igneous rocks, sedimentary rocks can be grouped according to how they form. There are three types of sedimentary rocks: clastic, chemical, and organic. Clastic sedimentary rocks are those in which pieces of rocks, minerals, and organic materials are cemented together. The bits of sediment that make up clastic rocks can be as small as single grains of mud or as large as boulders! As you might expect, sedimentary rocks are common on Earth's surface.

Clastic rocks are grouped according to the size of the sediments they contain. Conglomerate (kən gläm'ər it), shale, and sandstone are examples of clastic rocks. Study the photos of these rocks. How do their sediment pieces compare?

Most clastic rocks form when wind, water, or ice carry and then drop sediments. Over time, these materials

◄ **Conglomerate**

Sandstone ▶

▲ **Shale**

become compacted, or squeezed together. Minerals dissolved in water seep into spaces between the materials. As the water dries and the minerals grow, the minerals bind the loose sediments into solid rock. This binding of sediments is called **cementation** (sē men tā'shən).

Sandstone, as you might have guessed, is made of small, sand-sized rock bits. Sandstone often feels gritty, like sandpaper. Where on Earth do you think sandstone might be forming? Can you think of any uses for sandstone?

Chemical sedimentary rocks form when water rich in dissolved minerals evaporates, leaving the minerals behind, or when chemical changes form new minerals. Rock gypsum, rock salt, and some kinds of limestone are examples of chemical sedimentary rocks.

The type of limestone shown in the photograph below consists mostly of calcite, which formed when sea or lake waters evaporated. Limestone is ground and mixed with other ingredients to make certain cements.

▲ **Rock gypsum**

Rock gypsum forms when water evaporates, leaving behind the mineral gypsum. Gypsum is used in plaster of Paris and plaster walls.

Rock salt, which is almost pure halite, is known to you as table salt. It does, however, have other uses, as you can see in the photo below.

▼ **Limestone**

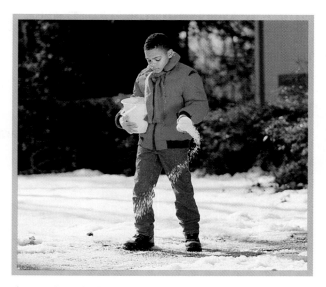

▲ **Rock salt is commonly used to melt ice and snow.**

The third type of sedimentary rock is called organic rock. Organic rocks form from the remains of plants and animals or from parts, such as shells, of organisms. One type of coal is an organic sedimentary rock that forms when bits of dead plants are compacted over long periods of time. The squeezing removes all the water, leaving behind the carbon that forms coal.

Limestone forms in different ways. Some limestones form when shells of dead sea animals become cemented together. Limestone consists mostly of calcite. Fine-grained limestones, such as chalk, form when calcite comes in contact with acid.

Features of Sedimentary Rocks

Scientists, including budding scientists like you, can learn about how a sedimentary rock was formed by observing the features preserved in the rock. When sediments are dropped by water, wind, or ice, the sediments build up in layers. A layer can be as thin as a sheet of paper or as thick as a few meters! The layers harden over time. And as more sediments are dropped, more layers are formed. So most sedimentary rocks are layered. This layering is often called bedding. Wind, water, and the shape of the land can all affect the formation of beds of sedimentary rock. Use the chart on page E46 to compare how sediment beds form.

SCIENCE IN LITERATURE

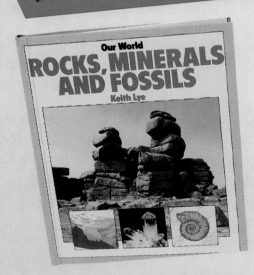

ROCKS, MINERALS AND FOSSILS
by Keith Lye
Silver Burdett Press, 1991

The sedimentary rocks of the Grand Canyon of the Colorado River are more than amazing scenery. The canyon is also a 3-D lesson on the history of Earth! Find out how to "read the rocks" on pages 32 and 33 of *Rocks, Minerals and Fossils*.

Then turn to pages 34 and 35 to see what creatures lived when each of the rock layers of the Grand Canyon formed. These fossils help scientists to read the history of life on Earth.

Sediment Beds

◄ Notice that the surface of this sediment layer looks wavy. These wavy lines are called ripple marks. They are formed by moving water or wind. You may have seen ripple marks near a stream or on a beach. How might they become sedimentary rock?

◄ Most sediment beds, like these in shale, were deposited horizontally, resulting in the characteristic layering of sedimentary rock.

◄ The beds in this sandstone show cross-bedding. They formed when wind dropped sand on the curved slopes of sand dunes. Eventually, the sand beds hardened to form sandstone. What kinds of places can you think of that have sand dunes?

◄ Mud cracks are another feature sometimes preserved in sedimentary rocks. Mud cracks are evidence of wet periods followed by dry periods during the formation of a rock.

If you've ever gone rock collecting or to a natural history museum, you've probably seen fossils. A **fossil** is any remains or evidence of an organism from the past. Sedimentary rocks sometimes contain fossils. The photograph shows a fossil fern. Based on this fossil, what conclusions might you draw about how this rock formed?

Refer to the Rock Key and the rocks that you identified in the activity on page E38. Which rocks in your collection are sedimentary rocks? (The Rock Key uses a letter *S* to show them.) Try to classify the sedimentary rocks in your collection as clastic, chemical, or organic, based on their properties. ■

Fossil fern ▶

Metamorphic Rocks:
A Change of Identity

The third major group of rocks is the metamorphic (met ə môr'fik) rocks. The word *metamorphic* is made of two word parts that mean "to change form." In some ways, metamorphic rocks are like sedimentary rocks because both kinds form from existing rocks. In other ways, metamorphic rocks are like igneous rocks because both kinds can form at high temperatures and pressures. So what qualities make metamorphic rocks different from both sedimentary and igneous rocks? Let's find out.

New Rocks

Metamorphic rocks are new rocks that form from existing rocks because of changes caused by heat, pressure, or chemicals. The existing rocks that are changed may be sedimentary, igneous, or other metamorphic rocks. The change from one rock type to another is called metamorphism.

Some changes that occur with metamorphism result in changes in texture. *Texture* refers to the size and shape of mineral grains and the way in which they are arranged in a rock. In other cases, changes in composition, or makeup, take place. The changes that occur during metamorphism can result from three different sets of conditions.

Contact metamorphism occurs when hot magma or lava comes in contact with rock. The rock gets "baked" by the molten

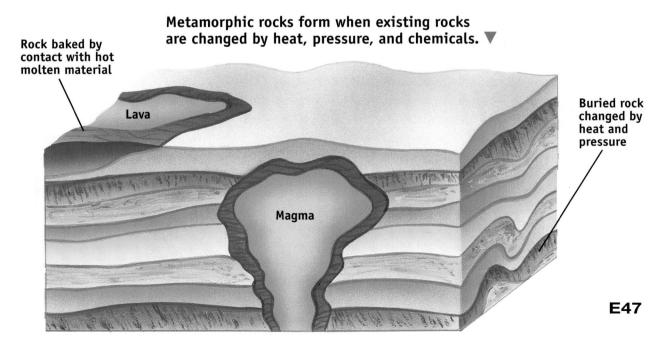

Metamorphic rocks form when existing rocks are changed by heat, pressure, and chemicals. ▼

Rock baked by contact with hot molten material

Lava

Magma

Buried rock changed by heat and pressure

material. So temperature alone, not pressure, causes the rock to change. Changes can occur in the kinds of minerals present and in the sizes of the grains. Liquids and gases escaping from the magma can also chemically change minerals in the surrounding rocks.

A second type of metamorphism is called regional metamorphism. It occurs in rocks that are buried deep below the surface, where temperature and pressure are high. The texture of the rocks changes, particularly in the way the minerals are arranged. Mineral grains tend to become lined up in the same direction because of high pressures. Also, high temperatures cause changes in the original mineral composition of the rocks.

Burial metamorphism causes the least amount of change in a rock. Burial metamorphism occurs when the weight of rocks and sediments burying a rock puts pressure on that rock. During burial metamorphism, the temperatures and pressures involved are low compared with those of other kinds of metamorphism. Low temperatures and pressures, for example, can cause new minerals to grow and textures to change slightly. Such changes cause

shale, a sedimentary rock, to become the metamorphic rock called slate.

Banded Metamorphic Rocks

Metamorphic rocks are grouped according to their textures as banded or nonbanded. As you would expect, rocks with a banded texture look as if they contain bands, or thin layers, which may look wavy or straight. You are probably familiar with some banded metamorphic rocks. Gneiss (nīs) is a banded metamorphic rock that contains quartz, mica, and feldspar. Which igneous rock is made of these same three minerals? Look at the photograph of gneiss. Note the bands of mineral grains. In which direction do you think the pressure was applied during metamorphism?

Another banded metamorphic rock is slate. Recall that slate forms when shale, a sedimentary rock, is exposed to changes in temperature and pressure. Slate is used as a roofing material. Some chalkboards are even made of slate. When exposed to more heat and pressure, slate can become another banded metamorphic rock, called phyllite (fil′īt).

▼ Gneiss

Phyllite ▶

Slate ▶

▲ Marble

▲ Quartzite

Nonbanded Metamorphic Rocks

In nonbanded metamorphic rocks the mineral grains have not been lined up by pressure. The texture of these rocks is described as massive. Look at the photographs of the nonbanded rocks above. Contrast them with the photographs of banded rocks. Can you infer the meaning of the term *massive* as used to describe metamorphic rocks?

Marble is a nonbanded metamorphic rock. Marble forms when limestone is changed by metamorphism. Marble can be white, black, pink, gray, or green with streaks of other colors.

Another nonbanded metamorphic rock is quartzite (kwôrts'īt). Quartzite forms when quartz-rich sandstone is exposed to high pressures and temperatures. ■

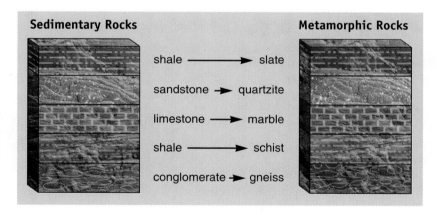

Sedimentary Rocks

Metamorphic Rocks

shale ⟶ slate

sandstone ⟶ quartzite

limestone ⟶ marble

shale ⟶ schist

conglomerate ⟶ gneiss

◀ **The drawing shows the different parent rocks of metamorphic rocks. Try to match metamorphic rocks in your collection with their parent rocks.**

INVESTIGATION 1

THINK IT WRITE IT

1. Name the three basic types of rocks and describe how each formed.

2. Fossils are found almost exclusively in sedimentary rocks. Suggest a hypothesis to explain this observation.

How Do the Properties of Rocks Make Them Useful?

Make a rock! Punch small holes in the bottom of a paper cup. Pour a handful of sand into the cup. Dilute some white glue with a little water. Pour it into the sand. Let the water drain out. After it has dried, tear off the paper and behold your "rock." What are its properties? Find a use for it!

Activity

Comparing Properties of Rocks

Different kinds of rocks have different properties, which make the rocks useful in different ways.

MATERIALS
- rock set
- hand lens
- *Science Notebook*

Procedure

1. Look at the Rock Key on page E39. The column at the far right lists the letters *I, S,* and *M*. These stand for igneous, sedimentary, and metamorphic.

2. Separate your rocks into three sets so that the first set has all the rocks labeled *I* on the Rock Key, the second set contains those labeled *S*, and the third, those labeled *M*.

3. Predict which sets will have layered rocks. Look for layered rocks and **record** your observations in your *Science Notebook*.

4. **Predict** which sets will have crystalline rocks (rocks with crystals). Look for crystalline rocks and **record** your observations.

5. **Predict** which rocks will be made of particles or fragments. Look for rocks that are made of particles or fragments. **Record** your observations.

6. **Compare and contrast** the rocks in your collection. **Record** as many properties as you can for each rock.

Analyze and Conclude

1. In which group(s) of rocks do you find layers, and in which do you not find layers?

2. In which group(s) of rocks do you find crystals, and in which do you not find crystals?

3. In which group(s) do you find particles or fragments, and in which do you not find particles or fragments?

4. Consider the properties of the rocks in your collection. Then make **inferences** about some uses for the rocks.

INVESTIGATE FURTHER!

RESEARCH

How's your rock collection coming? Do some research to find out how the types of rocks in your collection are used by people.

Rock Quarries

Have you ever seen a fireplace built of rocks? How about a rock wall or a path lined with stones? Chances are, the rocks that make up these things came from a quarry (kwôr'ē). A rock **quarry** is a mine, usually close to or at Earth's surface, from which certain rocks are removed. Billions of tons of granite, sandstone, limestone, slate, marble, and other types of rocks are removed each year from quarries all over the world.

Rock is removed from quarries in two forms. Dimension stones are slabs of rock that are removed from quarries in specific shapes and sizes. Most dimension stones are used to build things that will both last and look decorative, such as buildings. So the slabs must be solid and have an attractive texture, pattern, or color.

Most of the rock removed from quarries is in another form, called crushed stone. Crushed stone consists of bits and pieces of rocks that are primarily used in concrete, cements, and other construction materials.

You've probably tried to break or move a few big rocks at times. It isn't easy. So how do you suppose rocks are mined in quarries? How rocks are mined depends on how they'll be used. Most crushed stone gets blasted from solid rock with the use of explosives. First, holes are drilled into the rock. Then explosives are placed in the holes

Marble being cut at a quarry ▼

Marble slab being lifted by crane ▼

Transporting marble slabs ▼

and set off, causing the rock to break up. Of course, this wouldn't be a great way to quarry dimension stones, unless you are planning to cement the pieces back together!

In most quarries, dimension stones are cut from solid rock by using either a drill or a torch. Air moving through the drill makes the drill bit, or tip, spin rapidly. As it spins, the bit cuts away at the rock. A torch, on the other hand, cuts the rock by melting it. When cut with a torch, the edges of the slabs are smooth.

Once the dimension stones are cut, a huge crane is used to move them. The blocks of rock, which can weigh several tons each, are secured with hooks and chains. Then the crane is used to slowly lift and carry the stones.

From the quarry, loose slabs are transported to a processing mill. Many quarries that mine dimension stones have their own processing mills. At these mills, the rock slabs are cut to certain sizes by using steel wires and rock saws. The saw blades are often made with diamonds. As you learned in Chapter 1, diamonds are the hardest known minerals. They can cut through even the hardest rocks with the greatest of ease.

Once the rocks are cut and sized, they may be polished. Polishing gradually smooths out any wire or saw marks left from the cutting stage. When the dimension stones are highly polished, they are ready to be shipped around the corner, around the country, or around the world. The chart shows some common dimension stones, where they come from, and what they are used for. Do any quarried rocks come from your state? What states might produce the marble for a counter top? Which stones might be used in monuments? ∎

Rock	Where From	Uses
Granite	Vermont, Massachusetts, Maine, New Hampshire, Rhode Island, Minnesota, Wisconsin	monuments, buildings, grave markers
Sandstone	New York, Ohio, Pennsylvania, Kentucky, Connecticut	buildings, trim
Marble	Vermont, Georgia	monuments, buildings, flooring, counter tops, kitchen items
Limestone	Texas, Utah, Indiana, Missouri, Florida, Minnesota	decorative trims, buildings, monuments, park benches

A Ton of Bricks!

Is your home or school made of bricks? Do you think bricks are rocks? Although they are hard like most rocks and are made from minerals, bricks aren't actually rocks. "Well, why not?" you may be asking yourself. Rocks are made of one or more minerals, and they form naturally. Since rocks are formed by nature, bricks cannot be rocks because bricks are made by people!

Brick Making Today

What, then, *are* bricks? Bricks are small, rectangular blocks made from a mixture of clays and other sediments. To make bricks, different kinds and amounts of clays are dug from river bottoms or other places on Earth's surface.

To make bricks, clays and sediments are removed from Earth, ground into powder, mixed with water to form a paste, poured into molds, and hardened by baking in kilns. ▼

These minerals are taken to a factory where they are crushed into a fine powder. Sometimes the powder is sifted to remove any large pieces. Water is added to the powder to make a thick, gooey paste. The paste is pressed into molds that are coated with sand or water. The coating helps to prevent the mixture from sticking to the molds, much as butter helps to keep cake batter from sticking to a pan.

Next, molds are placed in a kiln, or drying oven. When the clay mixture is completely dry, the molds are fired in another kiln. Firing chemically changes the clay blocks by heating them for up to 12 hours at temperatures above 800°C (1,500°F). Once fired, the bricks are cooled and taken to other parts of the factory to be packed and shipped.

Brick Making in the Past

Scientists who study ancient cultures discovered that bricks have been used by people for at least 60 centuries! The first bricks were probably simple mud blocks dried in the sun. Adobe (ə dō′bē), or sun-dried brick, is thought to have first been made in dry areas of the world, including parts of Africa, Spain, Peru, and the southwestern part of the United States. Adobe bricks are made with a mixture of clay, sand, and sometimes, straw. The materials are mixed by hand, with bare feet, or with a simple tool. The mixture is then put into molds and allowed to dry for at least two weeks. When dry, the bricks are removed from the molds and used.

About 3,500 years ago, people began to fire bricks. They discovered that firing the clay blocks made them harder and longer-lasting.

Bricks are not rocks. But like sedimentary rocks, bricks are made of sediments. Also, with firing, clay is changed chemically to a different material. How is this similar to the way some metamorphic rocks form? ■

▲ **This structure is made from adobe brick.**

INVESTIGATION 2

1. Identify some ways in which rocks differ.

2. Suppose you were asked to recommend a type of rock that could be used to make a strong but attractive building. Use the Rock Key for help in making your suggestion. Give reasons to support your choice.

Coal:
A Fossil Fuel

How might you describe coal to someone who has never seen it or who knows nothing about it? You might explain that one kind of coal is a sedimentary rock and one kind is a metamorphic rock. You might also say that coal can be burned to heat your home. Would you describe coal as a fossil fuel?

As you might suspect from its name, a fossil fuel is a material formed from plant or animal remains that can be burned for energy. Over millions of years, pressures and temperatures have squeezed and changed the remains. Left behind are elements, such as carbon, hydrogen, and oxygen, that once made up the organisms. Coal is one kind of fossil fuel.

Millions of years ago

PEAT
60% Carbon
Coal begins to form when swamp plants die and are quickly buried beneath sediments and other plants. Tiny organisms called bacteria cause organic material to decay and change. Over time, a dark, watery organic material called peat forms.

Peat Layer

LIGNITE
70% Carbon
With time, the peat gets buried by more sediments. The weight of these sediments compacts the peat and squeezes water out. Eventually, the percent of carbon present increases and a sedimentary rock called lignite, a type of coal, forms.

Lignite Layer

All forms of coal are used as fuel. Coal is burned to provide energy to heat homes, offices, and other buildings. Some coal is used to fuel furnaces in factories. In fact, coal provides about 20 percent of the energy needs in the United States.

Bituminous (bi tōō'mə nəs) coal lights very easily and provides the most energy of all the types of coal. But burning this kind of coal produces a sooty residue and yellow smoke. Anthracite (an'thrə sīt) coal burns much cleaner and longer than bituminous coal, but does not provide as much energy. The diagram below shows the changes coal can go through. ∎

Peat ▼

Lignite ▼

▲ **Bituminous Coal**

▲ **Anthracite**

Present Day ➤

BITUMINOUS COAL

80% Carbon

As the rock becomes buried deeper, temperature and pressure increase. Nearly all of the water that was once in the plant parts gets forced out and bituminous coal forms. Recall that bituminous coal, or soft coal, is a sedimentary rock that is mostly carbon.

Bituminous Layer

ANTHRACITE

95% Carbon

With deep burying and great temperature and pressure, bituminous coal becomes metamorphosed to form anthracite. Anthracite is a metamorphic rock. It has the highest percent of carbon of all the forms of coal.

Anthracite Layer

Rocks in Circles

 You learned that high temperatures and great pressures can change any rock into a metamorphic rock. But did you realize that any kind of rock—igneous, sedimentary, or metamorphic—can be changed into another kind of rock, not just by metamorphism?

Melting and cooling are just two of Earth's agents of change. They act to change Earth's rock materials. The series of changes that rocks undergo is called the **rock cycle**.

Notice the ovals in the diagram of the rock cycle. They represent five kinds of rock materials: igneous rock, sedimentary rock, metamorphic rock, sediments, and molten rock (magma and lava). Between the ovals are things that cause rock materials to change—factors such as melting and pressure. When you play most board games, you can move in only one direction around the board. But with the rock cycle, rocks may "move," or change, in many ways. To use the diagram to see how one type of rock changes into another, start at any oval. Then move in the direction of any arrow coming out of the oval. Follow the arrows, and you can't go wrong.

Sedimentary to Metamorphic

As you can see from the diagram, there are many factors in the rock cycle that cause change. Find the words *Sedimentary Rock* on the diagram. What's one way in which sedimentary rock can change? You know that sedimentary rocks form at or near Earth's surface. What do you think happens when these rocks become buried? High temperatures and pressures deep below the surface change sedimentary rocks into metamorphic rocks. Follow this change on the diagram.

Metamorphic to Igneous

Now what do you suppose happens when the pressures and temperatures deep below the surface become very high? Melting, or the changing of a solid to a liquid, occurs to change metamorphic rock into molten rock. Find *Melting* on the diagram.

As magma or lava cools, minerals form. When minerals form, they grow into different-sized crystals, so this step is sometimes called crystallizing. Notice in the rock cycle diagram that magma and lava cool and crystallize to form igneous rock. On the diagram, follow the change from metamorphic rock to igneous rock.

The Rock Cycle

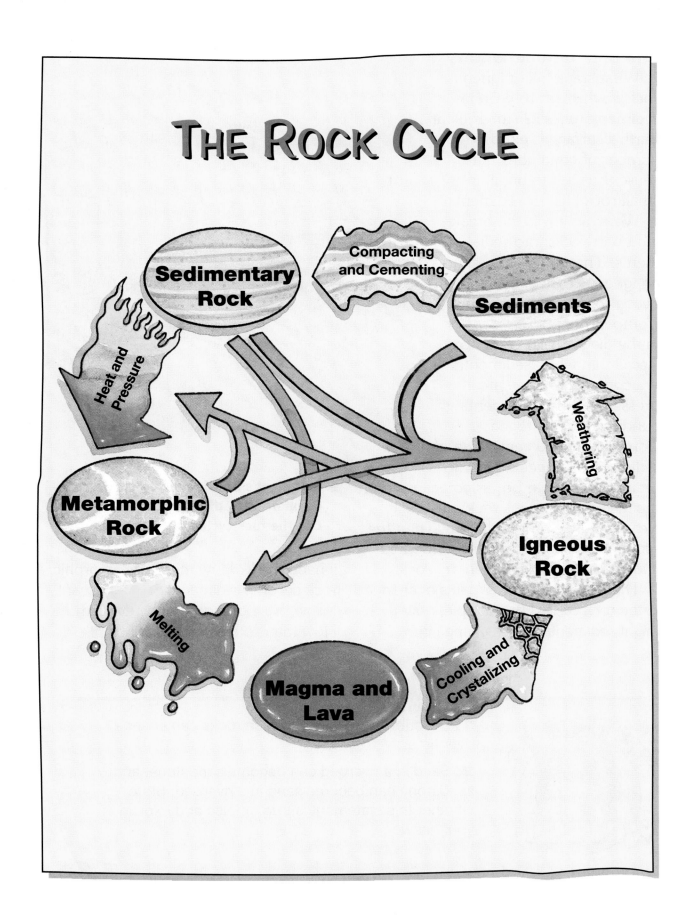

Sedimentary Rock

Compacting and Cementing

Sediments

Heat and Pressure

Weathering

Metamorphic Rock

Igneous Rock

Melting

Cooling and Crystalizing

Magma and Lava

Igneous to Sedimentary

What steps might igneous rock go through to become sedimentary rock? Any rock at Earth's surface is exposed to a number of conditions that cause the rock to break into small rock bits, or sediments.

Weathering is the breaking up of rocks into sediments. Through weathering, an igneous rock can eventually become sediment bits. Find *Compacting* and *Cementing* in the diagram on page E61. Recall that when sediments are compacted, they are pressed together. Cementing bonds sediments together. Compacting and cementing of sediments changes them into sedimentary rock. So, as you can see in the diagram, igneous rock must first weather to become sediment. Then the sediment is compacted and cemented and changed into sedimentary rock.

There are many other paths of change in the rock cycle. For example, how might sedimentary rock change into

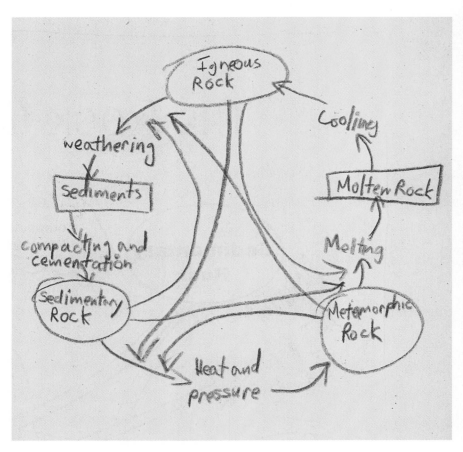

▲ **A student's drawing of the rock cycle. Compare it to the diagram on page E61. Can the rock cycle start at any point?**

igneous rock? How might metamorphic rock become sediment? See if you can follow these changes on the diagram. How many others can you find? ■

INVESTIGATION 3

1. Describe four ways by which rocks can change over time.

2. Sand in a riverbed can become sandstone, and sandstone can become sand in a riverbed. State whether this statement is true or false and explain your answer.

REFLECT & EVALUATE

WORD POWER

cementation
fossil
lava
magma
igneous rocks
metamorphic rocks
sedimentary rocks

quarry
rock cycle
rocks
sediments

On Your Own

Review the terms in the list. Then use as many terms as you can in a paragraph about how rocks are related.

With a Partner

Write a slogan for one of the terms. Do not use the term. (You may use other terms in the slogan.) Share the slogan with a group and have them guess the term.

BUILD YOUR PORTFOLIO

Write a story about the trip a rock material makes in one complete cycle through the rock cycle. Be sure to name all rock materials. Be creative, but base your fiction on scientific fact.

Analyze Information

Explain how the cycle shown could be never ending. Then describe an event that could break the cycle.

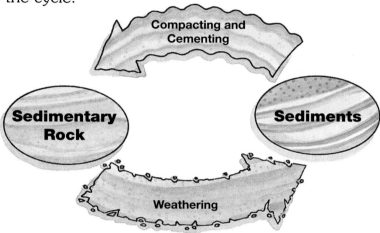

Assess Performance

Obtain several samples of unknown rock. Using a hand lens and the Rock Key on page E39, identify each sample and classify each as igneous, sedimentary, or metamorphic.

Problem Solving

1. You observe that a rock has large crystals and is unlayered. What type of rock would you infer it to be? Explain your inference.

2. How are the rock cycle and the yearly cycle of changing seasons alike and not alike?

3. Make a sketch that illustrates the rock cycle. Use examples of rocks from this chapter in your sketch.

CHAPTER 3

EARTH'S STRUCTURES

Did you know that you can float with both feet on the ground? In fact, you're always floating—even when you think you're standing still. Here's why. The ground under your feet is drifting on a layer of hot, gooey rock. This rock is only one of the remarkable materials that make up Earth. Sometimes the drifting movement leads to earthquakes.

A Deep, Deep Quake

On June 8, 1994, an unusual earthquake struck the country of Bolivia, in South America. The quake was severe, but it caused relatively little damage and no loss of life because the quake was located very deep beneath Earth's surface. Such rare, deep earthquakes usually cause little damage. And they come with a bonus for seismologists (sīz mäl'ə jists), the scientists who study earthquakes. The vibrations caused by a deep quake provide much information about Earth's interior. By measuring the activity from the Bolivia quake at different locations around the world, scientists learned a great deal about the materials that make up the inner Earth. You might say that the scientists received a picture of the interior structure of our planet.

What is inside Earth? What causes earthquakes? The investigations in this chapter will help you find out.

Coming Up

◄ A seismograph recording of the deep earthquake in Bolivia

WHAT IS EARTH'S STRUCTURE?

How do rocks make up the sphere you call Earth? What's at the center of that sphere? This investigation will help you answer such questions about Earth's structure by looking at what's inside as well as outside Earth.

Activity

A Model Earth

An apple makes a good model of Earth's structure. In science, a model is used to help us understand something else. Sometimes a model helps us to ask better questions. Let's look carefully at an apple.

MATERIALS
- apple
- plastic knife
- wax paper
- *Science Notebook*

Procedure

1. Place a piece of wax paper on your desktop. Put an apple on the wax paper.

2. Use the apple to model the interior of Earth. Cut the apple in half. Carefully observe the cut surface from the skin to the center of the apple. In your *Science Notebook*, sketch and describe what you see.

Step 2

3. Cut both halves in half again. The skin represents Earth's **crust,** or surface layer. The skin on three of the pieces is a model for the amount of Earth's crust that is covered by oceans.

4. Examine one of the pieces of apple carefully. **Compare** the thickness of the skin to the thickness of the rest of the piece.

Analyze and Conclude

1. Based on your model, how much of Earth's crust is covered by oceans? How much of the crust is land?

2. Earth has a layer below its crust called the **mantle**. The mantle covers a ball, called the **core**, in the middle of Earth. **Infer** which parts of the apple are models for the mantle and the core.

3. **Compare** the thicknesses of the crust, mantle, and core in your model. Based on your model, what conclusions can you draw about the depths, or thicknesses, of the layers of Earth?

Step 3

INVESTIGATE FURTHER!

RESEARCH

Earth's land includes mountains, plains, plateaus, and other types of landforms. Find out how much of Earth's surface is land on which people can plant crops. How much of the land is largely uninhabitable?

The Sphere We Live On

When you hear the word *model*, what do you think of? You may picture a model airplane or a fashion model. In science, a **model** is something used to represent an object or an idea. In the activity on pages E66 and E67, you used an apple as a model of Earth.

What would happen if you took a huge knife and sliced right through Earth instead of through an apple? You'd see four layers instead of three—so your model was a bit too simple. Now take a look at another Earth model, the diagram shown here.

The Crust

Earth's outer layer is called the **crust**. It is the thinnest of all the layers, but it varies in thickness around Earth. It can be as thin as 10 km (6 mi) under the oceans and as thick as 65 km (40 mi) below the continents.

The crust is made up of solid rock. It is mostly granite, gabbro, and basalt, but it also includes all the igneous, sedimentary, and metamorphic rocks you have learned about. Much of the crust is covered by oceans, lakes, rivers, sediments, plants, and soil.

Earth has four layers. ▼

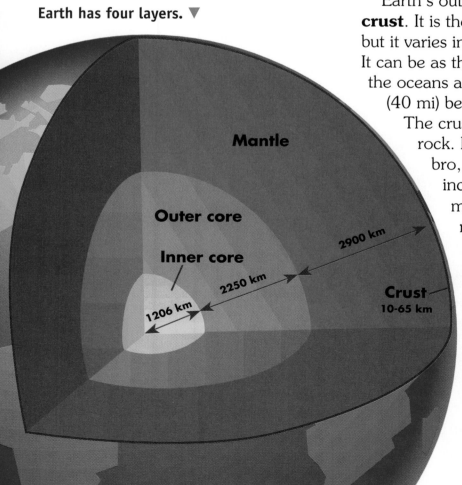

Mantle

Outer core

Inner core

2900 km

2250 km

1206 km

Crust
10-65 km

The crust is broken into many large and small pieces called plates. These plates float like rafts on the layer below the crust. So they can move very slowly around Earth's surface, carrying the continents and oceans with them.

Earth's crust is thicker beneath continents than beneath oceans. ▼

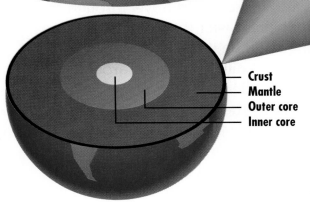

Crust
Mantle
Outer core
Inner core

The Mantle

Below the crust is the **mantle**. It is the thickest layer, taking up about 84 percent of Earth's volume. The part of this layer that is closest to the crust is made of solid rock that has the same properties as other solids. However, much of the mantle is solid rock that has some properties of liquids. It can flow like maple syrup or be stretched out like putty.

Much of the mantle is composed of an igneous rock called peridotite. This rock is dark in color and rich in the elements iron, magnesium, and silicon.

When you learned about metamorphic rocks, you found out that temperature and pressure increase as you go deeper below Earth's surface. Temperature and pressure are much greater in the mantle than in the crust. As a result, some rock in the mantle melts. This molten rock sometimes makes its way to the surface as lava.

The Inner and Outer Core

Below the mantle is Earth's core. The **core** consists of heavy material that sank to Earth's center billions of years ago. The core consists of a solid inner layer and a molten outer layer.

The outer core is made of molten iron and nickel. Scientists think the boundary between the outer core and the mantle is wavy. They think the hills and valleys in this boundary are caused by the movement of molten rock between the outer core and the mantle.

At Earth's center is the inner core, which is made of solid iron and nickel. Temperatures here may exceed 5,000°C (9,000°F)—almost as hot as the surface of the Sun! The extreme pressure here prevents the iron and nickel from melting, in spite of the high temperature.

How do you think the different layers of Earth developed? One hypothesis is that billions of years ago, energy released by the breakdown of elements inside Earth caused the planet to grow hotter and hotter. Much of the iron and nickel found in Earth's rocks melted. Because these are very heavy materials, the molten iron and nickel sank to the center of the planet. Extreme pressure turned these materials back to a solid. Lighter materials also melted, but they rose to the surface. As a result, a crust of light rock and a core of heavy metals formed, with the mantle layer in between.

Journeying to Earth's Center

You may have wondered how scientists know so much about Earth's deep layers. They certainly haven't been able to travel there! However, some rocks that have formed from magma make it possible for us to "see" the mantle. Rocks such as kimberlite that were once magma in the mantle give us clues about the composition of the mantle. But how do scientists know where the layers begin and end?

Think about the last time you tried to figure out what was inside a wrapped present. You couldn't see inside, but you could try to infer what was in the box. Scientists make inferences about Earth's layers by studying earthquake waves.

When you drop a stone in a pond, waves of energy move across the water's surface. In a similar way, when an earthquake occurs, waves of energy travel through Earth in all directions. Earthquake waves travel through some materials faster than others. By measuring the time it takes for the waves to arrive at different places around the world, scientists infer what kind of material the waves traveled through.

In 1909 the boundary between the crust and mantle was discovered by a scientist named Andrija Mohorovičic' (mō hō rō'və chich). He noticed that earthquake waves started to travel faster once they reached a certain depth below Earth's surface. Mohorovičic' inferred that there must be a different kind of rock at this depth. This boundary between the crust and the mantle, named after the man who discovered it, is called the Moho.

Two kinds of earthquake waves, called P waves and S waves, have also been used to make inferences about the properties of the core and its depth below the surface. Look at the figure on the next page to find out what scientists have learned from earthquake waves.

HOW EARTHQUAKE WAVES TRAVEL

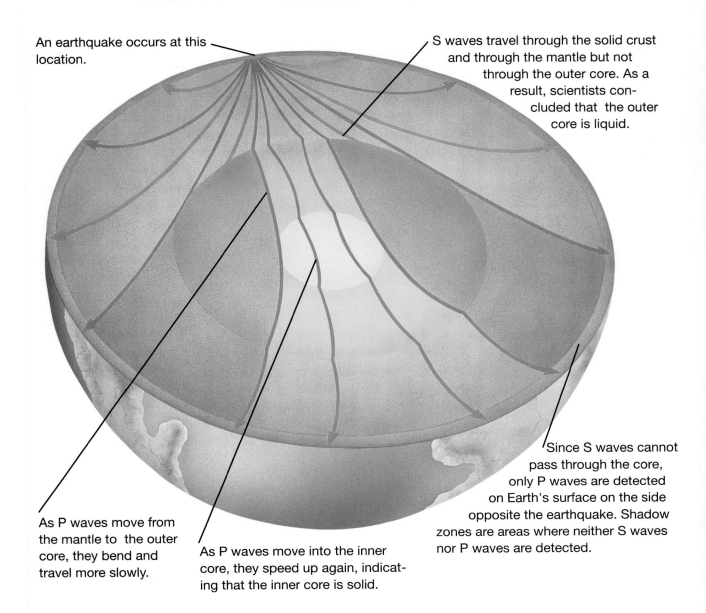

An earthquake occurs at this location.

S waves travel through the solid crust and through the mantle but not through the outer core. As a result, scientists concluded that the outer core is liquid.

Since S waves cannot pass through the core, only P waves are detected on Earth's surface on the side opposite the earthquake. Shadow zones are areas where neither S waves nor P waves are detected.

As P waves move from the mantle to the outer core, they bend and travel more slowly.

As P waves move into the inner core, they speed up again, indicating that the inner core is solid.

INVESTIGATION 1

1. Use materials of your choice to make a three-dimensional model showing Earth's layers. Make labels to identify the layers.

2. Scientists know the mass and the volume of Earth. How could this information help them make inferences about the kind of matter that makes up Earth's interior?

INVESTIGATION 2

HOW CAN FOSSILS HELP TELL US HOW OLD A ROCK IS?

Think of Earth as a book, with layers of rock stacked on top of one another like pages. How can you use the fossils in rocks to number the pages and read the book?

Activity
Layering Fossils

Scientists study rock layers and the fossils in them to learn about ancient forms of life. Find out what scientists can learn by doing this activity.

MATERIALS

- 3 different colors of clay
- shell
- leaf
- twig
- *Science Notebook*

Procedure

1. Flatten three pieces of clay, each a different color.

2. **Make a model** of a fossil imprint by making an impression of a shell in one piece of clay. Make an impression of a leaf in the second piece of clay and a twig in the third piece of clay. Set aside the shell, leaf, and twig.

Step 2

3. Each piece of clay represents a layer of sedimentary rock. Stack your rock layers one on top of the other. In your *Science Notebook*, **record** the order from top to bottom.

Analyze and Conclude

1. Based on what you have learned about how sedimentary rock forms, **infer** which of your "fossils" would be the oldest and which would be the youngest. Explain your reasoning.

2. If the twig is from a bush that lived after the shellfish died but before the tree from which the leaf was taken lived, which fossil would be on the top of the stack? Which fossil would be on the bottom?

3. **Compare** your stack of fossils with the stacks made by other students. Are the fossils in the same order? If not, **infer** the relative ages of the fossils in each of the other stacks.

UNIT PROJECT LINK

Find out about fossils that have been collected in your community or that were discovered in your state. If possible, obtain examples of such fossils for your collection. Be sure to note the exact location where each fossil was found. If you can't get examples, make drawings of the fossils.

Activity

Finding the Order

Geologists often try to find out the order in which rock layers formed. It isn't always easy. In this activity you'll make a model of rock layers and infer the order in which they were made.

MATERIALS
- paper cups
- plastic spoons
- white glue
- food coloring, 4 colors
- sand
- wooden stick
- milk carton (1 pt)
- *Science Notebook*

Procedure

1. In a paper cup, mix a spoonful of white glue with 4 drops of red food coloring. Mix the colored glue with half a cup of sand. In the same way, make blue sand in a second cup, green sand in a third cup, and yellow sand in a fourth cup.

2. Place a small wooden stick against the inside of a milk carton. Then pack one color of sand in the bottom of the carton. Pack a second color on top of the first, and a third on top of the second.

3. Carefully pull the stick out of the carton and fill the hole with the fourth color of sand. Set the carton aside until the next day. **Predict** what the sand layers will look like when you take them out of the milk carton. In your *Science Notebook*, **draw a diagram** of your prediction.

Step 1

4. Carefully tear the milk carton away from the layers. If the glue has not dried, let it set a while longer.

5. Compare your layers to the drawing that you made.

6. On your drawing, number the "rock" layers from 1 to 4, with 1 representing the oldest layer, or the layer that you made first.

Analyze and Conclude

1. Which "rock" layer was laid down first? Which one "formed" last?

2. For rock layers that are horizontal, what general statement can you make about where the oldest and youngest layers are located in the stack of layers?

3. What inference can you make about the age of a rock layer that cuts through other layers?

INVESTIGATE FURTHER!

EXPERIMENT

Trade rock layers with another student. Infer the order in which the layers were deposited.

Sorting Through Time

People have been digging up fossils for centuries. But not until the 1700s did the idea that fossils were the remains of creatures from the past begin to be accepted. You can bet that William Smith, an English geologist, never realized that his hobby of fossil collecting would show a way of matching rock layers by age! While surveying the land in western England, Smith had a chance to observe many rock layers and collect fossils. First, he noticed that rock layers lie "like slices of bread and butter," stacked in a set order. Next, he saw that each layer of sedimentary rock contained different types of fossils. He soon realized that fossils could be used to recognize rock layers of the same age in different places around the world. And scientists today use fossils to do just that! ■

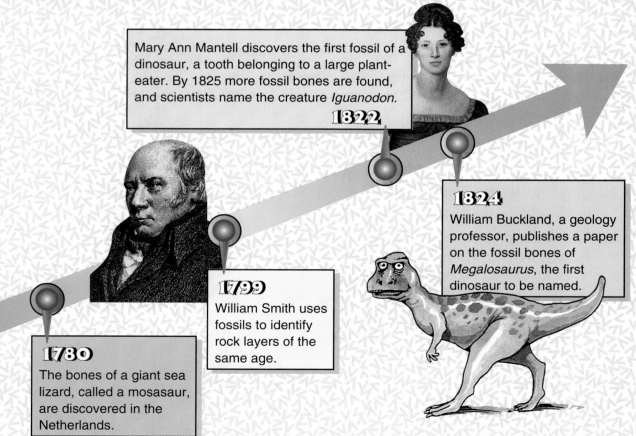

Mary Ann Mantell discovers the first fossil of a dinosaur, a tooth belonging to a large plant-eater. By 1825 more fossil bones are found, and scientists name the creature *Iguanodon*.
1822

1824
William Buckland, a geology professor, publishes a paper on the fossil bones of *Megalosaurus*, the first dinosaur to be named.

1799
William Smith uses fossils to identify rock layers of the same age.

1780
The bones of a giant sea lizard, called a mosasaur, are discovered in the Netherlands.

Fossils Tell Tales!

1. An organism dies.

2. The remains get buried quickly by sediment. The soft parts decay.

3. With time, the hard parts get replaced with minerals. The sediment layer gets buried deeper and is compacted and cemented to form sedimentary rock.

There aren't many things more exciting than coming face to face with a dinosaur—a dinosaur skeleton, that is. Our knowledge of dinosaurs has come from studying **fossils**, which are the remains and traces of living things preserved in rock. What clues do you think a fossil might provide about Earth's past? A fossil can give clues about where an organism once lived, how it may have moved, what it ate, and what it looked like, not to mention how old the rock it was found in might be.

You Old Fossil!

How does a fossil form? Many fossils form when plants and animals die and are quickly buried by clay, sand, and other sediments. Look at the drawings to see how a fossil might form.

In some cases, bone and other hard material is replaced by minerals. Other

4. A fossil is later exposed due to erosion.

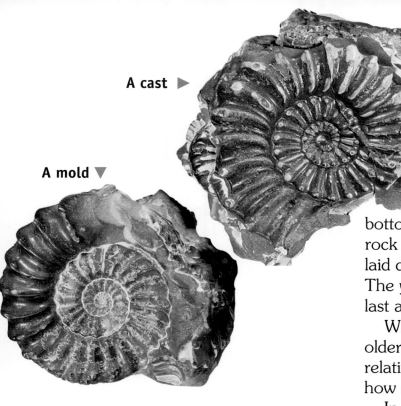

◀ A cast

▼ A mold

fossils form when plants and animals leave imprints in soft sediment. Over time, the organic material dissolves and the imprint gets filled with minerals or sediments. The imprint, or hollow part of the fossil, is called a mold. The material that fills in the imprint is called a cast. Remember when you pressed a shell, a leaf, and a twig into clay in the activity on pages E72 and E73? Did you make molds, or casts?

Relative Age

Scientists began studying fossils partly in the hope that fossils would help them estimate the age of Earth's rocks. There are many clues, including fossils, that you can use to learn about the ages of the rocks you see.

One clue to look for is the position of the rock layers. Recall that most sedimentary rocks begin as horizontal sediment layers. Think about books you might stack before putting them away. The first book you put down is on the

bottom of the stack. It's the same with rock layers. The oldest rock layer was laid down first and is on the bottom. The youngest rock layer was laid down last and is on the top.

When you can say that one rock is older than another, you have found its relative age. A rock's **relative age** is how old it is compared to other rocks.

In addition to a rock's position, scientists also use certain kinds of fossils, called **index fossils**, to help them tell the relative ages of rock. Plant and animal species that lived for only a short time (perhaps only a few million years) but that could be found in large numbers over much of Earth make very helpful index fossils.

▲ **The sequence of rock layers can be used to determine the relative ages of rocks.**

The fossil shown below is a trilobite. Many kinds of trilobites lived in oceans all over the world. Since certain kinds lived only at certain times in the past, they make good index fossils. When scientists find two rocks in two different places that both contain the same kind of trilobite fossils, they know that both rocks are about the same age.

Absolute Age

When someone asks how old you are, you probably don't answer with your relative age. You probably say, "I'm 11 years old," rather than "I'm older than my sister." At times, scientists need to know more than a rock's relative age. They need to know its **absolute age**, or how old the rock really is.

Some elements found on Earth are not stable. These elements decay, or break down, into other elements at a known rate. Scientists measure how much of a decaying element is present in a rock layer and how much of the new element into which it decays is present. The amount of time required for this level of decay provides the rock's absolute age.

Potassium is an element found in rocks. Some of the potassium found in igneous and metamorphic rocks is not stable. It breaks down to form a certain kind of argon, another element. Scientists have used the amount of potassium and argon in rocks to find the absolute age of those rocks. Some were as old as a few billion years! ■

▲ Trilobites are common index fossils.

INVESTIGATION 2

1. How are index fossils used to tell the ages of rocks?

2. Suppose you and a friend each found fossils in different layers of sedimentary rock. How could you tell which fossil is older?

HOW DO ROCKS BEND?

Tonight, before you climb into bed, put your hands flat on top of your covers and push them 10 or 20 cm (8 in.) across the bed. Make them push up into folds. How are these folds, or bends, like mountains?

Activity

Big Wrinkles

The Appalachian Mountains in the eastern United States are folded and eroded mountains. Geologists read them like a book. Here's how.

MATERIALS
- 3 different colors of clay
- metric ruler
- plastic knife
- *Science Notebook*

Procedure

1. Flatten three pieces of clay, each a different color, into slabs about 1 cm thick. Each slab represents a layer of rock. Stack the layers. In your *Science Notebook*, **make a sketch** to show the order of the colors from top to bottom.

2. Gently press the sides of the stack together, folding the layers upward into a mountain. Continue pressing until the sides come together.

Step 2

3. You are going to cut off the top your mountain but before you do, **predict** what the cut surface will look like. **Make a sketch** of your prediction.

4. **Model** erosion by cutting the top off your mountain with a plastic knife so you can see all three layers in the cut surface. Does it look like your prediction? **Sketch** the eroded top. Label the layers by color and title your drawing "Upward Fold."

5. Separate the three colors of clay, flatten each lump again, and make another stack. Keep the order of the colors the same as in step 1.

6. Fold the left and right sides of the stack upward until they meet, forming a mountain.

7. **Model** erosion by cutting the top off your mountain. **Make a sketch** of the eroded top. Label the layers and title your drawing "Downward Fold."

Step 6

Analyze and Conclude

1. Where was the oldest layer of rock in the stack in step 1? in the upward fold (step 4)? in the downward fold (step 7)?

2. If you know the relative ages of rock layers on an eroded surface, explain how you can tell if an upward folding of rocks or a downward folding of rocks has occurred.

UNIT PROJECT LINK

Walk around your community to observe natural landforms. Make a list of the landforms you observe. Try to identify the types of rocks that make up the different landforms. Can you tell which rock layers are oldest?

E81

Activity

Dome Questions

Some rocks get pushed up to form a geologic structure called a dome. Investigate how bending rocks can form this structure.

MATERIALS

- 3 different colors of clay
- small ball (table tennis or golf ball)
- plastic knife
- *Science Notebook*

Procedure

1. Flatten and stack three layers of clay, each a different color. Then press the stack down over a small ball to make a dome.

Step 1

2. **Predict** what the pattern of layers will be when you cut the top off the dome. In your *Science Notebook*, **make a sketch** of your prediction.

3. **Model** erosion by cutting the top off the dome, but do not cut so deep that you can see the ball. Does the pattern of layers match your prediction? **Make a sketch** of the actual pattern and title it "Dome." Be sure to label the order of the layers.

Analyze and Conclude

1. What does the pattern of layers in a dome look like?

2. **Infer** what forces could cause a dome to form. Explain your inference.

INVESTIGATE FURTHER!

EXPERIMENT

Get an ice-cream cone of fudge-ripple ice cream. Observe the pattern of chocolate and vanilla layers. Now erode the ice cream from the top down. How does the pattern change? What kinds of "geologic structures" are you observing?

All Bent Out of Shape

No matter how hard you try, you will probably never be able to bend a rock. But mountains all over the eastern United States formed because rocks can and do bend. Let's explore how this comes about.

Forces Bend Rocks

Every time you push open a door or pull a window shut, you apply a force. A force is a push or a pull. In the activity on pages E80 and E81, you applied forces to layers of clay. You did this with your hands by pushing the clay in different directions.

Sometimes forces in nature push on rocks in the same way. If the forces are strong enough and applied long enough, they can cause the rock layers to bend. A bend in a rock layer is called a **fold**.

Most forces that bend rock layers are caused by Earth's moving plates. As you know, Earth's crust consists of huge plates that move slowly around the surface. When two plates come together, the edges of the plates may become folded. Over millions of years the folds become higher and the folded rock forms mountains.

Folded mountains form as rock layers bend and are pushed upward. ▼

The Black Hills

Forces pressing on rock from opposite sides can cause rock layers to fold. Over time, the folds may form mountains such as the Appalachians. A mountain called a dome mountain can also form from folded rock layers. The Black Hills of western South Dakota and eastern Wyoming are an example of dome mountains.

A dome mountain forms when forces deep within Earth push rock layers upward. Recall that magma can flow into existing rock. Sometimes the magma pushes the rock layers above it upward, creating a dome.

When erosion wears down the top of a dome, new rock layers are exposed. If more erosion takes place, the rock formed from magma may be exposed.

In the Black Hills, the magma that created the domes is now granite and is exposed at the surface. The center of the dome is granite surrounded by schist. How do you think the schist formed? Around the center are rings of sedimentary rock, including limestone and sandstone. The sandstone is very hard and resists erosion, forming steep ridges sometimes called hogbacks. People have also shaped the Black Hills—by carving the faces of four presidents into Mount Rushmore! ■

1 A dome forms when a vertical force, such as rising magma, pushes up.

2 In a dome, the youngest rock is the igneous rock formed from the magma.

3 Erosion of a dome may expose the igneous rock formed from the magma.

MOUNT RUSHMORE

Mr. President...

How many of the likenesses of former presidents carved into this mountain's granite wall can you identify? The national memorial on Mount Rushmore's northeastern side is just over 1800m high. Each head is about 30m tall.

JEWEL CAVE

A Real Jewel...

Jewel Cave National Monument is a 100-km long maze of underground rooms and passageways. Its caves formed long ago when water seeped underground and eroded the limestone rock layers.

INVESTIGATION 3

1. How are folded mountains different from dome mountains?

2. Imagine that you come across some folded rock layers that have been exposed by erosion. How would knowing the ages of the layers help you determine if the folding was an anticline or a syncline?

Why do you think earthquakes don't occur all the time along the system of faults under California? Faults are jagged and rough. So as plates move, sections of rock on either side catch on each other and lock together. Eventually enough force builds up so that the rocks unlock and slip past each other. This sudden movement causes an earthquake.

Most earthquakes occur at shallow depths, above 650 km (400 mi). Below this depth, temperature and pressure are so high that all rock bends and flows rather than breaks. Along the famous San Andreas Fault, most earthquakes occur at depths less than 30 km (18 mi).

There have been major earthquakes along the San Andreas Fault. In 1857, a section of the fault 120 km (74 mi) from Los Angeles moved 9 m (30 ft). In 1906 the fault shifted 6 m (20 ft) and the earthquake that resulted destroyed San Francisco. Since scientists believe the San Andreas Fault is about 20 million years old, you can bet there were many more major earthquakes along this fault before such occurrences were recorded.

Slow movement occurs along the San Andreas Fault all the time. Each year, crust along the fault moves several centimeters. Scientists believe that in about 10 million years, Los Angeles will have moved so far north that it will sit just across the fault from San Francisco! In about 60 million years, it will be completely separated from the rest of California. As long as the crust along the San Andreas Fault continues to move, earthquakes will keep happening, and the residents of California must keep expecting them. ■

▲ **Signs of movement along the San Andreas Fault**

INVESTIGATION 4

1. How do faults result in the formation of mountains?

2. Along what type of fault is a mountain not likely to occur? Explain your answer.

REFLECT & EVALUATE

WORD POWER

fault
anticline
core
crust
erosion
fold
absolute age

fossil
index fossil
mantle
model
relative age
syncline

On Your Own
Review the terms in the list. Then use as many terms as you can in a paragraph about Earth's structure.

With a Partner
Write a definition for each term in the list. Have your partner match each definition to the correct term.

BUILD YOUR PORTFOLIO

Collect pictures from magazines that show rock formations of various kinds. Try to identify faults, folds, and other features in the pictures.

Analyze Information
Study the drawing. Then identify the layers of Earth shown.

Assess Performance
Using materials of your choice, model movement along the three types of faults. Describe the forces acting in each case.

Problem Solving

1. Compare and contrast folding and faulting.

2. A sandstone layer is found atop a shale layer. A thick section of gabbro, which hardened from magma, cuts upward through both layers. A fault cuts through all three rocks. What are the relative ages of the fault and the three rock layers? Explain your reasoning.

3. Make a sketch of a syncline and an anticline. Then make a sketch showing the eroded top of each formation. Label the rock layers from oldest to youngest in each sketch.

Throughout this unit, you've investigated questions related to Earth and its structures. How will you use what you've learned and share that information with others? Here are some ideas.

Hold a Big Event
to Share Your Unit Project

Set up a rock, mineral, and fossil exhibit using the collections your group and the other groups assembled. Prepare identification cards for each sample. Also publish a guide to rocks, minerals, and fossils for your area. Distribute copies to parents and friends who attend the exhibit and invite them to use the guide to learn about the types of rocks, minerals, and fossils present in your community.

Experiment

With the help of a mineral guide and a hand lens, classify your minerals based on crystal structure. You might also grow crystal gardens, using different materials—alum, salt, sugar, and so on. Try adding a few drops of food coloring to each solution. What happens to the crystals? When the crystals are grown, examine them with a microscope or hand lens. Which crystals look like the cubes? Which have six faces? What other shapes of crystals did you grow? Draw and label the characteristcs of the crystals in your *Science Notebook*.

Research

Which topic in this unit would you like to investigate further? Try finding out more about rock layers or erosion. (You might wish to ask a partner to work with you.) To do so, locate a rock face or any rock formation where you can observe layers of rocks. Study the rock formation as closely as you can. Sketch or photograph the layers. Take rock samples. If possible, ask a geologist to help you interpret what you see. Then assemble your research into an informative display.

UNIT F

LIGHT AND SOUND

Theme: Models

GET READY TO

OBSERVE & QUESTION

How is sound transmitted and recorded?

Today, sounds—and images—are transmitted in an instant to all parts of the world. Find out how this instantaneous transmission of music, voices, and images affects you.

EXPERIMENT & HYPOTHESIZE

How are lenses used in telescopes and microscopes?

Telescopes were first invented in the early 1600's. Build your own telescope much like the ones built hundreds of years ago.

INVESTIGATE!

RESEARCH & ANALYZE

As you investigate, find out more from these books.

- ***Tuning In: The Sounds of the Radio*** by Eve and Albert Stwertka, Illustrated by Mena Dolobrowsky (Julian Messner, 1992). How can music and information travel invisibly from a radio station to your house? Find out what radio waves are and how radios work.

- ***Extremely Weird Micro Monsters*** by Sarah Lovett (John Muir Publications, 1993). Discover how powerful microscopes can take pictures that make incredibly small creatures look gigantic!

- ***That's a Wrap: How Movies Are Made*** by Ned Dowd, Photography by Henry Horenstein (Silver Burdett Press, 1993). How are stunts and special effects recorded? How does sound make a film exciting? Find out how movies are made by reading this book.

WORK TOGETHER & SHARE IDEAS

How can you put together a sound and light show?

Working together, you'll have a chance to apply what you have learned. You and your class will stage a puppet show. You'll write, rehearse, and perform your own narration. Then you'll mix lights of different colors to achieve special effects. Finally you'll build models of musical instruments from around the world and provide the music for your show.

CHAPTER 1

PROPERTIES OF LIGHT

Black lamps don't seem to give off much light. But shine them on surfaces covered with a certain kind of paint and see what happens! What is light, anyway? How can light be black?

Lighten Up

Richard Green is founder of Wildfire Incorporated, a company in Los Angeles that creates lighting effects for music videos, television commercials, theme parks, and movies. Richard is a lighting specialist, someone who designs and produces just the right lighting for shows and other events.

One popular lighting technique involves making objects fluoresce, or glow. Richard covers objects with fluorescent paint and then shines a black light on them. The objects seem to glow! He says that people experience fluorescent objects in different ways. For some it is like stepping into an animated cartoon world of bright, crazy colors. For others the color and light seem to appear from nowhere.

Coming Up

◄ These people seem to glow because of fluorescent paint and black lights.

WHAT IS LIGHT AND WHERE DOES IT COME FROM?

Have you ever been home when the electric power went out? A power failure can make you stop and think about something you take for granted—light! In this investigation you'll find out about light you can see and its relatives you can't see.

Activity

Seeing the Light

There are lights all around you. Try a "scavenger hunt" to find some of them.

MATERIALS
• *Science Notebook*

Procedure

Work with a group of other students to investigate light sources in various places. Look for all possible light sources. List the locations and the light sources in your *Science Notebook*. **Record** the kind of energy you think is being used to produce the light.

Rank the light sources from brightest to dimmest, using 1 for the brightest. Note whether any heat was given off from each light source.

Analyze and Conclude

1. What were the light sources your group found?

2. For each source, what kind of energy change produces the light? What can you **infer** about the connection between light and heat?

Activity

All Aglow

A simple electric circuit contains one battery, a light bulb, and a couple of connecting wires. What changes can you see in the light as you experiment with the different parts of the circuit?

MATERIALS
- light bulb *A*
- 3 batteries (size D)
- insulated copper wire
- light bulb holder
- light bulb *B*
- tape
- *Science Notebook*

Procedure

1. Insert light bulb *A* into a light bulb holder. Connect one battery to light bulb *A*, using copper wire. Use tape to hold the wire in place.

2. **Observe** what happens when you complete the electric circuit. Carefully note if the bulbs are warm. **Record** your observations in your *Science Notebook*.

3. **Predict** what will happen if you add a second battery to the circuit. **Record** your prediction. Then add the second battery and **record** the results.

4. Add a third battery to the circuit and again **record** your observations.

5. Replace light bulb *A* with light bulb *B*. Repeat steps 1–4. **Record** the results.

Step 1

Analyze and Conclude

1. In step 3, how did your prediction match what happened?

2. What happened when you added more batteries to the circuit? **Suggest a hypothesis** to explain what you observed.

3. What change occurred when you replaced bulb *A* with bulb *B*? Why did this change occur?

4. What do you think is flowing from the battery to the bulb through the copper wire?

5. What causes the bulbs to glow? Were the bulbs warm?

6. What evidence do you have that light is energy?

Lighting the Way

Imagine that it is summertime and you are lying on a sandy beach. Through your sunglasses you can see the light of the Sun. You can feel the heat of the Sun on your bare skin. The Sun's rays provide Earth with light and heat, which are both forms of energy. You may recall that **energy** is the ability to do work or cause a change in matter.

The Sun, a star, supplies nearly all of Earth's natural light energy. From Earth you can see other stars during the night, but the amount of light from those stars is very small compared to the amount received from the Sun. Moonlight, the light Earth receives from the Moon, is really sunlight that has bounced off the Moon's surface.

Energy From the Sun

The Sun gives off huge amounts of energy that travel to Earth through the vacuum of space. The energy given off by the Sun is called **electromagnetic radiation** (ē lek trō mag net'ik rā dē ā'shən). There are many kinds of electromagnetic (E-M) radiation; some kinds you can see, and others you can't see. **Visible light** is the type of E-M radiation that you can see.

Most types of E-M radiation are invisible. For example, infrared radiation and ultraviolet radiation are two types of invisible E-M radiation. Infrared radiation from the Sun is what causes you to feel warm when you

X-rays

gamma rays

Electromagnetic radiation from the Sun includes visible and invisible radiation. ▶

stand in sunlight. Heat lamps also produce infrared radiation.

Ultraviolet radiation, or UV light, is sometimes called black light because an ultraviolet lamp looks dark to us when it is on. But some materials glow, or give off visible light, when UV light shines on them. That painful sunburn you get from lying too long on the beach is caused by ultraviolet radiation.

Electromagnetic radiation can cause changes in matter. For example, sunlight heats water in the oceans. Light can also be used to heat water in solar collectors. Have you ever seen a solar calculator? When light shines on the calculator's solar cells, electricity to run the calculator is produced. In each case, light is changed to other forms of energy.

▲ **Certain minerals glow under ultraviolet (UV) light (*left*). The same minerals are shown under normal light (*right*).**

Light starts many chemical reactions. One of the most important reactions started by light is photosynthesis, the food-making process of plants. During photosynthesis, plant cells convert carbon dioxide and water to oxygen and sugar. In this reaction, light energy is stored as chemical energy.

ultraviolet rays

visible light

infrared rays

microwaves

radio waves

INVESTIGATE FURTHER!

EXPERIMENT

Hold your hand above a lighted light bulb. What do you observe? Place a glass jar over the bulb. Hold your hand near the jar's side. What do you observe? Remove the jar. Is it as warm as your hand? How do you know energy waves passed through the glass?

Making Light

How many light sources can you think of other than the Sun? Light bulbs are the most common sources of artificial light. But fire was the first source of light that humans were able to control.

A campfire is a chemical reaction that gives off light. When a substance burns, the energy stored in it is given off as heat and light. The matter being burned is not used up. Instead, it is changed to other substances.

▲ **A campfire is a chemical reaction in which light and heat are given off.**

Most of the chemical reactions that give off light also produce heat. With a campfire, you may be more interested in the heat than in the light. If you light a candle, on the other hand, you're interested in the light that is released. If you burn a candle, less than 1 percent of the stored energy in the candle is changed to light. The rest is changed to heat.

Have you ever carried a "light stick"? People often take these along on camp-ing trips for emergency lights. The plastic tubes contain two sets of chemicals. When you bend the light stick, you break a small tube inside it. When the inner tube breaks, chemicals mix. A reaction occurs that gives off light. This reaction does not make much heat, so the tube does not get hot.

In an incandescent light bulb, there is a very thin wire, called a filament, that carries electricity. The wire gets very

A light stick before its chemical reaction (*left*); breaking the tube releases chemicals that mix, causing a chemical reaction (*center*); the glowing light stick (*right*)

Sources of light: fluorescent light bulbs (*left*); lightning bolt (*center*); sparks given off during welding (*right*)

hot when the electricity goes through it. This makes the wire glow. But only about 2 percent of the electrical energy is changed into light.

Your classroom probably is lighted by fluorescent (flo͞o res'ənt) lamps. These electric lights don't contain a filament. Instead, they contain a gas that gives off ultraviolet light when electricity flows through it. Remember that you can't *see* ultraviolet light. To make visible light, the fluorescent tube is lined with chemicals that glow when ultraviolet light strikes them. Ultraviolet lights do a much better job of changing electrical energy into light energy than do incandescent lights. About 30 percent of the electrical energy is changed into light. As a result fluorescent bulbs don't get as hot as incandescent bulbs do.

One familiar source of light doesn't last very long, but it can be very bright. What is it? Lightning! Lightning is a very bright electrical spark. Perhaps you've seen a lightning flash light up the night sky so that it's as bright as day. What are other examples of light coming from sparks? ■

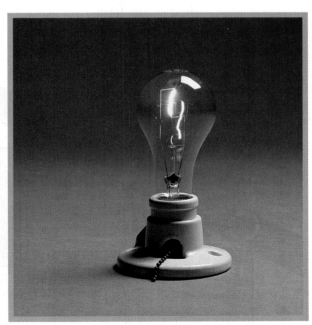

▲ **Incandescent light bulb with glowing filament**

CHAPTER 2

LIGHT, LENSES, AND COLOR

Scientists seek to understand our planet, our solar system, and even the universe. This often involves getting the best possible view of things. Telescopes extend our vision to the galaxies. Microscopes help us see the tiny, complex world that is invisible to our unaided eyes. How is it possible for us to see so far and so much?

A Young Astronomer

Marian Toro, 17, is a Native American of the Tohono O'odham Nation. She lives on a reservation about 96 km (60 mi) west of Tucson, Arizona, near Kitt Peak. According to Marian, long ago her people looked at the Moon and stars to tell if the harvest would be a good one. Now she studies those stars with the aid of a telescope.

Marian hopes to become an astronomer. She became an amateur astronomer at the astronomy camp of the University of Arizona. Using the Mount Lemmon telescope, Marian tracked satellites and observed planets. She watched scientists at the university make some of the world's largest telescope mirrors. Marian also built a small telescope.

Why is it important for an astronomer to know about light and lenses?

Coming Up

◀ A student observes the stars through the Mount Lemmon telescope.

INVESTIGATION ①

HOW DO LENSES HELP CONTROL LIGHT?

Do you know someone who wears contact lenses? A contact lens changes the direction of light passing through it. This investigation should help you understand how lenses help a person see more clearly.

Activity
Becoming Focused

You've seen that as light passes from one material to another it can change direction. When a material such as glass is shaped into a lens, it directs—or redirects—the path of light. Explore how lens shape affects the way light passes into and out of the lens.

Procedure

1. In your *Science Notebook* make a chart titled "Comparing Convex and Concave Lenses." Record all observations during this activity in the chart.

2. Take a piece of lens paper and feel the shape of the convex lens through it. Make a sketch of the lens.

3. Darken the room. Using a manila folder as a screen, place a flashlight about 30 cm from the screen. Point the flashlight toward the screen.

4. Place the convex lens between the flashlight and the screen so that the light passes through the lens and shines onto the screen.

Step 4

5. **Observe** what happens on the screen as you move the lens back and forth between the light and the screen. **Infer** how the lens is affecting the light. **Record** your inference.

6. Stand with your back toward a window. Hold the lens in one hand and extend your arm so that the light from the window passes through the lens.

7. Have a classmate hold the screen so that the light passing through the lens shines on the screen. Move the screen and lens as needed until a clear image appears on the screen. Look at the image carefully and **record** your observations.

8. Place the convex lens on the print on a piece of newspaper. Raise the lens slowly and **observe** the print. **Record** your observations.

9. Repeat steps 2–8, using a concave lens. In the chart, **record** your observations about the concave lens.

Step 7

Analyze and Conclude

1. In step 5, how did the appearance of the beam of light on the screen change for each lens?

2. Describe the image you saw on the screen as you moved each lens back and forth in step 7. What was unusual about the image?

3. How does a convex lens affect light when it focuses light to a point? How do convex and concave lenses differ in the way they affect light?

UNIT PROJECT LINK

Your group is going to put on a puppet show, using different colored lights to produce special visual effects. Cover a flashlight with cellophane of different colors. Experiment with blue, red, and green, in turn. Create situations to act out, using your puppets. Decide which colors of light to use to create the right emotion for each situation. Then give your show.

WHAT IS SOUND?

Have you ever sat perfectly still and listened to the sound around you? Try it sometime and you may be amazed at what you hear. In this investigation you'll see how sound is produced and how it travels. In the process, you may hear some sweet—and sour— sounds!

Activity
Rubber-Band Banjo

How are sounds produced? Construct a simple banjo and use it to find out.

Procedure

Stretch a rubber band lengthwise over a ruler. Then insert a pencil under the rubber band at each end of the ruler so that the rubber band is lifted away from the surface of the ruler. Pluck the rubber band at any point between the two pencils. Observe what happens. Record what you see and hear in your *Science Notebook*. Press your finger at different points along the rubber band, plucking it each time. Describe the sounds produced.

Analyze and Conclude

1. Hypothesize how the rubber band produces sound.

2. How did the sound change when you pressed the rubber band at different points on the ruler?

Activity
Waves and Sound

Sound is a form of energy that travels through different objects and materials. In this activity you'll build a model of the way a sound wave moves.

Procedure

1. Use a piece of string to tie one end of a coil spring to a table leg. Stretch the coil spring and use another piece of string to tie the other end to another table leg. Make sure that the spring is stretched tightly enough so that it doesn't touch the floor.

2. Fold pieces of yarn in half. Starting at one end of the spring, hang a piece of yarn on every tenth coil.

3. **Predict** what will happen to the yarn if you pinch five end coils together and then release them. **Discuss** your prediction with your group. **Record** your prediction in your *Science Notebook*.

4. Pinch together five coils at one end of the spring and quickly release them. **Record** your observations of the coil spring and the yarn.

5. Repeat step 4 several times. **Record** your observations each time.

Step 1

Analyze and Conclude

1. Write a general statement about the way the spring coil behaved when you pinched and then released the five end coils.

2. What evidence did you observe that energy was transferred along the coil?

F55

Noise Pollution

The growth of cities and technology has led to sounds and sound volumes that were unknown until recent centuries. Studies have shown that exposure to loud noise or loud music can damage a person's hearing. Besides causing damage to the ear itself, noise can cause stress-related disorders such as hives, ulcers, or high blood pressure. The occurrence of damaging sound in the environment even has a name—**noise pollution**!

An understanding of the properties of sound can help you reduce noise pollution. Like light, sound is absorbed by some materials and reflected by others. Materials that are hard, such as concrete or brick, reflect most of the sound that reaches them. Highway engineers

▲ **In a recording studio a complex control panel allows the sound engineers to control sounds produced by the recording artists.**

SCIENCE IN LITERATURE

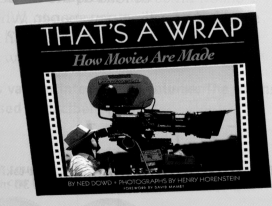

THAT'S A WRAP: HOW MOVIES ARE MADE
by Ned Dowd
Books for Young Readers, Simon & Schuster, 1991

You may say that you want to see a movie, but *seeing* is only half the experience. Try enjoying a movie with your hands over your ears! Movie makers know that the sound of a film is just as important as its images. That's why there are sound designers, boom operators, and sound mixers on movie crews. That's why the director yells, "Quiet on the set!"

Find out how a movie is made by reading *That's a Wrap: How Movies Are Made* by Ned Dowd. You'll learn how the stunts and special effects are recorded. From a whispered secret to an explosion, sounds make movies thrilling.

take advantage of this property by building wooden or concrete barriers between highways and surrounding homes. These barriers help reduce noise by reflecting it.

Materials that are soft, such as cloth, plastic foam, and acoustical plaster, absorb much of the sound that reaches them. These materials are useful in reducing noise within buildings. In many buildings, ceilings and walls are built of such sound-absorbing materials. The hanging banners in school gymnasiums help absorb sound so that you can hear the gym teacher speaking. ■

A large cafeteria can be a very noisy place if it has no materials to absorb sound (*left*). A restaurant is often a quiet place because its chairs, floors, and walls have sound-absorbing materials (*right*).

INVESTIGATION 1

1. Describe at least two specific ways that people can control sound.

2. What is a decibel? Draw and explain a scale that shows sounds around you expressed in decibels.

INVESTIGATION 2

HOW DO PEOPLE HEAR?

Every day you are bombarded by sound. You may wake up to the jarring noise of an alarm clock. On the street, recyclers may be collecting your used glass. How can you tell one sound from another? This investigation explores hearing—and not hearing.

Activity

Identifying Sounds

How distinctive are sounds? Are there any two voices—or sounds—that are exactly alike? In this activity you'll test how well you can tell one sound from another.

MATERIALS
- blindfold
- assorted sound makers (bells, whistles, rattles)
- *Science Notebook*

Procedure

1. Blindfold one member of your group. Then have each student in your group, one by one, say a word or phrase. Have the blindfolded student identify each person who speaks. **Record** in your *Science Notebook* whether the blindfolded student could identify each person.

2. Repeat step 1. This time, have each student *whisper* the same word or phrase. **Record** whether each person was identified. **Discuss** your findings with your group.

3. Blindfold a different group member. Have each student, one by one, make a sound with a different sound maker.

4. **Record** whether the blindfolded student identified each sound maker. **Discuss** your findings as a group.

Step 3

Analyze and Conclude

1. In step 1, could the student correctly identify each person who spoke? What do you think allowed the blindfolded student to identify the speakers? If the student couldn't identify each person, give a reason why not.

2. In step 2, could the blindfolded student identify each student who spoke? Why might it have been difficult to identify the speakers?

3. Could the blindfolded student identify each sound maker? Which ones couldn't be easily identified?

4. In general, what properties of a sound can be used to identify it?

UNIT PROJECT LINK

Plan a soundtrack for the folk tale you have begun rehearsing. Include the instruments and other devices needed for the sound effects. Choose a narrator to tell the story. Decide how long the show will last. Then make an audiotape of the soundtrack, including the narration. Make sure the puppets' movements are synchronized with the soundtrack.

magnetic
tape

record/play-
back head

erase head

magnetic
tape

recorded iron oxide particles

erased iron
oxide particles

audiocassettes—miniature versions of the older reel-to-reel tapes. When you record sound on tape, as you did on page F89, electric currents produced by sound waves entering a microphone are sent through the coil of an electromagnet (the recording head). The changing electric current in the coil causes changes in the magnetic field of the recording head. As the tape moves through the changing magnetic field of the head, a magnetic pattern is formed in the tiny crystals of iron oxide on the surface of the tape. The tape can then be passed through another head, called the playback head. This causes it to produce weak electrical signals that are then amplified. When these amplified electrical signals are fed to a loudspeaker, they reproduce the sounds that first entered the microphone.

By the mid-1980s audiocassettes were outselling records. This was due

A compact disc (CD), showing an
enlargement of "pits" (holes)
and "flats" (flat surfaces) ▶

◀ **An audiocassette, showing the
magnetic tape on small reels**

mainly to their convenience. Tapes could be played anywhere—even in a moving car.

Compact Discs (CDs)

Tapes store a magnetic "image" of sounds. Today, digital signals can also be used to store sound. In a digital recording, the electrical signal from the microphone is changed to a series of on-or-off electrical pulses that are recorded as strong or weak magnetic fields.

A **compact disc**, or CD, contains a digital recording. Along the very thin recording track of the disc, the "offs" are recorded as pits. The "ons" are recorded as the flat surface of the disc. As the disc spins on a CD player, the codes of offs and ons along the track are scanned by a laser beam and changed to electrical signals. These signals are then sent to the speakers. Today, CDs are fast replacing audiocassette tapes. What do you think might replace CDs? ■

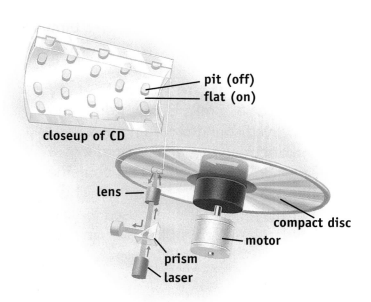

pit (off)
flat (on)

closeup of CD

lens

compact disc

motor

prism

laser

Delivering
Information

SCIENCE TECHNOLOGY & SOCIETY

Television provides the world with an amazing variety of entertainment. You can enjoy comedy, drama, music, and sports all on the same day in the comfort of your home. Satellites in orbit above Earth make it possible for people in nearly all parts of the world to view an Olympic event as it happens.

Through TV, you can see world leaders in action and observe the effects of wars and natural disasters. You can also see that even though people have different backgrounds and cultures, people all over the world have many of the same needs and interests.

The Information Superhighway

Your television will soon be part of the communication system of the future— the **information superhighway**. The telephone,

computer, and television will be combined to link people together in a way that was not possible before. Imagine being part of a worldwide network joining communication, entertainment, and information. Your telephone line will be your link to the information superhighway.

Small but powerful computers linked by telephone lines and television cable systems will take you to any stop you choose along the information superhighway. Even now, many personal-computer users browse through libraries and databases and communicate with

Fiber-optic bundles ▶

other users on Internet. **Internet** is a data highway made up of more than 10,000 computer networks.

In the future the information superhighway will let you access over 500 TV channels and watch almost any movie ever made. You will also be able to make airline and hotel reservations, as well as shop at your favorite stores, while sitting in your living room. You'll be able to buy whatever you wish by inserting a credit card into a slot beside your TV screen.

Your doctor will be able to provide you with better care because he or she will be able to reach the medical special-

▲ **The information superhighway**

ist you need through the information superhighway. The specialist will be able to view, examine, and talk with you and your family doctor.

What lies beyond the information superhighway? In another two or three decades you'll know! ■

INVESTIGATION 3

1. Choose a sound-recording system, either old or new, and describe how sound is recorded on this device.

2. Describe how you think your life may be changed if your home or school is linked to the information superhighway.

REFLECT & EVALUATE

WORD POWER

audiocassette

auditory nerve

compact disc

decibel

eustachian tube

information superhighway

noise pollution

phonograph

semicircular canal

intensity

Internet

hearing aid

volume

On Your Own

Review the terms in the list. Write one new thing you learned about each term.

With a Partner

Write each term in the list on one side of an index card and the definition on the other side. Use the cards to quiz your partner.

BUILD YOUR PORTFOLIO

Design a poster to make people aware of the danger of loud noises. Show why loud noises are dangerous and suggest ways people can protect themselves.

Analyze Information

Look at the graph below. How does the sound shown at 50 dB compare with the sound at 60 dB? Suggest a sound that could be placed at 0 dB.

dB 0   10   20   30   40   50   60

Assess Performance

Some rooms in your home or school might be very noisy because they have few sound-proofing materials in them. Choose such a room and plan a way to reduce the noise level of the room.

Problem Solving

1. One thing actors must learn is to speak loudly enough to be heard by the audience. This skill is called "projecting the voice." Why do actors have to project more when an audience is present than at rehearsals?

2. One type of frequently used hearing aid was not worn in the ear. Instead, it was hooked over the ear and rested against the bone behind the ear. How, do you think, did this hearing aid help a person hear?

3. Devices such as LPs, cassette tapes, and CDs do not actually "store" sound itself. Explain what is meant by this statement.

Throughout this unit, you've investigated questions related to light and sound. How will you use what you've learned and share that information with others? Here are some ideas.

Hold a Big Event
to Share Your Unit Project

You and your class have been putting together a sound and light show using puppets as the characters. You've written and rehearsed the narration and worked on the special lighting effects. You've made models of musical instruments from different parts of the world and have rehearsed the songs played on the instruments. Now is the time to put the finishing touches on your show. Go over all the details until everything is perfect—the narration, the lighting, and the music. Then put on the show for another class or the entire school. You may even wish to invite your family and friends to enjoy the show!

Experiment

In this unit, you investigated the effects of mixing different colors of light. Create an experiment to discover if mixing different colors of paint pigments yields the same results as mixing different colors of light. Make a poster showing the results of your experiment.

Research

Choose a topic in this unit to investigate further at the library. You might want to learn more about musical instruments of different cultures. You might want to explore how the colors and sounds in fireworks are created. Or, you might want to find out what sound pollution is and why it can be dangerous. Find an interesting way to share what you learn.

MOVEMENT AND CONTROL

Theme: Systems

GET READY TO

OBSERVE & QUESTION

How can you respond to things around you?

What if there was a wheelchair that could be completely controlled by a disabled person's brain waves? Learn how scientists are making connections between mind and body by using new technologies.

EXPERIMENT & HYPOTHESIZE

What are the parts of the skeletal system?

Make a bone model and discover how bones move at a joint. Can you predict where each type of joint is found in your body? Check out your predictions with a model of the human skeleton.

INVESTIGATE!

RESEARCH & ANALYZE

As you investigate, find out more from these books.

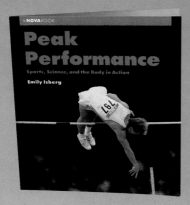

- **Peak Performance** by Emily Isberg (Simon & Schuster Books for Young Readers, 1989). Discover how up-to-the-minute scientific technology helps athletes all over the world. Read about the workings of the U.S. Olympic Training Centers.

- **Native American Doctor: The Story of Susan LaFlesche Picotte** by Jeri Ferris (Carolrhoda Books, 1991). This biography takes you to the Great Plains in the 1860's. Learn how alcohol abuse was fought by the first Native American woman to earn a medical degree.

WORK TOGETHER & SHARE IDEAS

What's your plan for a sports event that involves three systems of your body?

You'll design a series of activities to show how your skeletal, muscular, and nervous systems all work together. Have fun planning and competing in your Bone, Muscle, Brain Triathlon!

Triathlon

CHAPTER 1

BONES AND MUSCLES

Watch the ways athletes move. They use their legs to run and jump in the air. They use their hands to catch balls of different shapes. It's a blur of motion. What systems of the body allow for these amazing movements? How do these systems work together?

Will I Walk Again?

In 1992, New York Jets defensive lineman 270-lb Dennis Byrd collided with a 275-lb teammate on the field. Byrd shattered a vertebra, one of the 33 bones of the spine. This caused injury to the nerve tissue of the spinal cord. The muscles in his arms and legs didn't work, and Dennis Byrd couldn't move.

"Am I going to be paralyzed?" Byrd kept asking. The Jets team doctor feared that the answer would be "Yes." But Dennis Byrd was determined not to give up. Two weeks after extensive surgery on his spine, he began physical therapy. At first, therapists had to move Byrd's limbs for him. But after several weeks of intensive exercises, he was not only moving his limbs on his own but was racing around in a wheelchair. Gradually, Dennis Byrd learned to walk again.

In this chapter you'll learn how the bones and muscles of the body make walking and other movements possible.

◄ Dennis Byrd prepares for his physical therapy.

INVESTIGATION 1

WHAT ARE THE PARTS OF THE SKELETAL SYSTEM?

How many bones do you think make up the human skeleton? Would you say 50? 100? You might be surprised to learn that the human skeleton has 206 bones! These range from the long bone in your thigh to the tiny bones in your ears. Find out more about your skeletal system in Investigation 1.

Activity

A Closer Look at Bones

Although you have a full set of bones, you really can't study them. But in this activity you'll get a chance to look closely at a bone.

MATERIALS
- goggles
- gloves
- paper towels
- hand lens
- bone specimen
- *Science Notebook*

SAFETY ///////
Wear goggles and gloves when handling the bone specimen.

Procedure

Observe the outside covering and features of the bone. Describe the bone in your *Science Notebook*. Next, observe the inside of the bone. Notice how the inside structure differs from the outside structure. Describe the inside of the bone. Make a drawing of the bone. Talk with your group. What can you infer about the material that makes up the bone?

Analyze and Conclude

1. Compare and contrast the inside structure of the bone with the outside structure of the bone.

2. Do you think that bones are living material? What evidence supports your conclusion?

Activity

Where Bones Meet

What would happen if all of your bones were fixed in place? How would you move? Find out what structures allow movement of your skeleton.

MATERIALS

- bone diagrams
- scissors
- tape
- posterboard
- paste
- brass fastener
- model of a human skeleton
- *Science Notebook*

Procedure

1. Work with a partner. Cut out the bone diagrams and tape them together to form two long bones. Paste the bones on posterboard and cut them out.

2. Use a fastener to attach an end of one bone to an end of the other bone. Observe the ways in which the bones of your model move. Describe in your *Science Notebook* how the bones move.

3. Predict where in the human skeleton bones move in a similar way to your model. Record your predictions.

4. Examine your own body or a model of a human skeleton to find places where bones move in a similar way to your model. Record these places.

Step 2

Analyze and Conclude

1. Compare your observations of your skeleton or the human skeleton model with your predictions. How are they alike? How do they differ?

2. The place where two bones meet is called a joint. What can you infer about the functions of joints?

3. Did you find additional bones in your body or in the skeleton model moving like your long-bone model? Where were they located?

4. How did bones in your body move differently from your model?

HOW DO BONES AND MUSCLES CAUSE MOVEMENT?

Smack! You hit the ball far out into center field. You run as fast as you can—past first, past second, past third. Home run! Your skeletal system made it around the bases, but not without help from another system. Can you name it? It's your system of muscles!

Activity

Push or Pull?

To make something move, you can either push it or pull it. Do your muscles push your bones to make them move, or pull them?

Procedure

1. The biceps is the muscle on the front of the upper arm. The triceps is the muscle on the back of the upper arm. Locate your biceps and triceps.

2. Wrap the fingers of your right hand around your left upper arm so you can feel both the top and bottom of your arm at the same time. Bend and straighten your fore-arm slowly several times. Describe in your *Science Notebook* how your biceps and triceps changed as you moved your arm.

Step 2

3. Have a group member measure the length of your biceps and triceps when your arm is straight and when it is bent. Make a chart and record the measurements.

4. Have a group member measure the thickness around your arm when it is straight and when it is bent. Measure halfway between your elbow and shoulder. Record these measurements in your chart.

Analyze and Conclude

1. How did your biceps and triceps change as you bent and straightened your arm?

2. Based on your data, hypothesize how your muscles cause your bones to move. Make a drawing to show your hypothesis.

3. How do the biceps and triceps work together to cause your arm to move?

INVESTIGATE FURTHER!

EXPERIMENT

Add two rubber bands to the model you made for the activity on page G7. One rubber band should act like a biceps and one should act like a triceps. Compare your model with other students' models.

Step 3

Step 4

G15

CHAPTER 2

THE NERVOUS SYSTEM

Have you ever been nervous? Your hands tremble, your stomach muscles tighten, and your mouth gets dry. Your nervous system senses things about your surroundings and causes your body to respond. How does the nervous system control and coordinate what your body does?

Snails on the Scent

What can you smell? Burning leaves? Sour milk? Chocolate cake? You may think you have a keen sense of smell. But among the creatures of the animal kingdom, humans have a rather dull sense of smell.

Ronald Chase is a neurobiologist (nōō'rō bī äl'ə jist), a scientist who studies the nervous system. At McGill University in Montreal, Canada, he has investigated the land snail's sense of smell. Land snails have been around for about 350 million years. Half of the brain of a land snail deals mainly with smells and tastes.

Dr. Chase has spent years training snails to follow different smells by rewarding them with food. He has even taught snails to follow smells they don't like! Chase claims to have set a record by training snails to remember particular scents for as long as 120 days.

Do you think humans' sense of smell would improve if it were the only way to find food?

▶ Dr. Ronald Chase tests the land snail's sense of smell.

WHAT ROLE DO THE BRAIN AND NERVES PLAY?

Think about the operation of a clothing-store chain. Workers in each store call Headquarters with reports on what's selling. Headquarters makes decisions and calls back, saying, "Put slacks on sale; order more shirts!" Now investigate what goes on in your body's "headquarters" and how messages get there and back.

Activity

Walk Straight and Tall

How do muscles and bones work together with the brain and nerves? This activity will help you understand how.

MATERIALS
- book
- *Science Notebook*

Procedure

Try to balance a book on your head and walk across the room without dropping it. Before you do this, **predict** what you think will happen. **Record** your prediction in your *Science Notebook*. Have a partner **observe** you as you walk while balancing the book. Each of you **record** your own observations. Next, **observe** as your partner walks across the room. Again, each **record** your own observations.

Analyze and Conclude

1. How did your observations compare to your prediction?

2. How did muscles and bones enable you to balance a book on your head and to walk across the room? **Infer** what role your nervous system played in this activity.

Activity

Measuring Reaction Time

How are your brain and nerves needed for you to react to a falling object? How long does it take them to "get the message"?

MATERIALS
- meterstick
- *Science Notebook*

Step 2

Procedure

1. Hold out your arm and spread your thumb and forefinger slightly apart.

2. Have your partner hold a meterstick above your hand so that the 0-cm end of the stick is between your thumb and finger.

3. Without warning, your partner will let go of the meterstick. **Predict** at which centimeter mark you will catch the falling meterstick. **Record** your prediction in your *Science Notebook*.

4. Catch the meterstick as it falls. Look at the centimeter mark where you caught it. **Record** that number in a chart.

5. Repeat steps 1 through 4 nine more times. **Compare** your data with that of other groups.

Step 4

Analyze and Conclude

1. The time it takes the body to recognize and react to something is called reaction time. How did your reaction time change as you did this activity? Why do you think it changed?

2. What do you think happens between your eyes, brain, and hand from the time the meterstick starts to fall until you catch it?

3. **Infer** why there was a reaction time between when you saw the meterstick fall and when you caught it.

The Path of a
Nerve Impulse

Do you think you responded quickly to the falling meterstick in the activity on page G27? No matter how fast you grabbed the meterstick, there was still a little time that passed after you saw it fall. This time—your reaction time—was the time it took for a nerve impulse to make its way through your nervous system.

A **nerve impulse** is a message carried through your body by nerve cells, or **neurons** (nōō'ränz). Neurons are found throughout your body.

Certain neurons, the **sensory neurons**, pick up signals from the environment. These signals, or **stimuli**

(stim'yōō lī), start a nerve impulse. Your muscles move in reaction to the messages carried to them by another type of neuron, the **motor neurons.** Bundles of neurons are called nerves.

What happens between a stimulus and your response? To answer this question, follow the path of the nerve impulse in the illustration on page G29.

Now you know the path of a nerve impulse. These impulses are similar to electrical signals and are caused by changes in chemicals in the neurons. A nerve impulse can travel through your nervous system at speeds from 10 to 120 m/s. That's why you can respond so quickly to a stimulus. ■

In a neuron, impulses travel along extensions to other neurons. ▼

direction of impulse

FOLLOWING THE NERVE IMPULSE

The nerve impulse begins with a stimulus. The impulse travels through sensory neurons either directly to the brain, or to the spinal column and then to the brain. The brain analyzes the message and decides what action to take. Then the brain sends an impulse back down the spinal column and out through motor neurons to the muscles. As the muscles contract, the body makes the proper response.

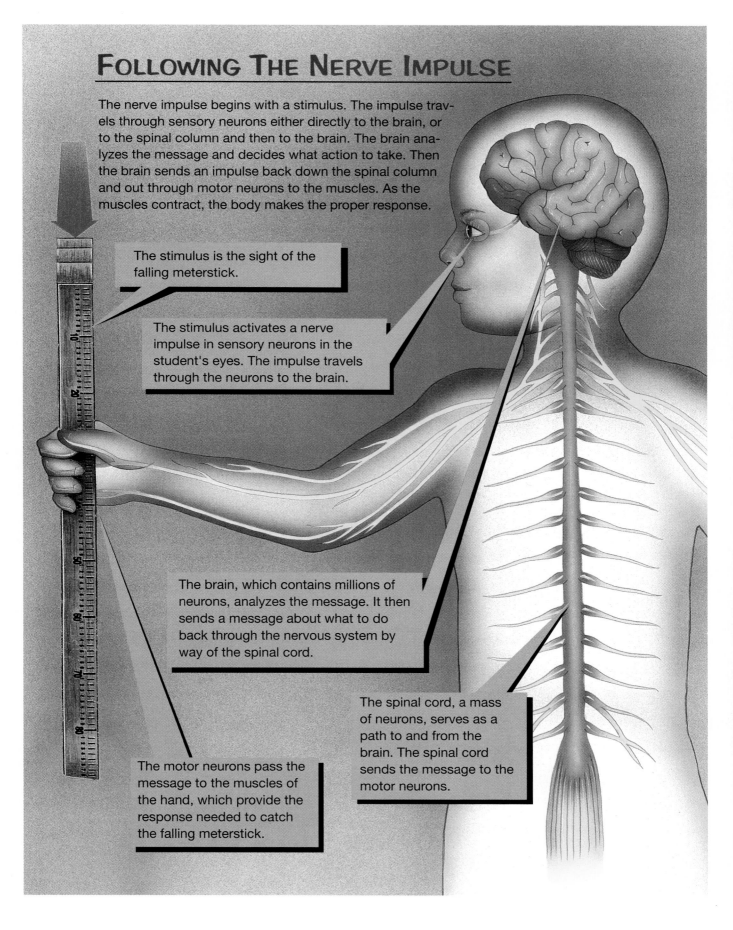

The stimulus is the sight of the falling meterstick.

The stimulus activates a nerve impulse in sensory neurons in the student's eyes. The impulse travels through the neurons to the brain.

The brain, which contains millions of neurons, analyzes the message. It then sends a message about what to do back through the nervous system by way of the spinal cord.

The spinal cord, a mass of neurons, serves as a path to and from the brain. The spinal cord sends the message to the motor neurons.

The motor neurons pass the message to the muscles of the hand, which provide the response needed to catch the falling meterstick.

A Tour of the Brain

"All aboard for a tour of the brain! Check all sharp objects at the gate. Once we get past the skull, we must ensure that the soft tissue of the brain remains uninjured by our journey. Take your seats, please. Here we go!"

Off to a Bony Start

What if you could take a tour of the brain? You'd have to shrink yourself down to board a miniature inner-space ship that will make its way through the complex structure of this control center of the nervous system.

Your first obstacle will be getting through the brain's protective covering, the skull. The brain is composed of very soft tissue. Without the skull the brain could be seriously injured by the slightest bump. In addition to the bony covering, the brain is protected by three layers of membranes, one of which is tough and leathery. Finally, a watery fluid surrounds the brain, cushioning it from any impact.

Once inside, you'll find an extremely complex organ containing about 15 billion neurons—not surprising, considering the important role the brain plays in the body! You'll see that the brain has three main parts: the cerebrum, the cerebellum, and the medulla.

The three main parts of the brain together weigh about 1.5 kg (3 lb). ▼

skull

cerebrum

cerebellum

medulla

G30

Rolling Gray Hills and Valleys

Once inside the skull, you'll find yourself in the **cerebrum** (sə rē′ brəm), the largest part of the brain. You can easily get lost in the cerebrum, since its outer layer—the cortex—contains many folds and grooves. These folds give the brain an increased surface area—more thinking space. Your first impression will be one of total grayness. The outer part of the cerebrum contains the gray matter of the brain.

The cerebrum is divided into two halves, or hemispheres. A band of neurons connects the halves, carrying nerve impulses from one to the other.

Thinking takes place in your cerebrum. It is where you store memories and make decisions. The cerebrum is also the place where your emotions and

▲ **In general, the right half of the cerebrum controls the left side of the body, and the left half controls the right side.**

attitudes originate. Notice on the map the cerebral areas controlling different parts of the body.

Body parts and functions controlled by areas of the cerebrum ▼

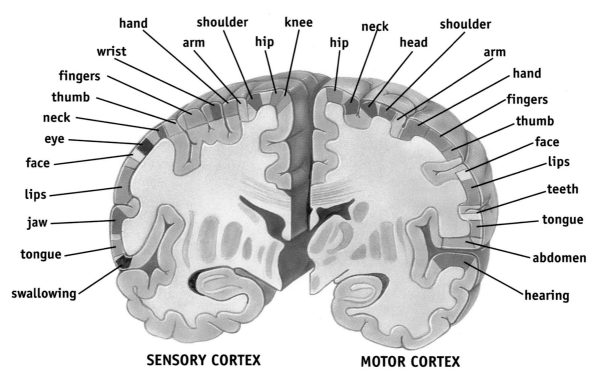

SENSORY CORTEX   MOTOR CORTEX

South of the Cerebrum

After exploring the gray matter, you'll go to the cerebellum, below and to the rear of the cerebrum. The **cerebellum** (ser ə bel'əm), the second largest part of the brain, coordinates the body's muscles. Your sense of balance comes from the cerebellum.

When you first learn a physical activity—a dance routine or swim stroke—you are really training the cerebellum. The nerve impulses that direct your muscles start in the cerebrum but pass through the cerebellum on their way to your muscles. The cerebellum makes sure your movements are smooth and coordinated.

Last Stop

No trip to the brain would be complete without a stop at the medulla. The **medulla** (mi dul'ə) connects the brain to the spinal column. You'll probably notice that, in addition to some gray neuron groups, the medulla contains white matter.

The medulla controls the involuntary actions of the body—the actions that you don't think about. These include heart rate, blood pressure, breathing, blinking, and coughing. Imagine if you had to think about all those actions all the time! The medulla directs such basic functions, leaving your cerebrum free to take care of other things.

SCIENCE IN LITERATURE

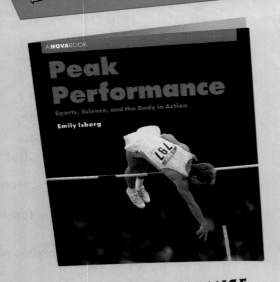

PEAK PERFORMANCE
by Emily Isberg
Simon & Schuster, 1989

How do you get your brain in shape for an athletic competition? Use your imagination! That's the advice of psychologists who teach athletes how to "visualize" a race, or other sports event, before it happens.

Read page 13 of *Peak Performance* by Emily Isberg to find out how this technique affects the brain, motor nerves, and muscles. Then read pages 27–32 to find out in what ways the bodies of top athletes differ from the rest of ours.

brain

spinal cord

nerves

▲ The brain is the control center for the nervous system. Nerves connect the brain to all parts of the body.

Side Trips Optional

You could end your tour here, since you've visited the three main parts of the brain. Or you could keep on going, following the path of a nerve impulse out of the brain. First, you would travel through the spinal cord. From there, you could choose any number of nerves that lead to all of the other parts of the body.

"Next stop, spinal column. After that, we head down to the toes." Good luck. You've got a long, exciting journey ahead of you! ■

INVESTIGATE FURTHER!

TAKE ACTION

The brain can become injured, just as other parts of the body can. But when the brain is injured, the effects can also show up in other parts of the body. Interview a doctor or nurse to find out about the consequences of head injuries. What are some of the best ways for you to avoid head injuries?

INVESTIGATION 1

THINK IT WRITE IT

1. Compare the functions of the three main parts of the brain.

2. A skier had a severe injury to her lower back, damaging the spinal cord. As a result, her legs and feet are paralyzed. Explain her condition, based on what you've learned about the nervous system.

HOW CAN YOU RESPOND TO THINGS AROUND YOU?

It's time for lunch! You smell food and hear laughter from the lunchroom. Hungry kids bump into you as they join the line. You eye the choices and decide on a bowl of soup. Find out how the senses work with your nerves and brain to respond to all the choices in your environment.

Activity
Test Your Mind

How does the brain get the information it needs to learn and remember? Try this activity to find out how memory is related to how quickly you respond.

MATERIALS
- index cards
- marker
- timer
- *Science Notebook*

Procedure

1. With a marker, write a large letter *A* on one side of an index card. Do the same for the letters *B* through *F*. Then make another set of cards to match the first. You will have six pairs of cards when finished.

2. Have a partner mix up the cards and lay them on a table, letter-side down, in three neat rows of four cards each. Don't watch!

3. Your partner will tell you when to begin and will time you. You should select two cards to turn over, trying to match similar letters. If the cards don't match, place them face down in position again. When you make a match, leave the cards face up in their places.

Step 1

Step 3

4. Continue until you have matched all the pairs of cards. **Record** in a chart in your *Science Notebook* the time it took you to do this.

5. **Predict** what will happen when you do this test again with the cards in the same places. **Record** your prediction.

6. Repeat steps 3 and 4. **Compare** your times.

7. Now your partner will mix the cards around, keeping three rows. **Predict** what will happen when you do the test this time.

8. Repeat steps 3 and 4. **Compare** your times. **Compare** your data with the data of other groups.

Analyze and Conclude

1. In which case did you match all the letters in the shortest amount of time?

2. How did your time for the third test compare with your times for the other tests?

3. What role do you think learning and memory played in this activity? **Tell what evidence** you can cite to support your answer.

INVESTIGATE FURTHER!

EXPERIMENT

Make pairs of cards for six more letters and repeat the activity with six rows of four cards in each row. How do your times compare to those with twelve cards? Explain why this happened.

Activity
Reflex Action

MATERIALS
- chair
- *Science Notebook*

Have you ever touched something hot and pulled your hand away before you felt any pain? This is another way your nervous system can respond to your environment.

- -

Procedure

1. Sit in a chair and cross your legs so that the top leg can swing freely.

2. **Predict** what will happen if your top leg is gently tapped just below the kneecap. **Record** your prediction in your *Science Notebook*.

3. Have a partner use the side of his or her hand to gently tap your top leg just below the kneecap. **Record** the results.

Step 3

4. Repeat step 3, but this time try to keep your top leg from moving.

Analyze and Conclude

1. What happened to your leg when your partner tapped it? How did this compare to your prediction?

2. What happened when you concentrated on controlling your leg? Why did this happen?

3. A reflex is an automatic response that you can't control. In what ways do voluntary actions, which you can control, differ from reflex actions?

The Senses

Can you name your five senses? Reread the description on page G34 of standing in the lunch line and try to identify the senses. Your senses let you collect information from your environment. When your brain receives this information, it analyzes it and decides on the proper actions by your body.

Your senses work because of sense **receptors,** which are special sensory neurons that can receive stimuli from the environment. These receptors are found in your five sense organs—the skin, tongue, nose, eyes, and ears.

Touch

The skin is the body's largest organ. Your skin protects you, but it also provides you with your sense of touch. Under the skin's surface are receptors that can sense the texture of objects. Other receptors deeper in the skin sense pressure. Still other receptors sense heat, cold, and pain.

These receptors collect this information and pass it along to sensory neurons. The information reaches the brain through nerve impulses, as you saw in the diagram on page G29.

Receptors in the skin provide you with your sense of touch. ▼

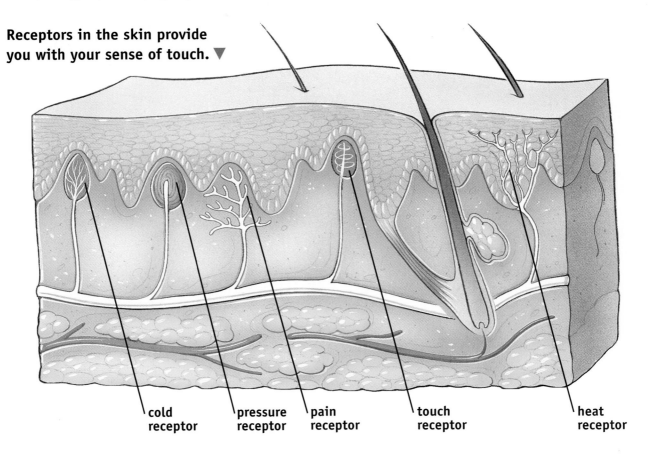

cold receptor pressure receptor pain receptor touch receptor heat receptor

Taste

Your sense of taste is centered in your tongue, which has taste receptors on its surface. These receptors are bunched together in small round bumps called **taste buds.** Most taste buds lie on the tip and back of the tongue.

Your taste buds only respond to four basic tastes: bitter, sour, sweet, and salty. The many combinations of these four tastes produce the wide variety of tastes you experience.

Smell

Your sense of smell results from receptors in your nose that sense chemical particles floating in the air. These receptors have tiny hairs that extend into the air passages in your nose.

When they sense chemicals, the receptors send nerve impulses to a smell center in the brain. The brain uses its memory bank and interprets these nerve impulses from the nose as odors, or smells.

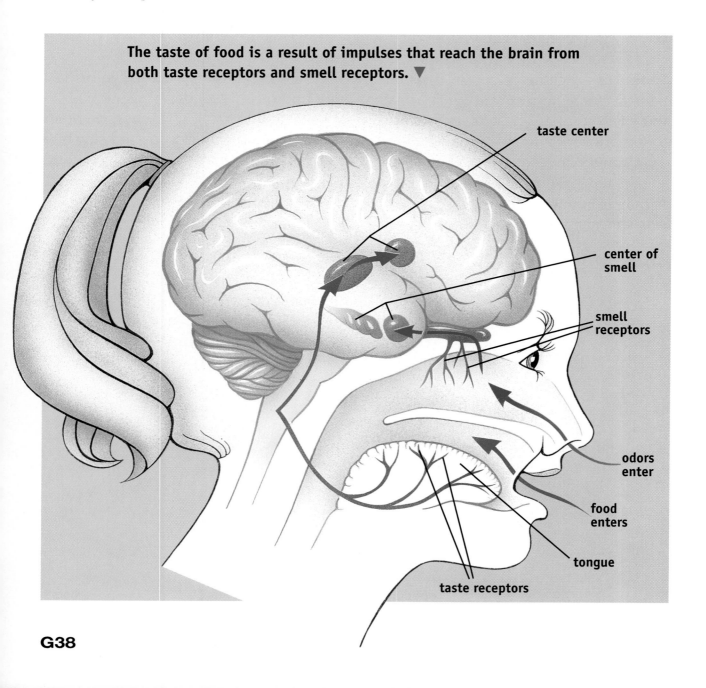

The taste of food is a result of impulses that reach the brain from both taste receptors and smell receptors. ▼

taste center

center of smell

smell receptors

odors enter

food enters

tongue

taste receptors

Sight

Your sense of sight—your vision—is a result of sense receptors within your eyes. These receptors gather information from light rays.

Light enters the eye through the lens, which focuses an image on the surface of the retina (ret''n ə), at the back of the eye. The light affects receptors on the retina, producing nerve impulses. These nerve impulses travel to the brain along a bundle of neurons called the **optic nerve**. So you actually "see" with your brain.

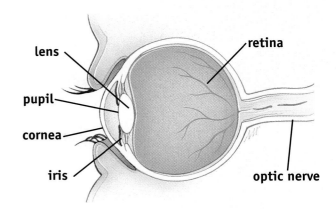

▲ **Light rays are focused by the lens onto the retina. Receptors sense the light and send impulses to the brain through the optic nerve.**

Hearing

Your sense of hearing is a result of receptors in your ears. These receptors sense vibrations in the air.

Sounds are really vibrations that move through the air in waves. Your outer ear collects these sound waves and funnels them in through your ear canal. At the end of the ear canal is a membrane called the eardrum, which vibrates with the sound waves. These vibrations are passed into the inner ear, where receptors turn them into nerve impulses. The impulses travel to the brain through the **auditory nerve.** Your brain interprets these impulses as sound. ■

Your ears are organs that can translate sound waves into nerve impulses. ▼

Stages of Mental Development

You've grown quite a bit in the last few years. You're probably much stronger now than you were in the second grade, and you can do things today that you couldn't do before.

Your brain has been growing along with the rest of your body. As you experience more of life and as your brain grows, you gain the ability to think in more complex ways. This process has been going on since you were born.

Everyone is different, and each person's mental abilities develop in different ways. But in some ways we're all alike. We all gain certain mental abilities at about the same stage of life, as you can see in this time line.

Remember, every person develops differently in both physical and mental abilities. Because you're still growing, you can be sure that some things you can't do or understand now will become easier as you grow older. Isn't it nice to know you have things to look forward to!

When a baby is born, its brain has already been growing for nine months. Although the brain will grow much more, even a newborn has an active, exploring mind.

BIRTH

INFANCY

In the first few months of life, a baby is aware only of its immediate surroundings. When something disappears from view, it's just gone—the baby has no understanding that things exist apart from what he or she sees. Therefore, to develop fully, an infant needs to be provided with a rich and varied environment.

Children become much more logical at this stage of mental development. They begin to better understand concepts such as time and geography. They not only can find their way around but also can draw a map for others to use. They can now predict how others might think or feel in a situation.

MIDDLE CHILDHOOD

LATE CHILDHOOD

When a young person reaches this stage, he or she can think in terms of symbols and can solve complex mental problems. A person at this stage can approach a problem by forming hypotheses—and testing those hypotheses in a logical way. This is also when a person can begin to reflect upon his or her own life and thoughts.

EARLY CHILDHOOD

As children pass into this stage of life, they master language ability. Using language, they can talk and think about the past—and anticipate the future. This is the time when a child seems always to be asking, "Why?" Children are discovering the world, though at this stage they think the world revolves around them.

UNIT PROJECT LINK

Just as there are stages of mental development, your body too develops over time. And all physical activities are controlled by the nervous system. With your group, think of a physical activity that demonstrates the coordination of the skeletal and muscular systems by the nervous system. The activity should be challenging but not impossible. Make a flowchart to show the pathways of nerve impulses during the activity.

The Path of a Reflex

In Investigation 1 you learned about the path a nerve impulse takes—from a sensory neuron to the spinal cord, to the brain, and then back to a motor neuron. But sometimes there isn't time to think about the action. In those cases, the body responds with a **reflex,** or an automatic reaction to a stimulus.

You investigated your own reflexes in the activity on page G36. Now compare the path of a reflex, pictured below, with the path of a nerve impulse, shown on page G29. The boy's brain is informed that he has taken this reflex action, because another nerve impulse goes up the spinal cord to his brain. But in this instance the brain isn't involved in pulling the hand away.

Can you see why reflexes are important for our survival? Reflexes protect our bodies from harm by allowing us to quickly react to pain or danger. ■

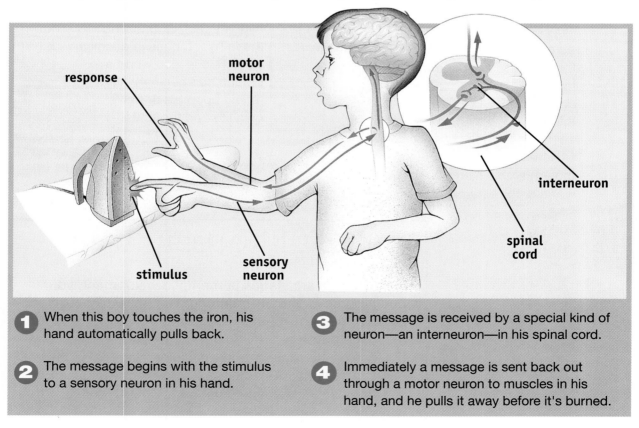

response
motor neuron
interneuron
spinal cord
sensory neuron
stimulus

1 When this boy touches the iron, his hand automatically pulls back.

2 The message begins with the stimulus to a sensory neuron in his hand.

3 The message is received by a special kind of neuron—an interneuron—in his spinal cord.

4 Immediately a message is sent back out through a motor neuron to muscles in his hand, and he pulls it away before it's burned.

Brain Power

 As you've already read, nerve impulses are electrical in nature. Neurons have a chemical makeup that gives them the ability to send nerve impulses. The brain contains billions of neurons, and they all produce nerve impulses. In fact, the nerve impulses from your brain—called brain waves—can be measured and recorded by machines. Doctors often record brain waves if they think a patient may have an illness that has affected the brain.

▲ **Doctors measure brain waves to discover the source of some illnesses.**

Using Brain Waves

Some scientists are now working to develop ways to use brain waves in performing simple tasks. This notion may not be so far-fetched. This task involves using a machine to detect brain waves and having a computer respond by signaling electricity to flow.

The first difficulty faced by these scientists has been to figure out how to identify just the brain waves for a specific action. The brain produces so many impulses—so many things are going on at once in a person's head—that it's not clear which brain wave is connected to which mental activity.

Recording Brain Waves

To record brain waves, scientists attach a number of electrodes to a person's head. Electrodes are small metal disks that can pick up electric currents. Wires connect the electrodes to a piece of machinery.

With practice, some people have actually been able to direct a piece of machinery to do certain tasks, such as making a line on a computer screen. The scientists are not sure exactly which impulses from the brain are actually causing the computer to respond and the task to be done. But one thing is clear: Sometimes a thought can be used to direct the action of a machine.

▼ "Look, Mom, no hands!" Could this be you in the not-too-distant future?

Brain-Actuated Technology

What these scientists have been developing is called brain-actuated technology, meaning the machines used are directed by brain waves. The first application of this technology may be in devices for people who have lost the use of parts of their bodies. If a wheelchair could be steered by brain waves, then a person without the use of arms and legs could live a much fuller life. If this technology is perfected, the future might see all kinds of fantastic technologies. Imagine flying a plane just by thinking about what the plane should do! ■

▲ A brain-actuated wheelchair would be a tremendous help to someone who has lost control of the arms and legs.

INVESTIGATION 2

1. Describe how your nervous system allows you to sense your environment and respond to it. What are the major organs involved?

2. In a physical examination a doctor usually uses a small rubber mallet to test a patient's reflexes. Explain why you think this procedure is important in assessing a person's health.

REFLECT & EVALUATE

WORD POWER

auditory nerve
cerebellum
cerebrum
medulla
motor neurons
nerve impulse
optic nerve
sensory neurons
taste buds

neurons
receptors
reflex
stimuli

On Your Own
Review the terms in the list. Then use as many terms as you can to make a labeled diagram of the nervous system.

With a Partner
Write a clue for each term in the list. Then design a crossword puzzle, using the terms. Trade puzzles with your partner.

BUILD YOUR PORTFOLIO

Draw a diagram of the brain. Label each part and tell what it does.

Analyze Information

Study the drawing. Then describe the path of a nerve impulse during a reflex. Compare this path with the normal path of a nerve impulse.

Assess Performance

Design an experiment to measure reaction time when there are distracting noises. Work with a partner to carry out the experiment. Compare your results to the results from the activity on page G27.

Problem Solving

1. The brain is one of the best-protected organs in the body. Why is this protection important?

2. Dogs have a very keen sense of smell, and bats have highly developed hearing. Which senses are most developed in humans? How are these an advantage? Which senses are not so highly developed? How are these a disadvantage?

3. Reflexes are a means for your body to protect itself. Imagine that you don't have reflexes. What are some things that could happen to you?

CHAPTER 3

STAYING IN CONTROL

Drug abuse. What images come to your mind when you read this phrase? Perhaps you see a person who is out of control, ranting wildly. Or maybe you imagine a dazed person staring blankly into the distance. Now think about an ordinary drugstore and its over-the-counter and prescription medicines. Can even these legal drugs be abused?

Getting the Point

Sally Dan practices acupuncture (ak′yo͞o puŋk chər), an ancient Chinese technique. She uses thin needles to probe points on her patients' bodies. These points seem to be linked with certain functions, such as breathing, or with certain organs, such as the liver. Only a mild tingling or sometimes a stinging sensation is felt.

Acupuncture has long been used to treat pain. But today it also helps addicts break the habit of using heroin, cocaine, nicotine, or alcohol. Recent studies show that those addicts who use acupuncture along with regular rehabilitation techniques stay drug-free longer than those who do not.

Why would people put into their bodies substances that can block awareness and lead to life-threatening disease? What decisions will you make about your own use of drugs?

◄ Acupuncture points are found throughout the body.

INVESTIGATION 1

HOW DO DRUGS AFFECT THE BODY?

Many diseases that commonly killed people in the past are now easily treated with modern drugs. Drugs can be very helpful when they are properly used. What happens to the systems of the body when drugs are misused?

Activity

Ad Power

Both helpful drugs and harmful drugs are common in today's society. How do magazine advertisements influence people about drugs? Find out!

MATERIALS
- posterboard
- marker
- magazines
- scissors
- paste or tape
- *Science Notebook*

Step 2

Procedure

1. Work in groups of three or four. In your *Science Notebook,* write survey questions to find out people's attitudes about taking medicines and about using tobacco and alcohol. Do people think medicines, alcohol, and tobacco are safe? Do people think these products are safe all the time?

2. With your group, survey ten students and tally the results. Then **create a chart** on posterboard. Show the result of each survey question.

3. Look through magazines to find ten advertisements for medicines, alcohol, and tobacco products. Cut out the ads and display them on another piece of posterboard.

4. Show the ads to the same students you surveyed in step 2. Then ask them the survey questions again.

Step 4

5. Tally the results from the second survey and add them to the chart. Compare your data from the two surveys. Discuss your results with your group and other groups.

Analyze and Conclude

1. Describe the results of your first survey in your *Science Notebook*.

2. Did the results of your second survey differ from those of your first survey? If so, how?

3. Consider the methods the magazine advertisements used to influence readers. What can you conclude about how the ads influenced the students you surveyed?

INVESTIGATE FURTHER!

TAKE ACTION

Survey at least ten adults, using the same survey questions. Create charts to display your results. Then compare the adults' responses with the students' responses. How do the results compare? What can you conclude?

The Misuse of Drugs

Drugs are a common part of our lives. When you are sick, you hope that taking a drug will provide a cure—or at least give some relief. But drugs can also be misused. And when they are misused, they can be very dangerous—even life threatening.

Drugs and Drug Abuse

A **drug** is a substance that can affect the function of body cells and tissues. The kinds of drugs that people can buy in stores are called over-the-counter medicines. To obtain certain types of medical drugs, you need permission from a doctor. Those drugs are called prescription medicines.

Of course, it is very important that you be extremely careful with all drugs. You should not take *any* type of drug—either over-the-counter or prescribed—unless it is given to you by a doctor or by another adult whom you trust. Don't *ever* take even a small amount of a drug on your own.

Certain drugs are found in products that some people use every day. **Caffeine** (ka fēn') is a drug found in coffee, some teas, chocolate, and some soft drinks. **Alcohol** is a drug found in beer, wine, and other, similar beverages.

Nicotine (nik'ə tēn) is a drug found in tobacco products, such as cigarettes, chewing tobacco, and snuff. Alcohol and nicotine are legal for adults, although their use is regulated.

Finally, there is a whole group of drugs classified as **illegal drugs**. The use of any of these drugs by a person of any age is against the law at all times.

The misuse of any drug is called **substance abuse**. Because drugs affect the function of the body's cells and tissues, the abuse of *any* drug is dangerous.

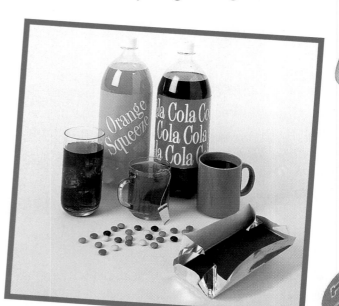

▲ **Caffeine is found in many familiar food products.**

Alcohol and Tobacco

In our society, adults can legally drink alcoholic beverages and use tobacco products. It is *not* legal for young people to *ever* use these substances. Drinking alcohol in moderate amounts is generally considered to be "socially acceptable" by some people. But when drinking is done to excess, alcohol can cause tremendous problems. You will look closely at alcohol abuse later in this chapter.

Using tobacco is also considered "socially acceptable," but it has become less so in recent years. To many people, smoking cigarettes, cigars, or pipes seems dirty and annoying. Smoking is also *extremely* unhealthy.

Smoking is a factor in the deaths of over 400,000 Americans *every year*. It is the major cause of lung cancer and contributes to heart disease. Even when tobacco is chewed rather than smoked, it can cause disease. Cancers of the mouth and throat are related to the use of chewing tobacco and snuff.

If tobacco is so bad, why do so many people use it? Nicotine, the drug found in tobacco, causes an addiction. An **addiction** is a condition in which a person has extreme difficulty in stop-

ping the use of a drug. The addicted person feels powerless to stop because of the physical or mental problems that would result. Many drugs besides nicotine are addictive.

Most adults who smoke began smoking at a young age, usually as teenagers. In most places it is now illegal to sell tobacco products to children and young teenagers. Although many smokers have been able to quit smoking, many more have been unsuccessful, even with help. Don't let yourself be fooled into starting smoking.

UNIT PROJECT LINK

You've read that the use of drugs affects the function of body cells and tissues. The misuse of drugs can impair the body's coordination. With your group, think of an activity, such as a three-legged race, that demonstrates such impaired coordination. The activity should be safe and easy to do. Make up an advertising slogan about your activity. Warn others of the effect of losing physical control due to the misuse of drugs.

DRUGS AND THEIR EFFECTS

Drug Type	Action	Example	Effects of Abuse
Stimulants	Increases activity of the nervous system	Nicotine	Lung disease; damage to heart, throat
		Amphetamines	Extreme nervousness; damage to nervous system; mental capacity diminished
		Cocaine, crack*	Heart attack; damage to nervous system; damage to lining of nose; death from overdose
Depressants	Decreases activity of the nervous system	Barbiturates, methaqualone*, tranquilizers	Damage to nervous system; tiredness; slurred speech; depression; convulsions; death from overdose
		Alcohol	Damage to nervous system, liver, and other organs; mental capacity diminished
Hallucinogens	Alters perception and awareness	Marijuana*, hashish*, LSD*	Lung disease; damage to nervous system; panic; distorted reality; personality changes; mental capacity diminished
Narcotics	Depresses the functions of the brain and nervous system	Morphine, heroin*	Damage to nervous system, liver, and other organs; heart attack; lung disease; personality changes; mental capacity diminished; death from overdose
Inhalants	Increases activity of the nervous system	Glues, paints, aerosol sprays, nitrous oxide	Damage to brain, lungs, liver, bones, kidneys, and nervous system; possible death
Steroids	Increases body mass and strength	Dianabol, Anavar, Winstrol-V	Damage to heart, liver, brain, bones; personality changes; death from overdose

*an illegal drug

Illegal Drugs

As you know, drugs affect the body's cells and tissues. The short-term effects of many drugs might seem good to the user. Drugs can relax, excite, or give energy. People take illegal drugs to experience these effects.

But illegal drugs have been made illegal because they also have bad effects. Many drugs are extremely addictive. And most, when used for even a short time, can damage vital body organs, such as the liver, brain, and heart. People who abuse illegal drugs are ignoring the long-term harm simply to get short-term pleasure.

Some illegal drugs are taken by using a needle to inject the drug into the bloodstream. There are many risks associated with injections involving unclean needles. AIDS—a fatal disease of the body's immune system—can be spread by improper use of needles.

Taking illegal drugs involves more than just a health risk. People are arrested and jailed for using illegal drugs. If you think about all that you could lose by using illegal drugs, you won't even be tempted for a minute.

Avoiding Drug Abuse

At some point you may be offered some kind of drug to use. First, you should know exactly what is being offered. Study the table of Drugs and Their Effects on page G52 to gain an understanding of the different kinds of drugs that people use and abuse.

Second, think about the reasons *not* to use drugs. Consider both the health risks and the legal risks.

Third, decide now what you would say if someone offered you an illegal drug or suggested you misuse a legal product. You could simply say, "That's trouble, and I don't want any part of it!" ■

▲ **People can learn to overcome their addiction to drugs at treatment centers such as this.**

INVESTIGATE FURTHER!

TAKE ACTION

For one week, go through newspapers to find articles on drug abuse. Also find articles that in some way relate to drug abuse, such as drug-related crimes. Discuss your findings with the class.

Drugs and Sports

At the sound of the gun, the runners exploded from the starting blocks. This was the 100-meter dash at the 1988 Summer Olympics in Seoul, South Korea. The winner of the race would be called the fastest human alive.

No one who saw the event will ever forget the scene. The sprinters ran in a pack for about half the distance. Then Canada's Ben Johnson seemed to take off like a jet. He crossed the finish line in a burst of speed as the excited crowd cheered its new hero.

But within a few days, Johnson's prized gold medal had been taken back, and his name had been erased forever from the record books. Medical tests showed that Johnson had taken certain drugs to build up his muscles and make himself run faster.

Why Athletes Use Drugs

Athletes feel great pressure to perform. They want to make the first team or win the big race. They know the coach is counting on them. They want to impress their families and friends. Also, winning often means big money.

For those reasons, some athletes try to improve their performances by using drugs. These drugs might help in building muscles, or they might take away the pain of an injury. They might even help the athlete run faster or run longer.

The pressure to use steroids is greatest in sports where strength makes a big difference, such as weight lifting and football. ▼

Kinds of Drugs Used

Athletes who abuse drugs mainly use three kinds of drugs—stimulants, narcotics, and steroids. **Steroids** (stir'-oidz) are drugs that act like certain natural chemicals found in the body called hormones. Steroids can help an athlete build up muscles and gain strength. This is the kind of drug that Ben Johnson took. He did get short-term benefits, but he also put himself at risk for long-term damage. The use of steroids can harm the heart and other organs as well as cause personality changes and possible death.

Athletes also use **stimulants**, which speed up the nervous system. A stimulant may make an athlete more active and alert. But abuse over a long period can damage the nervous system.

Finally, athletes with injuries may be tempted to use **narcotics**—heroin, for example. Narcotics can lessen pain, but they're also very addictive. And they can damage many body systems.

Banned From Sports

Athletic organizations forbid the use of steroids, stimulants, and narcotics for two reasons. First, the drugs can be

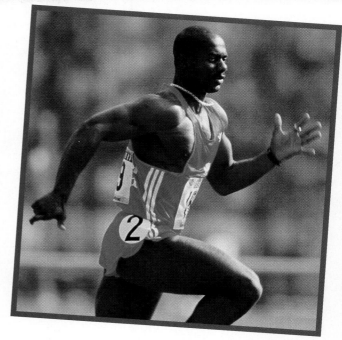

▲ **Although Ben Johnson was the greatest sprinter in Canadian history, his use of steroids cost him an Olympic gold medal.**

very harmful to those who take them. And second, they give an unfair advantage to those who use the drugs over those who don't. Ben Johnson cheated, and for that reason he lost his medal.

Sports organizations test athletes for drugs, usually just after a performance or event. A person caught using drugs may be banned from the sport.

Most athletes don't use drugs. With hard work, a good diet, and proper rest, they are able to win fairly and without risking their health. ■

INVESTIGATION 1

1. A friend has just asked you to help her convince young people not to smoke. How would you try to encourage your classmates to avoid tobacco?

2. Explain the difference between the short-term and the long-term effects of drugs. Why should you consider the long-term effects over the short-term effects if you're ever tempted to try drugs?

INVESTIGATION 2

How Does Alcohol Affect the Body?

When a person takes a drink of alcohol, it goes into the bloodstream almost immediately. Within a few minutes, the alcohol causes changes in the way the person feels and acts. Find out more about the effects of alcohol in Investigation 2.

Activity

Alcohol Advertising: Pro and Con

MATERIALS
- reference materials
- *Science Notebook*

Billboards, magazines, and newspapers all show ads for alcohol, even though it is a drug. What's your stand on whether these ads should be allowed?

Procedure

1. Your teacher will divide your class into teams for a debate. Your team will be either for or against alcohol advertising.

2. **Discuss** your side of the debate with your team members. Divide research responsibilities among members.

3. Use reference materials to find information to support your side of the debate. Also **talk** to people who might give you helpful information. **Record** your information in your *Science Notebook*.

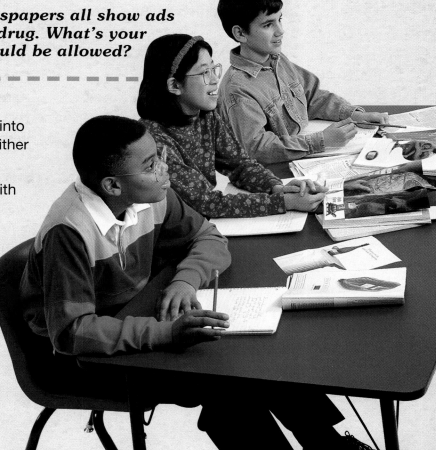

4. **Talk** with your team members and share information. Decide on your strongest points. **Predict** what points the other side will make. Plan your arguments.

5. Debate the other team. Your teacher will act as a moderator.

Analyze and Conclude

1. What were the strongest points your team made? What arguments against these points did the other team use?

2. What were the strongest points made by the other team? What arguments against these points did your team members use?

3. Which team do you think won the debate? Explain.

INVESTIGATE FURTHER!

TAKE ACTION

Use the best points from your debate to write a letter to an editor of a newspaper or magazine. Explain how you feel about the issue of alcohol advertising.

Step 5

Alcohol in the Body

Have you ever seen adults who have been drinking beer or wine? They can seem pretty silly, with a little too much laughter and loud talking.

Actually, people may drink alcoholic beverages just to get those kinds of effects. Sometimes, alcohol can seem to lift a person's spirits. Shyness falls away, and it seems easier to relax.

The problem is that alcohol can be very dangerous to the body, especially when abused. You may decide you want to drink when you become an adult. But before you do, you should learn what alcohol does to the body.

What Happens to the Body

Alcohol is a part of every alcoholic beverage, including beer, wine, and the various liquors. When a person drinks one of these beverages, the alcohol in the drink is absorbed directly into the bloodstream through the walls of the stomach. Unlike food, alcohol does not need to be digested, and so it quickly moves throughout the body.

In the body, alcohol increases both the heart rate and the blood pressure. The blood vessels in the skin expand. That effect often results in a reddishness of the drinker's nose and cheeks. Sometimes people think the drinker

looks warm, and maybe the face is. But alcohol actually causes a loss of heat from the body. No one should ever drink alcohol to keep warm.

Another misunderstanding is that drinking alcohol adds fluids to the body. Actually, alcohol causes the tissues of the body to lose water. So despite drinking even a large amount of alcohol, a person could end up with less fluid than his or her body needs.

Alcohol is a depressant drug. It depresses the workings of the nervous system. It affects how well the brain functions and how well the neurons throughout the body carry messages.

This effect on the nervous system is what causes people to become less shy, for example. But the effect also accounts for many of the dangers of drinking alcohol. Physically, people become slow and clumsy. All kinds of accidents can result. Also, thinking is affected. Bad judgment can lead to accidents as well as to lost friendships and missed opportunities.

A Drinker's Fate

Bad things can happen to a person in just a few hours of drinking. A person who has been drinking is more likely than others to cause accidents.

WHAT ALCOHOL DOES TO THE BODY

Alcohol affects every part of the body because it is carried throughout the body by the bloodstream.

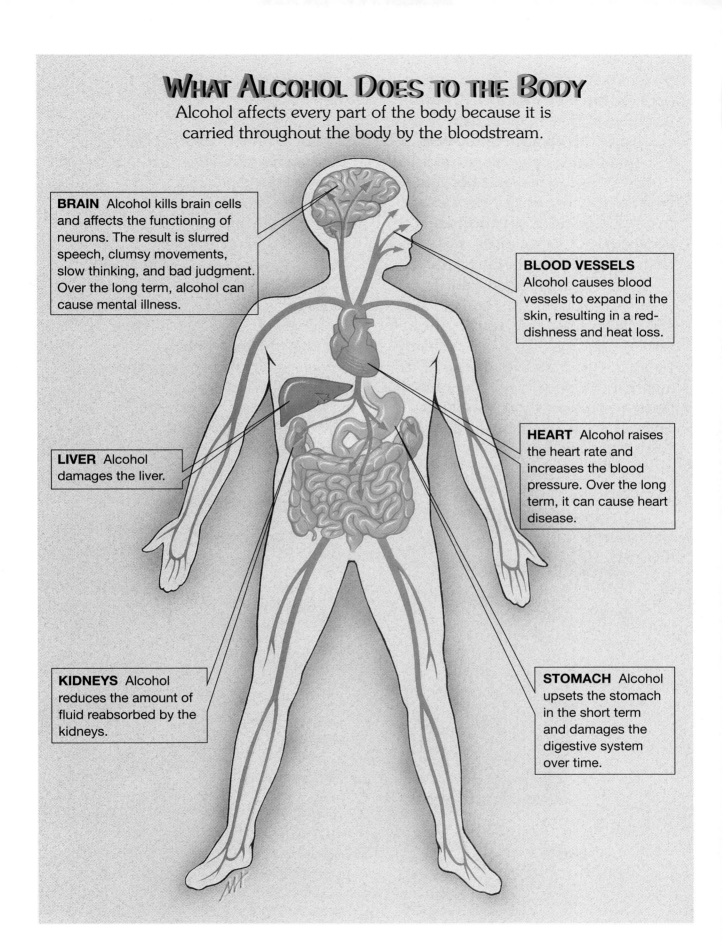

BRAIN Alcohol kills brain cells and affects the functioning of neurons. The result is slurred speech, clumsy movements, slow thinking, and bad judgment. Over the long term, alcohol can cause mental illness.

BLOOD VESSELS Alcohol causes blood vessels to expand in the skin, resulting in a reddishness and heat loss.

LIVER Alcohol damages the liver.

HEART Alcohol raises the heart rate and increases the blood pressure. Over the long term, it can cause heart disease.

KIDNEYS Alcohol reduces the amount of fluid reabsorbed by the kidneys.

STOMACH Alcohol upsets the stomach in the short term and damages the digestive system over time.

Violent behavior often accompanies drinking too much alcohol. A person who abuses alcohol over many years causes serious damage to the body.

Some people can become addicted to alcohol just as they can become addicted to other drugs. The disease that results is called **alcoholism**. The alcohol addict, or alcoholic, may suffer from many illnesses or disorders.

Alcohol destroys brain cells. The alcoholic gradually loses brain function and may become mentally ill. Alcohol severely damages the liver, and many alcoholics die from liver disease. Over a period of time, alcohol also causes digestive problems and heart disease. There is no question that alcohol has destroyed many lives.

Perhaps more tragic is that alcohol can also affect an unborn child. When a pregnant woman drinks alcohol, the alcohol also enters her baby's system. This can then result in fetal alcohol syndrome, a condition in which the baby is born deformed or with a damaged nervous system.

Avoiding Alcohol Use

Sometimes it might seem like most adults drink alcohol. Actually, only about half do. Many adults have decided that the long-term risks to health are not worth any short-term pleasure.

Certainly it is more risky for young people to drink, because their bodies are still growing. It is also illegal for a person your age to drink alcohol. ■

SCIENCE IN LITERATURE

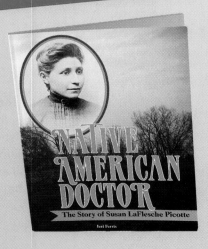

**NATIVE AMERICAN DOCTOR:
THE STORY OF SUSAN
LaFLESCHE PICOTTE
by Jeri Ferris**
Carolrhoda Books, 1991

By the 1860s the Native Americans of the Great Plains had lost their best hunting and farming lands to white settlers. White traders had slaughtered the buffalo. Many Native American traditions seemed meaningless. But then a new hero emerged. Susan LaFlesche Picotte—an Omaha Indian, the first Native American woman to receive a medical diploma—worked to build bridges between her people and the white world.

Native American Doctor by Jeri Ferris is the story of this remarkable woman. She was a doctor, advisor, and translator to the Omaha of Nebraska. In all her roles, she fought against alcohol abuse, which she saw as the greatest medical problem of her people.

Alcohol and Driving

A leading cause of death among teenagers is drunk driving. ▶

STS
SCIENCE
TECHNOLOGY
& SOCIETY

The leading cause of death among American teenagers is accidents. Alcohol is a factor in about half of all accidents that are auto-related. It contributes to the deaths of as many as 20,000 people every year.

The high number of auto deaths involving alcohol has caused Americans to take a harsh view of anyone who drinks and then drives. Penalties for such lawbreaking are severe.

Highway Safety

Every state has laws against driving under the influence of alcohol. When an accident occurs, the police check whether a driver has been drinking by testing the person's **blood alcohol concentration (BAC)**. A BAC test shows how much alcohol is in the person's blood, and that tells how many drinks the person has had.

The table on page G62 shows how a certain number of drinks changes the BAC and affects the drinker. In most states a person is considered legally intoxicated, usually known as being drunk, when the BAC is 0.1 percent or more. But no one should drive after having even one drink, because judgment will have been impaired.

Young People and Drunk Driving

Teenagers who are old enough to drive are just gaining experience at that skill. Imagine adding the effects of illegal alcohol consumption to their inexperience! The result of this combination is that a large number of alcohol-related traffic accidents involve teenagers.

What does this mean for you? Don't *ever* get into a car with anyone who has been drinking. And when you're on a bike or crossing a street, watch carefully for reckless drivers. Stay alert so that you won't become involved in an alcohol-related accident. ■

▲ **Police may use a BAC-testing device if they suspect a driver has been drinking.**

Drinks in 1 hr	BAC (%)	Effects on a Driver (weight, 120 lb)
1	0.03	Increase in heart rate; decrease in coordination
2	0.05	Reduced ability to make good decisions; reduced coordination
3	0.08	Decrease in attention and alertness; slurred speech; slowness in reactions; further decrease in ability to make good decisions
4	0.10	Legally intoxicated; very slow reaction time; terrible coordination; loss of balance; further decrease in ability to make good decisions
5	0.13	Visibly intoxicated; vomiting; poor body control and decision making
6	0.16	Limited awareness; almost no control of body or decision making

INVESTIGATION 2

THINK IT WRITE IT

1. Describe some of the short-term and long-term effects of alcohol on the body. How are some of the short-term effects dangerous not only to drinkers but also to others around them?

2. Why is a warning to avoid drinking alcohol often shown on medicines that depress the activity of the nervous system?

REFLECT & EVALUATE

WORD POWER

addiction
alcohol
alcoholism
blood alcohol concentration
caffeine
drug
illegal drugs
narcotics
nicotine
steroids
stimulants
substance abuse

On Your Own
Write a definition for each term in the list.

With a Partner
Make up a quiz, using all the terms in the list. Challenge your partner to complete the quiz.

BUILD YOUR PORTFOLIO

Make a concept map, starting with the word *drug*. On your concept map, include both legal and illegal drugs and some of their effects.

Analyze Information

Study the drawing. Then identify the organs that are affected by alcohol and explain how alcohol reaches those organs.

Assess Performance

Design a test to find out how advertisements for drugs influence people. You might want to have people answer questions about various ads or challenge them to match slogans to the correct products, or you may have a different idea. Discuss your findings with your classmates.

Problem Solving

1. Imagine there's a debate over whether to allow members to smoke at your youth center. What arguments could you use to convince others that it's not a good idea to allow smoking?

2. Why might it be harmful for you to take some of another family member's leftover prescription medicine when you have similar symptoms?

3. How could you discourage a friend on your team from using steroids when he or she feels a lot of pressure to succeed in a sport?

4. You've arranged to ride home from a party with a friend. Your friend's sister picks you up, and you haven't gone far before you realize that she's been drinking. What should you do?

Throughout this unit you've investigated questions related to movement and control. How will you use what you've learned and share that information with others? Here are some ideas.

Hold a Big Event
to Share Your Unit Project

Work with your classmates to plan The Bone, Muscle, Brain Triathlon. This competitive athletic meet will have three categories: Movement Events, Coordination Events, and Impaired Coordination Events. Use the physical activities that your group planned for the Unit Project Links. Gather any props and equipment you may need. Then invite families and friends to come enjoy the Triathlon...and have fun!

Experiment

Explore this test of muscular control. Tape your thumb to the side of your hand. Then use that hand to pick up a pencil. Can you control your fingers well? What adjustments do you have to make? What can you conclude about the importance of having an opposable thumb?

Research

Choose a sport that you enjoy or would like to learn. Find out which muscles must be developed to excel in this sport. Does a baseball player, for example, need to stretch, build upper or lower body strength, or need aerobic exercise? Write and share a report about your sport.

Take Action

Think of a way to educate others about the dangers of tobacco, alcohol, and other drugs. You might write a story or poem, produce radio announcements, design posters, or do something else that will discourage people from using drugs. Carry out your plan yourself or with some classmates.

SCIENCE Handbook

THINK LIKE A SCIENTIST

You don't have to be a professional scientist to act and think like one. Thinking like a scientist mostly means using common sense. It also means learning how to test your ideas in a careful way.

In other words, you can think like a scientist.

Make a Hypothesis

Plan and Do a Test

Make Observations

To think like a scientist, you should learn as much as you can by observing things around you. Everything you hear and see is a clue about how the natural world works.

Ask a Question

Look for patterns. You'll get ideas and ask questions like these:

- Do all birds eat the same seeds?
- How does the time that the Sun sets change from day to day?

Make a Guess Called a Hypothesis

If you have an idea about why or how something happens, make an educated guess, or *hypothesis*, that you can test. For example, let's suppose that your hypothesis about the sunset time is that it changes by one minute each day.

Plan and Do a Test

Plan how to test your hypothesis. Your plan would need to consider some of these problems:

- How will you measure the time that the Sun sets?
- Will you measure the time every day?
- For how many days or weeks do you need to measure?

Record and Analyze What Happens

When you test your idea, you need to observe carefully and write down, or record, everything that happens. When you finish collecting data, you may need to do some calculations with it. For example, you might want to calculate how much the sunset time changes in a week or a month.

Ask a Question

Make Observations

Draw Conclusions

Record and Analyze What Happens

Draw Conclusions

Whatever happens in a test, think about all the reasons for your results. For example, you might wonder what causes the time of sunset to change. You might also ask when the earliest and latest sunsets occur during the year. Sometimes this thinking leads to a new hypothesis.

If the time of the sunset changes by one minute each day, think about what else the data shows you. Can you predict the time that the Sun will set one month from now?

WHAT CAUSES THE ROCK IN STATUES TO WEAR AWAY?

Make Observations

Ask a Question

D onelle and Ramon were walking through downtown when Ramon pointed to a statue, laughed, and said, "Look, that poor guy's nose has fallen off." Donelle laughed and as they both took a closer look at the statue, they could see that most of the statue's face was missing. Even the statue's body was pitted.

Donelle thought she knew why. She suspected that rain, snow, and ice were destroying the statue. "But it's stone," Ramon argued. "Stone doesn't dissolve in water. Does it?" "But don't we get acid rain here?" Donelle replied. "Maybe acid rain destroys stone."

The next day in school, Donelle described the "melting" statue to the class. Mr. Reynolds, their teacher, suggested that the class set up an experiment to find out what might be causing the damage to the statue. To begin, they came up with some questions that they wanted to answer.

What is destroying this statue?

Is rain destroying this statue?

Are cold winter temperatures destroying this statue?

The class decided that the first question was not specific enough. They

Make Observations

Make a Hypothesis

Here's an example of an everyday problem and how thinking like a scientist can help you explore it.

Before the class could begin setting up an experiment, there were some things they had to find out about the problem. First, they had to find out what the statue was made of. Ramon contacted City Hall and found out that the statue was made out of a stone called limestone.

Donelle told her classmates that she thought that the rain that fell on their town was sometimes acid. So Donelle and her classmates took samples of rainwater. They tested the rainwater with litmus paper and discovered that the rain was acidic.

The class thought about the new information they now had. It was time to use this information to formulate a hypothesis that they could test. Their hypothesis was "Acid rain eats away limestone."

decided to test whether rain could be destroying the statue. Students were curious about whether pollution in the air, and thus in the rain, might be affecting the statue.

Scientific investigations usually begin with something that you have noticed or read about. As you think about what you already know, you'll discover some ideas that you're not sure about. This will help you to ask the question that you really want to answer.

When you use what you have observed to suggest a possible answer to your question, you are making a *hypothesis*. Be sure that your hypothesis is an idea that you can test somehow. If you can't think of an experiment or a model to test your hypothesis, try changing it. Sometimes it's better to make a simpler, clearer hypothesis that answers only part of your question.

Plan and Do a Test

Make Observations

Ramon, Donelle, and their classmates designed a way to test their hypothesis. First, Mr. Reynolds got some fairly equal-sized lumps of limestone for the class to use. Donelle set up three flat-bottomed beakers big enough to hold the chunks of limestone. Ramon created a table for recording information.

The students had discussed what kind of solutions they should use in each beaker. They decided to put rainwater they'd collected in one beaker. They decided to put a more acidic solution in the second beaker. Mr. Reynolds provided them with a solution of weak sulfuric acid. The students knew that the third beaker should contain only pure, distilled water.

The third beaker served as the students' control. The control part of an experiment is almost identical to the other parts of the experiment. It is different in just one way: it doesn't have the condition that is being tested. In this case, the class was testing the effects on limestone of water that is acidic. To make sure that their results only reflect the effects of acid, and not something else that might be in water, the students set up a control in which acid was missing.

After the three beakers were each filled with their specific liquid and labeled, the students found the mass of each chunk of limestone and then put one in each beaker.

The students placed the beakers on a lab table at the back of the classroom. A square piece of glass was placed over each beaker to keep out dirt and dust that might affect the results.

One way to try out your hypothesis is to use a test called an experiment. When you plan an experiment, be sure that it helps you to answer your question. But even when you plan, things can happen that make the experiment confusing or make it not work properly. If this happens, you can change the plan or the experiment, and try again.

Record and Analyze What Happened

Make Observations

After seven days, the mass of each limestone chunk was found again. The mass was recorded on the chart on the board. The chunk was replaced in the same beaker. This was repeated every seven days.

The students recorded the mass of the limestone chunks for fourteen weeks. At the end of the experiment, their chart looked like the one on the next page.

The students analyzed the data on their chart. Donelle noted that the more acidic the solution in the beaker, the more mass the limestone "lost." Ramon noted that the mass of the limestone in the beaker containing distilled water remained the same. The limestone in the rainwater beaker "lost" some mass, but not as much as the limestone chunk in the beaker containing sulfuric acid.

Mass of Limestone Each Week (in grams)

	Week													
	1	**2**	**3**	**4**	**5**	**6**	**7**	**8**	**9**	**10**	**11**	**12**	**13**	**14**
Rainwater	83	83	82	82	81	80	80	79	79	78	77	77	76	75
Sulfuric acid solution	76	74	71	69	68	65	63	60	59	55	53	50	48	45
Distilled water	79	79	79	79	79	79	79	79	79	79	79	79	79	79

When you do an experiment, you need to write down, or record, your observations. Some of your observations might be numbers of things that you counted or measured. Your recorded observations are called data. When you record your data, you need to organize it in a way that helps you to understand it. Graphs and tables are helpful ways to organize data. Then think about the information you have collected. Analyze what it tells you.

Draw Conclusions

Both Ramon and Donelle thought that it looked like their hypothesis was supported. Water containing an acid, or acid rain, did eat away limestone. But Ramon was still not completely satisfied. He wondered if acid rain affected all kinds of stone in the same way, or if it destroyed only limestone. Ramon posed his question to Mr. Reynolds and the other students. Then Patrick added, "And I wonder if cold weather makes the effects of acid rain even worse."

It was soon evident that though their experiment had showed that acid rain does affect limestone, a whole new set of questions occurred to them.

After you have analyzed your data, you should use what you have learned to draw a conclusion. A conclusion is a statement that sums up what you learned. The conclusion should be about the question you asked. Think about whether the information you have gathered supports your hypothesis or not. If it does, figure out how to test out your idea more thoroughly. Also think about new questions you can ask.

SAFETY

The best way to be safe in the classroom is to use common sense. Prepare yourself for each activity before you start it. Get help from your teacher when there is a problem. Most important of all, pay attention. Here are some other ways that you can stay safe.

Stay Safe From Stains

- Wear protective clothing or an old shirt when you work with messy materials.
- If anything spills, wipe it up or ask your teacher to help you clean it up.

Stay Safe From Flames

- Keep your clothes away from open flames. If you have long or baggy sleeves, roll them up.
- Don't let your hair get close to a flame. If you have long hair, tie it back.

Stay Safe During Cleanup

- Wash up after you finish working.
- Dispose of things in the way that your teacher tells you to.

Stay Safe From Injuries

- Protect your eyes by wearing safety goggles when you are told that you need them.
- Keep your hands dry around electricity. Water is a good conductor of electricity, so you can get a shock more easily if your hands are wet.
- Be careful with sharp objects. If you have to press on them, keep the sharp side away from you.
- Cover any cuts you have that are exposed. If you spill something on a cut, be sure to wash it off immediately.
- Don't eat or drink anything unless your teacher tells you that it's okay.

MOST IMPORTANTLY

If you ever hurt yourself or one of your group members gets hurt, tell your teacher right away.

DON'T MAKE A MESS If you spill something, clean it up right away. When finished with an activity, clean up your work area. Dispose of things in the way your teacher tells you to.

EYES Wear safety goggles when you are told to.

HAIR Keep it out of the way of a flame.

HANDS Keep your hands dry around electricity. Cover any cuts. Wear gloves when told to. Wash up after you finish.

MOUTH Don't eat or drink ANYTHING unless your teacher tells you it's okay.

CLOTHES Keep long sleeves rolled up. Protect yourself from stains. Stay away from open flames.

Using a Microscope

A microscope makes it possible to see very small things by magnifying them. Some microscopes have a set of lenses to magnify objects different amounts.

Examine Some Salt Grains

Handle a microscope carefully; it can break easily. Carry it firmly with both hands and avoid touching the lenses.

1. Turn the mirror toward a source of light. **NEVER** use the Sun as a light source.

2. Place a few grains of salt on the slide. Put the slide on the stage of the microscope.

3. While looking through the eyepiece, turn the adjustment knob on the back of the microscope to bring the salt grains into focus.

4. Raise the eyepiece tube to increase the magnification; lower it to decrease magnification.

Using a Calculator

After you've made measurements, a calculator can help you analyze your data. Some calculators have a memory key that allows you to save the result of one calculation while you do another.

Find an Average

The table shows the amount of rain that was collected using a rain gauge in each month of one year. You can use a calculator to help you find the average monthly rainfall.

1. Add the numbers. When you add a series of numbers, you don't need to press the equal sign until the last number is entered. Just press the plus sign after you enter each number (except the last one).

2. If you make a mistake while you are entering numbers, try to erase your mistake by pushing the clear entry (CE) key or the clear (C) key. Then you can continue entering the rest of the numbers you are adding. If you can't fix your mistake, you can push the (C) key once or twice until the screen shows 0. Then start over.

3. Your total should be 1,131. You can use the total to find the average. Just divide by the number of months in the year.

| Rainfall | |
Month	Rain (mm)
Jan.	214
Feb.	138
Mar.	98
Apr.	157
May	84
June	41
July	5
Aug.	23
Sept.	48
Oct.	75
Nov.	140
Dec.	108

These keys run the calculator's memory functions.

This key erases the last entry.

Using a Balance

A balance is used to measure mass. Mass is the amount of matter in an object. Place the object to be massed in the left pan. Place standard masses in the right pan.

Measure the Mass of an Orange

1. Check that the empty pans are balanced, or level with each other. The pointer at the base should be on the middle mark. If it needs to be adjusted, move the slider on the back of the balance a little to the left or right.

2. Place an orange on the left pan. Notice that the pointer moves and that the pans are no longer level with each other. Then add standard masses, one at a time, to the right pan. When the pointer is at the middle mark again, the pans are balanced. Each pan holds the same amount of mass.

3. Each standard mass is marked to show the number of grams it contains. Add the number of grams marked on the masses in the pan. The total is the mass in grams of the orange.

Using a
Spring Scale

A spring scale is used to measure force.
You can use a spring scale to find the weight
of an object in newtons. You can also use
the scale to measure other forces.

Measure the Weight of an Object

1. Place the object in a net bag, and hang it from the hook on the bottom of the spring scale. Or, if possible, hang the object directly from the hook.

2. Slowly lift the scale by the top hook. Be sure the object to be weighed continues to hang from the bottom hook.

3. Wait until the pointer on the face of the spring scale has stopped moving. Read the number next to the pointer to determine the weight of the object in newtons.

Measure Friction

1. Hook the object to the bottom of the spring scale. Use a rubber band to connect the spring scale and object if needed.

2. Gently pull the top hook of the scale parallel to the floor. When the object starts to move, read the number of newtons next to the pointer on the scale. This number is the force of friction between the floor and the object as you drag the object.

Using a
Thermometer

A thermometer is used to measure temperature. When the liquid in the tube of a thermometer gets warmer, it expands and moves farther up the tube. Different units can be used to measure temperature, but scientists usually use the Celsius scale.

Measure the Temperature of a Cold Liquid

1. Half-fill a cup with chilled liquid.

2. Hold the thermometer so that the bulb is in the center of the liquid.

3. Wait until you see the liquid in the tube stop moving. Read the scale line that is closest to the top of the liquid in the tube.

Measuring Volume

A graduated cylinder, a measuring cup, and a beaker are used to measure volume. Volume is the amount of space something takes up. Most of the containers that scientists use to measure volume have a scale marked in milliliters (mL).

Measure the Volume of Juice

1. Pour the juice into a measuring container.

2. Move your head so that your eyes are level with the top of the juice. Read the scale line that is closest to the surface of the juice. If the surface of the juice is curved up on the sides, look at the lowest point of the curve.

3. You can estimate the value between two lines on the scale to obtain a more accurate measurement.

▲ The bottom of the curve is at 50 mL.

This graduated cylinder has marks for every 1 mL. ▶

This beaker has marks for each 25 mL. ▼

This measuring cup has marks for each 25 mL. ▼

Each container above has 50 mL of juice.

MEASUR

Area
A basketball court covers about 4,700 ft². It covers about 435 m².

Volume
1 L of sports drink is a little more than 1 qt.

Temperature
The temperature at an indoor basketball game might be 25°C, which is 77°F.

SI Measures

Temperature
Ice melts at 0 degrees Celsius (°C)

Water freezes at 0°C

Water boils at 100°C

Length and Distance
1,000 meters (m) = 1 kilometer (km)

100 centimeters (cm) = 1 m

10 millimeters (mm) = 1 cm

Force
1 newton (N) =
1 kilogram x meter/second/second
(kg x m/s²)

Volume
1 cubic meter (m³) = 1 m x 1 m x 1 m

1 cubic centimeter (cm³) =
1 cm x 1 cm x 1 cm

1 liter (L) = 1,000 milliliters (mL)

1 cm³ = 1 mL

Area
1 square kilometer (km²) = 1 km x 1 km

1 hectare = 10,000 m²

Mass
1,000 grams (g) = 1 kilogram (kg)

1,000 milligrams (mg) = 1 g

EMENTS

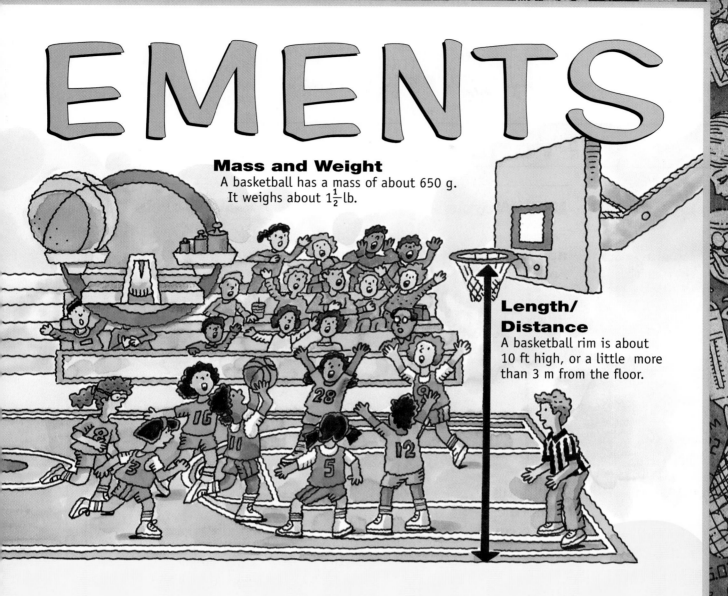

Mass and Weight
A basketball has a mass of about 650 g.
It weighs about $1\frac{1}{2}$ lb.

Length/ Distance
A basketball rim is about 10 ft high, or a little more than 3 m from the floor.

Rates (SI and English)

km/h = kilometers per hour

m/s = meters per second

mph = miles per hour

English Measures

Volume of Fluids

8 fluid ounces (fl oz) = 1 cup (c)

2 c = 1 pint (pt)

2 pt = 1 quart (qt)

4 qt = 1 gallon (gal)

Temperature

Ice melts at 32 degrees Fahrenheit (°F)

Water freezes at 32°F

Water boils at 212°F

Length and Distance

12 inches (in.) = 1 foot (ft)

3 ft = 1 yard (yd)

5,280 ft = 1 mile (mi)

Weight

16 ounces (oz) = 1 pound (lb)   2,000 pounds = 1 ton (T)

GLOSSARY

Pronunciation Key

Symbol	Key Words
a	cat
ā	ape
ä	cot, car
e	ten, berry
ē	me
i	fit, here
ī	ice, fire
ō	go
ô	fall, for
oi	oil
o͞o	look, pull
o͞o	tool, rule
ou	out, crowd
u	up
ʉ	fur, shirt
ə	a in ago
	e in agent
	i in pencil
	o in atom
	u in circus
b	bed
d	dog
f	fall

Symbol	Key Words
g	get
h	help
j	jump
k	kiss, call
l	leg
m	meat
n	nose
p	put
r	red
s	see
t	top
v	vat
w	wish
y	yard
z	zebra
ch	chin, arch
ŋ	ring, drink
sh	she, push
th	thin, truth
th	then, father
zh	measure

A heavy stress mark ′ is placed after a syllable that gets a heavy, or primary, stress, as in **picture** (pik′chər).

absolute age The actual age of an object. (E79) The *absolute age* of this statue is 3,500 years.

absolute magnitude The measure of a star's brightness, based on the amount of light it actually gives off. (B61) The Sun's *absolute magnitude* is less than that of many stars, but its apparent magnitude exceeds that of any other star.

adaptation (ad əp tā'shən) A structure or behavior that enables an organism to survive in its environment. (A70, A86) The thick fur of some animals is an *adaptation* to cold environments.

addiction (ə dik'shən) A condition in which a person has extreme difficulty in stopping the use of a drug. (G51) Sometimes it takes only a short time to develop an *addiction* to a drug.

alcohol (al'kə hôl) A drug that is found in some beverages, such as beer and wine. (G50) If a person drinks *alcohol* to excess, problems can occur.

alcoholism (al'kə hôl iz əm) A disease that results from the continual misuse of alcohol. (G60) Doctors continue to learn more about *alcoholism*.

amplitude (am'plə tōōd) A measure of the amount of energy in a sound wave. (F57) The *amplitude* of a loud sound is greater than the amplitude of a soft sound.

anticline (an'ti klīn) An upward fold of rock layers. (E84) Bending layers of rock formed an *anticline*.

eroded anticline

apparent magnitude The measure of a star's brightness as seen from Earth. (B61) A star's *apparent magnitude* depends on the amount of light it gives off and on its distance from Earth.

asexual reproduction (ā sek'shōō əl rē prə duk'shən) A process in which offspring are produced from one or more cells of a single parent. (A62) In *asexual reproduction*, the offspring is identical to the parent.

audiocassette (ô'dē ō kə set) A small container holding magnetic tape that is used for playing or recording sound. (F92) We inserted an *audiocassette* into the tape recorder.

auditory nerve (ô'də tôr ē nʉrv) A nerve in the ear that carries nerve impulses to the brain. (G39, F85) The *auditory nerve* contains sensory neurons.

axis The imaginary line on which an object rotates. (B13) Earth's *axis* runs between the North and South poles.

H19

Big Bang Theory A hypothesis, supported by data, that describes how the universe began with a huge explosion. (B39) The *Big Bang Theory* holds that everything in the universe was once concentrated at one tiny point.

biodiversity (bī ō də vʉr′sə tē) The variety of organisms that live in Earth's many ecosystems; the variety of plants and animals that live within a particular ecosystem. (D58) The *biodiversity* of an ecosystem quickly changes after a natural disaster.

biome (bī′ōm) A major land ecosystem having a distinct combination of plants and animals. (D48) Some *biomes*, such as the tundra, do not easily support human populations.

biosphere (bī′ō sfir) A self-sustaining natural system of living things and their environment. (B87) For humans to survive in space, they must bring along a version of their *biosphere.*

black dwarf The cool, dark body that is the final stage in the life cycle of a low-mass star. (B66) When the Sun dies, it will become a *black dwarf.*

black hole An extremely dense, invisible object in space whose gravity is so great that not even light can escape it. (B67) Scientists think that the remains of a very massive star can collapse following a supernova explosion to form a *black hole.*

blood alcohol concentration A test that determines the level of alcohol in a person's blood. (G61) A police officer can easily find out if a driver is drunk by giving a *blood alcohol concentration* test.

bone The hard tissue that forms the skeleton. Also, one of the organs that makes up the skeleton. (G8) The human hand contains many small *bones.*

caffeine (ka fēn′) A drug that acts as a stimulant and is present in coffee, many teas, cocoa, and some soft drinks. (G50) Many people prefer to drink herbal teas that do not have *caffeine* in them.

carbon dioxide–oxygen cycle *See* oxygen–carbon dioxide cycle.

cardiac muscle (kär′dē ak mus′əl) Involuntary muscle tissue that makes up the heart. (G17) *Cardiac muscle* contracts rhythmically.

carnivore (kär′nə vôr) A consumer that eats only other animals. (D19, D30) Lions are *carnivores* that prey on zebras and other large plant eaters.

cartilage (kärt′əl ij) Tough, flexible tissue that is part of the skeleton. (G8) *Cartilage* helps protect bones as they move at joints.

cell The basic unit of structure of all living things. (A24) Even though plant *cells* can be different sizes, they still have many of the same structures.

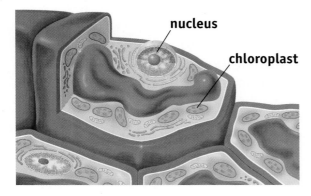

nucleus

chloroplast

cell membrane A thin layer that surrounds all cells and allows water and dissolved materials to pass into and out of the cell. (A24) In plant cells, the *cell membrane* lies inside the cell wall.

cell respiration The process of using oxygen to release energy from food. (A35, A45, D34) Animals and plants release carbon dioxide as a waste product of *cell respiration.*

cell wall The tough outer covering of a plant cell that gives the cell its rigid shape. (A24) A *cell wall* is not found in animal cells.

cementation (sē men tā'shən) A process in which minerals, deposited as water evaporates, bind sediments into solid rock. (E44) Sandstone is a sedimentary rock formed by *cementation.*

cerebellum (ser ə bel'əm) The second largest part of the brain, coordinating the body's muscles. (G32) The *cerebellum* allows smooth movement.

cerebrum (sə rē'brəm) The largest part of the brain in which the processes of thinking, learning, and reasoning take place. (G31) The *cerebrum* is the part of the brain that allows people to understand and remember ideas.

chloroplast (klôr'ə plast) A structure in plant cells that captures light energy that is used in the food-making process. (A24, A33) *Chloroplasts* are located within cells in the leaves of a plant.

cleavage (klēv'ij) The tendency of some minerals to split along flat surfaces. (E15) Salt, or halite, shows *cleavage* in three planes.

clone (klōn) An exact copy of a parent organism produced by asexual reproduction. (A62) One way to *clone* a parent plant is to place a cutting from that plant in water.

coastal ocean A saltwater ecosystem that is relatively shallow and close to the shoreline and that supports an abundance of life. (D54) The *coastal ocean* is an ecosystem that lies beyond the shoreline.

comet (käm'it) A small object in space, made of ice, dust, gas, and rock, that orbits a star and that can form a gaseous tail. (B24) As a *comet* approaches the Sun, it begins to melt.

commensalism (kə menʹsəl iz əm) A close relationship between two kinds of organisms that benefits one of the organisms while neither benefiting nor hurting the other. (D21) The way that some insects use their resemblance to plants to hide from predators is an example of *commensalism*.

community (kə myo͞oʹnə tē) All the organisms living together in a particular ecosystem. (D10) Raccoons, deer, and trees are part of a forest *community*.

compact disc (kämʹpakt disk) A small disk on which sounds are digitally recorded and played back when read by a laser beam. (F92) This *compact disc*, or CD, contains one hour of music.

compound machine A machine that is made up of two or more simple machines. (C62) A pair of scissors is a *compound machine* because it contains two kinds of simple machines—a lever and a wedge.

compound microscope A viewing instrument that uses two lenses to magnify objects many times. (F41) The human hair appeared 1,000 times larger than actual size under the *compound microscope*.

compression (kəm preshʹən) A region in a sound wave where particles have been pushed together. (F57) The *compressions* produced by a vibrating tuning fork are areas of greater than normal air pressure.

concave lens (känʹkāv lenz) A lens that is thicker at the edges than it is in the middle and that causes light rays to spread apart. (F32) A *concave lens* is used to correct nearsightedness.

concave mirror A mirror that curves inward at the middle. (F23) A *concave mirror* is used in a reflecting telescope.

concrete (känʹkrēt) A mixture of rock material and cement that is used as a building material. (E24) This sidewalk is made of *concrete*.

condensation (kän dən sāʹshən) The process by which water vapor is changed to liquid water. (D36) *Condensation* can occur on a glass containing ice cubes.

conduction (kən dukʹshən) The transfer of heat energy by direct contact between particles. (C13) Heat travels through a metal by *conduction*.

conifer (känʹə fər) A tree or shrub that bears its seeds in cones. (A80) The cones of each species of *conifer* are distinct and different from each other.

constellation (kän stə lāʹshən) A group of stars that form a fixed pattern in the night sky. (B10) The *constellation* Orion is best seen in the winter.

consumer (kən so͞omʹər) A living thing that obtains energy by eating other living things. (A36, D19) Meat eaters and plant eaters are *consumers*.

contact lens A thin lens worn over the cornea of the *eye*, usually to correct vision problems. (F35) Some people use *contact lenses* rather than eyeglasses to improve their vision.

convection (kən vek′shən) The transfer of heat energy through liquids and gases by moving particles. (C13) Heat is carried throughout water in a pot on the stove by *convection*.

convex lens (kän′veks lenz) A lens that is thicker in the middle than at the edges and that brings light rays together. (F32) A *convex lens* is used to correct farsightedness.

convex mirror A mirror that curves outward at the middle. (F23) The side-view mirror of a car is a *convex mirror.*

core The innermost layer of Earth, which consists of a molten outer part and a solid inner part. (E69) Temperatures inside the *core* of Earth are nearly as hot as those on the Sun's surface.

crest The highest point of a wave. (F57) The top of a water wave is its *crest.*

crust The outer layer of Earth. (E68) Earth's *crust* is a thin layer of rock.

cytoplasm (sīt′ō plaz əm) The jellylike substance that fills much of the cell. (A24) The nucleus, vacuoles, and many other cell structures float in the *cytoplasm.*

decibel (des′ə bəl) A unit used to measure the loudness or intensity of sound. (F79) Sounds that have an intensity greater than 120 *decibels* (db) can hurt your ears.

decomposer (dē kəm pōz′ər) A living thing that breaks down the remains of dead organisms. (A37, D19) *Decomposers*, such as bacteria, get their energy from the dead plants and animals they break down.

deciduous forest (dē sij′oo əs fôr′ist) A biome that contains many trees and in which rainfall is moderate. (D51) *Deciduous forests* support a great variety of animal life.

deforestation (dē fôr is tā′shən) A mass clearing of a forest. (A93) *Deforestation* is a major concern of environmentalists.

desert A biome in which plant life is not abundant and rainfall is low. (D50) Because *deserts* are dry, desert plants have adaptations to conserve water.

dicot (dī′kät) A flowering plant that produces seeds with two seed leaves, or food-storing leaves. (A81) A trait of a *dicot* is that its leaves have netlike veins.

drug A substance, other than food, that can affect the function of body cells and tissues and that produces a change in the body. (G50) A person sometimes takes a pain-killing *drug* after suffering a back injury.

ecosystem (ek'ō sis təm) An area in which living and nonliving things interact. (D10) An oak tree and the organisms that inhabit it can be thought of as a small *ecosystem*.

effort force The force that must be applied to an object to move the object. (C30) The tow truck applied enough *effort force* to pull the car away.

electromagnetic radiation (ē lek trō-mag net'ik rā dē ā'shən) Wave energy given off by the Sun and some other objects. (F8) Visible light is a form of *electromagnetic radiation*.

electron microscope (ē lek'trän mī'krə skōp) A viewing instrument that magnifies objects thousands of times by using a beam of electrons instead of a beam of light. (F43) Doctors studied the virus through an *electron microscope*.

embryo (em'brē ō) An organism in its earliest stages of development; in most plants it is found inside a seed. (A61) When conditions for growth are suitable, the *embryo* inside the seed develops into a young plant.

endangered In danger of becoming extinct. (A92, D61) As the destruction of the Amazon rain forest continues, the number of *endangered* species increases.

energy The ability to do work or cause change. (C9, F8) *Energy* from the Sun warms the air.

erosion (ē rō'zhən) The wearing away and removing of rock and soil caused by such forces as wind and flowing water. (E84) The pounding waves caused *erosion* of the sandy shoreline.

eustachian tube (yo͞o stā'kē ən to͞ob) A tube that connects the throat and the middle ear. (F85) The *eustachian tube* equalizes the air pressure on both sides of the eardrum.

evaporation (ē vap ə rā'shən) The process by which liquid water changes to water vapor. (D36) One phase of the water cycle is the *evaporation* of water from lakes, rivers, and oceans.

extinct (ek stiŋkt') No longer living as a species. (A92, D61) Traces of some *extinct* species can be found in fossils.

extraterrestrial (eks trə tə res'trē əl) A being from outer space; any object from beyond Earth. (B90) It would be extraordinary for scientists to discover that there is *extraterrestrial* life.

fault A break in rock along which rocks have moved. (E91) Forces within Earth's crust produce *faults.*

fern A nonseed plant that has roots, stems, and leaves and that is found mostly in moist, shady areas. (A79) On *ferns* that grow in tropical places, the fronds grow to a very tall size.

fertilization (fŭrt ′l ə zā′shən) The process by which a male sex cell joins with a female sex cell. In flowering plants, fertilization takes place in the pistil. (A60) *Fertilization* occurs after a pollen tube reaches the ovary.

filter A device that lets certain colors of light pass through while absorbing others. (F48) The stage manager placed a red *filter* over the spotlight.

flower The reproductive structure of a flowering plant. (A16) Petals protect the reproductive parts of a *flower.*

flowering plant Living organisms that reproduce by seeds formed in flowers and that have roots, stems, and leaves. (A81) *Flowering plants* are the most common group of plants on Earth today.

focal point The point at which light rays passing through a lens come together. (F32) Rays of light meet at the *focal point.*

fold A bend in a layer of rock. (E83) Forces within Earth can cause a *fold* to form in rock layers.

food chain The path of energy transfer from one living organism to another in an ecosystem. (A36, D29) Energy moves from producers to consumers in a *food chain.*

food web The overlapping food chains that link producers, consumers, and decomposers in an ecosystem. (A37, D30) Some consumers in a *food web* eat both plants and animals.

force A pull or a push. (C28) When you open a door, you apply a *force.*

fossil (fäs′əl) The remains or traces of a living thing from the past, preserved in rock. (E46, E77) *Fossils* can include imprints of animal skeletons pressed into rock.

fracture (frak′chər) A break or crack in a bone. (G20) The skier suffered a leg *fracture* when he hit an icy patch.

free fall The motion of a freely falling object, such as a spacecraft in orbit around Earth. (B79) Astronauts experiencing *free fall* in space feel weightless.

frequency (frē′kwən sē) The number of waves (such as light or sound) produced in a unit of time, such as a second. (F18, F57) The *frequency* of light waves varies with the color of the light.

friction (frik′shən) Force produced by the rubbing of one thing against another; a force that acts to oppose motion. (C31) *Friction* prevents sneakers from slipping on a gym floor.

fruit The enlarged ovary of a flower that protects the developing seeds. (A61) Some *fruits*, such as peaches or mangoes, contain only one seed.

fulcrum (ful′krəm) The fixed point around which a lever pivots. (C50) If you use a lever to lift an object, the *fulcrum* is located between you and the object you are lifting.

galaxy (gal′ək sē) A vast group of billions of stars that are held together by gravity. (B70) The Milky Way is a typical spiral *galaxy*.

gas giant A large planet that is made up mostly of gaseous and liquid substances, with little or no solid surface. (B47) Jupiter is a *gas giant*.

geocentric model (jē ō sen′trik mäd′′l) A representation of the universe in which stars and planets revolve around Earth. (B37) Ptolemy proposed a *geocentric model* of the universe.

glucose (gloo′kōs) A sugar produced by plants that is the main source of energy for cells. (A33) *Glucose* is produced during photosynthesis.

grassland A biome containing many grasses but few trees and having low to moderate rainfall. (D50) Taller grasses occur in *grasslands* that have more abundant rainfall.

hardness A measure of how easily a mineral can be scratched. (E13) The *hardness* of diamond is greater than that of any other mineral.

hearing aid A small battery-powered electronic device that makes sounds louder. (F86) Most people who wear a *hearing aid* have improved hearing.

heliocentric model (hē lē ō sen′trik mäd′′l) A representation of the relationship between the Sun and planets in which the planets revolve around the Sun. (B37) Copernicus hypothesized a *heliocentric model* of the solar system.

herbivore (hur′bə vôr) A consumer that eats only plants or other producers. (D19, D30) Panda bears are *herbivores* that have a very limited diet because they only eat bamboo.

hertz (herts) A unit used to measure wave frequency. (F18, F68) If 100 waves are produced per second, the frequency of the wave is 100 *hertz*.

igneous rock (ig'nē əs räk) A type of rock that forms from melted rock that cools and hardens. (E40) *Igneous rock* forms from both magma and lava.

illegal drug A substance whose use is prohibited by law. (G50) One *illegal drug* in the United States is heroin.

inclined plane A simple machine with a sloping surface. It allows objects to be raised or lowered from one level to another without lifting them. (C43) A ramp is a kind of *inclined plane*.

index fossil (in'deks fäs'əl) A fossil used to determine the relative age of rock. (E78) The remains of a living thing that lived only at a certain time in the past makes a good *index fossil*.

information superhighway The futuristic concept of communications as an electronic highway system in which telephones, computers, and televisions are linked. (F93) The *information superhighway* will let students do library research from their homes.

intensity (in ten'sə tē) A measure of the amount of energy of sound. (F78) A sound that has high *intensity* is loud enough to be heard from a distance.

Internet (in'tər net) A system of interconnected computer networks. (F94) Telephone lines link computer users with the *Internet*.

joint The place where two bones meet. (G8) Your elbow *joint* enables you to bend your arm.

joule (jōōl) The basic unit of energy and of work. (C19) Scientists measure amounts of energy in *joules*.

kinetic energy The energy that something has because of its motion. (C20) As a boulder rolls down a steep hill, it gains *kinetic energy*.

lake A freshwater ecosystem characterized by still, or standing water. (D53) *Lakes* support fish, birds, algae, and other forms of life.

lava (lä'və) Melted rock material that reaches Earth's surface before it cools and hardens. (E41) A volcano carries *lava* to Earth's surface.

leaf A plant part in which photosynthesis takes place. (A14) In a plant such as cabbage, it is the *leaf* that people eat.

lens A piece of glass or other transparent material with at least one curved surface that brings together or spreads apart light rays passing through it. (F32) The *lens* in a camera focuses an image on the film.

lever (lev'ər) A simple machine made up of a bar that pivots around a fixed point (a fulcrum). (C50) A *lever* can help lift a heavy object with less effort.

ligament (lig'ə mənt) A band of strong tissue that connects bones and holds them in place. (G8) A *ligament* holds bones together at a joint.

light-year A unit of measurement representing the distance that light travels in one year. (B61) Scientists use the unit called a *light-year* when measuring the distances to stars.

luster (lus'tər) The way that the surface of a mineral looks when it reflects light. (E13) Silver and gold have a shiny, metallic *luster.*

machine A device that makes work easier by reducing the amount of force needed to do a job. (C43) A *machine* can make it easier to move, lift, carry, or cut something.

magma (mag'mə) Melted rock material that forms deep within Earth. (E40) Some igneous rocks, such as granite, form from *magma.*

mantle A thick layer of rock between the crust and the core of Earth. (E69) The top of the *mantle* is solid rock but below that is a section of rock that can flow.

mechanical advantage (mə kan'i-kəl ad vant'ij) The number of times that a machine multiplies the effort force applied to it. (C44) To find the *mechanical advantage* of an inclined plane, divide the length of its sloping surface by its height.

medulla (mi dul'ə) The part of the brain that controls the involuntary functions of the body, such as heart rate and breathing. (G32) The *medulla* is located in the brain stem and controls many things you do without thinking.

metamorphic rock (met ə môr'fik räk) A type of rock that forms from existing rocks because of changes caused by heat, pressure, or chemicals. (E47) Slate is a *metamorphic rock* that forms from the sedimentary rock shale.

meteor (mēt'ē ər) A piece of rock or metal from space that enters Earth's atmosphere. (B25) A *meteor* appears as a streak of light, which is why it is also called a shooting star.

meteorite (mēt'ē ər īt) The remaining material of a meteor that has landed on the ground. (B25) In 1902, scientists were able to examine the largest *meteorite* ever known to land in the United States.

Milky Way Galaxy A gigantic cluster of billions of stars that is home to our solar system. (B70) The Sun is located in one of the arms of the *Milky Way Galaxy*.

mineral A solid element or compound found in nature and having a definite chemical composition and crystal structure. (E12) Quartz is a *mineral*.

model Something used or made to represent an object or an idea. (E68) The plastic *model* was a miniature copy of the actual airplane.

monocot (män′ō kät) A flowering plant that produces seeds with a single seed leaf, or food-storing leaf. (A81) About one third of all flowering plants are *monocots*.

moon A natural object that revolves around a planet. (B44) The planet Mars has two known *moons*.

moss A small nonseed plant that lacks roots, stems, and leaves and grows mostly in moist areas in woods or near stream banks. (A78) The leaflike part of a *moss* only grows a few centimeters above ground.

motor neuron (mōt′ər noo′rän) A nerve cell that carries impulses from the brain and spinal cord to muscles and glands in the body. (G28) When people exercise, *motor neurons* carry impulses from the spinal cord to different muscles in the body.

mutualism (myoo′choo əl iz əm) A close relationship between two or more organisms in which all organisms benefit. (D22) Bees carrying pollen from flower to flower as they obtain nectar is an example of *mutualism*.

narcotic (när kät′ik) A habit-forming drug that depresses the function of the nervous system. (G55) Morphine is a *narcotic* drug that is often given to cancer patients.

nebula (neb′yə lə) A huge cloud of gas and dust found in space. (B64) A *nebula* can form when a supernova explodes.

nerve impulse (nʉrv im′puls) A message carried through the body by neurons. (G28) *Nerve impulses* pass from one neuron to another as they move through the body.

neuron (noo′rän) A nerve cell. (G28) The brain is connected to all parts of the body by *neurons*.

neutron star (nōō'trän stär) The remains of a massive star that has exploded in a supernova. (B67) A typical *neutron star* is less than 20 km in diameter.

newton A unit used to measure force. (C29) About 300 *newtons* of force was applied in moving the rock.

nicotine (nik'ə tēn) A drug found in the tobacco plant. (G50) People become addicted to cigarettes because of the *nicotine* in the tobacco.

nitrogen cycle The cycle through which nitrogen gas is changed into compounds that can be used by living things and then is returned to the atmosphere. (D42) The *nitrogen cycle* is of great importance to all life forms because nitrogen is needed to make protein.

noise pollution The occurrence of loud or unpleasant sound in the environment. (F80) The sounds of city traffic are a form of *noise pollution*.

nonseed plant A plant that reproduces without forming seeds. (A78) Mosses are *nonseed plants*.

nucleus (nōō'klē əs) The cell structure that controls all of a cell's activities. (A24) The *nucleus* was clearly visible after it was stained.

octave (äk'tiv) The series of eight notes that makes up a musical scale. (F69) The music student practiced playing *octaves* on the piano.

omnivore (äm'ni vôr) A consumer that eats both plants and animals. (D19, D30) Because they eat both meats and vegetables, many humans are *omnivores*.

opaque (ō pāk') Not letting light through. (F47) The *opaque* curtains kept out the sunlight.

open ocean A large saltwater ecosystem containing both floating and free-swimming organisms. (D55) The *open ocean* covers much of Earth's surface.

optic nerve A bundle of neurons that carries impulses from the *eye* to the brain. (G39) If there is damage to the *optic nerve*, messages from the *eye* cannot be received by the brain.

ore (ôr) A mineral or rock that contains enough of a metal to making mining the metal profitable. (E27) Hematite is an *ore* mined for its iron content.

overtone A fainter, higher tone that harmonizes with the main tone produced by a musical instrument or the human voice. (F58) The blending of *overtones* gives the flute its unique sound.

oxygen–carbon dioxide cycle A natural cycle in which plants and other producers use carbon dioxide and produce oxygen, and living things use oxygen and produce carbon dioxide. (B86, D34) The *oxygen–carbon dioxide cycle* must be duplicated in space if humans wish to make long voyages to other planets.

--- P ---

parasitism (par′ə sīt iz əm) A relationship between two organisms in which one organism lives on or in the other, feeds upon it, and usually harms it. (D21) The way in which fleas live off dogs is an example of *parasitism.*

phloem cell (flō′əm sel) A plant cell that, when linked with other similar cells, forms a system of tubes for carrying nutrients from the leaves down through the stem and root. (A11) The *phloem cells* form a major transport system in plants.

phonograph (fō′nə graf) A device that reproduces sounds recorded on a disk. (F90) We played old records on the *phonograph.*

photosynthesis (fōt ō sin′thə sis) The process by which producers, such as plants, make their own food by using energy from the Sun. (A33) *Photosynthesis* takes place primarily in the leaves of plants.

pistil (pis′til) The female reproductive structure of a flower. (A16) A *pistil* consists of three main parts—the stigma, the style, and the ovary.

pitch The highness or lowness of a sound. (F68) A tuba produces sounds with a low *pitch.*

plane mirror A mirror that has a flat surface. (F22) The mirror over the bathroom sink is a *plane mirror.*

planet A large body in space that orbits a star and does not produce light on its own. (B17) Earth is one of nine known *planets* that revolve around the Sun.

plant kingdom A major group of living things that are multicellular and that carry out photosynthesis. (A78) Living organisms in the *plant kingdom* make their own food.

pollination (päl ə nā′shən) The transfer of pollen from the male part of one flower to the female part of another flower. (A60) Some *pollination* is done by insects.

population (päp yōō lā′shən) A group of the same kind of organisms that live in an area. (D10) There is a huge *population* of frogs in that marsh.

potential energy The energy that an object has because of its position or structure; stored energy. (C18) A coiled spring has *potential energy.*

precipitation (prē sip ə tā'shən) The process by which water from clouds falls back to the Earth. (D36) *Precipitation* falls to the Earth in the form of rain or snow.

producer (prō dōōs'ər) An organism that makes its own food through photosynthesis. (A36, D18) Plants and algae are examples of *producers*.

protein (prō'tēn) Organic compounds that form the structure and control the processes that take place in living things. (D41) *Proteins* provide the body with materials that help cells grow and repair themselves.

protostar (prōt'ō stär) A concentration of matter found in space that is the beginning of a star. (B64) When the temperature inside a *protostar* becomes high enough, nuclear reactions begin and it turns into a star.

pulley (pōōl'ē) A simple machine made up of a wheel around which a rope or chain is passed. (C53) A *pulley* helps lift objects that would be too heavy to lift directly.

quarry (kwôr'ē) A mine, usually near or at Earth's surface, from which rock is removed. (E52) Granite, sandstone, limestone, slate, and marble are some rocks that come from a *quarry*.

radiation (rā dē ā'shən) The transfer of energy by waves. (C11) Energy given off by the Sun travels as *radiation* through space.

radio telescope A gigantic antenna designed to receive radio signals from space. (B92) *Radio telescopes* are important tools for studying distant stars and galaxies.

rarefaction (rer ə fak'shən) A region in a sound wave where there are fewer particles than normal. (F57) The *rarefactions* that a vibrating violin string produces are areas of lower than normal air pressure.

receptor (ri sep'tər) A sensory neuron that receives stimuli from the environment. (G37) Sensory *receptors* in the skin make it possible for people to feel heat, cold, pressure, touch, and pain.

red giant A very large old reddish star that has greatly expanded and cooled as its fuel has begun to run out. (B65) As the Sun reaches old age, it will turn into a *red giant*.

reflecting telescope An instrument for viewing distant objects that uses a curved mirror at the back of its tube to gather light and produce an image. (B22, F39) This observatory uses a *reflecting telescope* to observe faraway galaxies.

reflection (ri flek′shən) The bouncing of light or sound off a surface. (F22) The *reflection* of sunlight off the snow made us squint.

reflex (rē′fleks) A simple behavior pattern involving an automatic response to a stimulus. (G42) The girl's automatic *reflex* quickly got her foot out of the hot water.

refracting telescope An instrument for viewing distant objects that uses two lenses to gather light and produce an image. (B21) The *refracting telescope* gave us a closer look at the Moon.

refraction (ri frak′shən) The bending of light as it passes from one material into another. (F24) Light traveling from air into water will undergo *refraction*.

relative age The age of an object as compared to other objects. (E78) The order of layers of rock shows the *relative ages* of the layers.

resistance force A force that resists, or opposes, motion. (C30) Friction is a *resistance force*.

retina (ret′′n ə) The light-sensitive area at the back of the eye on which an image is formed. (F32) The *retina* contains two kinds of cells.

revolution (rev ə loo′shən) The movement of an object around another object or point. (B14) It takes about 365 days for Earth to make one *revolution* around the Sun.

river A freshwater ecosystem characterized by running water. (D52) Salmon are able to swim against the current in a *river*.

rock The solid material composed of minerals that forms Earth's crust. Also, the material, sometimes molten, that forms Earth's inner layers. (E40) *Rocks* are weathered by wind and rain.

rock cycle The continuous series of changes that rocks undergo. (E60) In the *rock cycle*, changes are brought about by factors such as weathering, melting, cooling, or pressure.

root The underground part of a plant that anchors the plant and absorbs water and nutrients. (A10) Carrots and turnips have only one large single *root*.

rotation (rō tā′shən) The spinning motion of an object on its axis. (B14) It takes about 24 hours for Earth to make one complete *rotation*.

S

sapling (sap′liŋ) A young tree. (A67) The year after a tree seed germinates, the young plant is called a *sapling*.

satellite (sat′′l īt) A natural or human-built object that revolves around another object in space. (B44) The Moon is a natural *satellite* of Earth.

H33

sediment (sed′ə mənt) Bits of weathered rocks and minerals and pieces of dead plants or animals. (E43) Over time, *sediments* can form sedimentary rocks, such as sandstone and limestone.

sedimentary rock (sed ə men′tər ē räk) A type of rock that forms when sediments harden. (E43) Most *sedimentary rocks* form in layers.

seed coat A tough, protective covering on a seed, enclosing the embryo and its food supply. (A 61) When the leaves on a young plant start to grow and open up, the *seed coat* falls off.

seed dispersal The scattering of seeds away from the parent plant. (A88) The wind is one way in which *seed dispersal* is carried out.

seed leaf A first leaf found inside a seed, providing food for the tiny developing plant. (A66) A monocot seed contains one *seed leaf*.

seedling (sēd′liŋ) A young growing plant after it first sprouts and develops new leaves. (A66) In spring the forest floor is covered with green *seedlings*.

seed plant A plant that reproduces by forming seeds. (A78) Corn and wheat are *seed plants*.

semicircular canal Any of three curved tubelike structures of the inner ear that help the body to maintain balance. (F85) The *semicircular canals* respond to movements of the head.

sensory neuron (sen′sər ē nōō′rän) A nerve cell that carries impulses from the senses to the brain and spinal cord. (G28) *Sensory neurons* carry impulses from your eyes to your brain.

sexual reproduction The production of offspring that occurs when a male sex cell joins a female sex cell. (A59) The *sexual reproduction* of flowers is greatly aided by insects.

shoreline The ecosystem where land and ocean meet. (D54) The *shoreline* varies in width around the world.

simple microscope A microscope that uses a single lens to magnify objects. (F41) A magnifying glass is a *simple microscope*.

skeletal muscle Voluntary muscle tissue; also, one of the muscles that moves bones. (G17) Tendons attach *skeletal muscles* to bones.

skeletal system The system of bones and tissues that supports and protects the body. (G8) The human *skeletal system* contains 206 bones.

smelting (smelt′iŋ) The process of melting ore to remove the metal from it. (E28) Workers obtain iron by *smelting* iron ore in a blast furnace.

smooth muscle Involuntary muscle tissue that lines the inside of blood vessels, intestines, and other organs. (G17) *Smooth muscles* move food through the digestive system.

solar system The Sun and the planets and other objects that orbit the Sun. Also, any star and the objects that revolve around it. (B34) Our *solar system* consists of the Sun, nine known planets, and many smaller objects.

sound A form of energy that travels through matter as waves. (F56) The *sound* made the floor vibrate.

sound synthesizer (sound sin'thə-sī zər) An electronic device that can produce a wide variety of sounds. (F71) The composer used a *sound synthesizer* to create a new musical composition.

sprain An injury in which the ligament at a joint is torn or twisted. (G19) An ankle *sprain* can take weeks to heal.

stamen (stā'mən) The male reproductive structure of a flower. (A16) Pollen is produced in the *stamens*.

star A huge object in space, made up of hot gases, that shines by its own light. (B17) Many *stars* are believed to have systems of planets.

starch (stärch) A substance found in plants that is a storage form of glucose. (A35) Potatoes contain a lot of *starch*.

stem The part of a plant that supports the leaves and flowers and carries water to these parts of the plant. (A12) The trunk of a tree is a *stem*.

steroid (stir'oid) A drug that helps to build up muscle tissue and strength. (G55) Some athletes have used *steroids*.

stimulant (stim'yoo lənt) A drug that increases the activity of the nervous system. (G55) Many people drink coffee because it acts as a *stimulant*.

stimulus (stim'yoo ləs) An event or environmental condition that triggers a nerve impulse, thus causing an organism to respond. (G28) The *stimulus* of a loud sound can make a person jump.

stoma (stō'mə; *pl.* stō ma'tə) One of many small openings, or pores, usually on the underside of a leaf, through which gases enter and leave a plant. (A46) The *stomata* on a water lily are on the top of the leaf.

strain An injury in which a muscle or tendon is torn slightly or stretched too far. (G20) Lifting the heavy couch gave me a back *strain*.

streak (strēk) The colored powder made by rubbing a mineral against a ceramic surface. (E15) Although pyrite is yellow, it produces a black *streak*.

substance abuse (sub'stəns ə-byoos') The improper use, or abuse, of alcohol or drugs. (G50) *Substance abuse* can damage a person's health.

supernova (soo'pər nō və) An exploding star. (B66) When a red giant star uses up all its fuel, it collapses and explodes in a *supernova*.

syncline (sin'klīn) A downward fold of rock layers. (E84) Forces in Earth pushing on rock formed a *syncline*.

taiga (tī′gə) A biome that contains many coniferous trees and in which rainfall is moderate. (D51) The *taiga* is south of the tundra.

taste bud A receptor on the surface of the tongue that responds to different substances and makes it possible to taste. (G38) There are only four basic types of *taste buds.*

tendon (ten′dən) A strong cord of tissue that joins a muscle to a bone. (G17) *Tendons* pull on bones like strings pull on the limbs of a puppet.

terrestrial planet (tə res′trē əl plan′it) An object in space that resembles Earth in size, in density, and in its mainly rocky composition. (B44) Mars is a *terrestrial planet.*

timbre (tam′bər) The quality of sound that sets one voice or musical instrument apart from another. (F58) The same note played on a violin and on a trumpet differ in *timbre.*

translucent (trans lōō′sənt) Letting light through but scattering it; objects cannot be clearly seen through translucent material. (F48) The *translucent* glass dimmed the room.

transparent (trans per′ənt) Letting light through; objects can be clearly seen through transparent material. (F47) Window glass is usually *transparent* so that people can see through it.

transpiration (tran spə rā′shən) A process in which a plant releases moisture through its stomata. (A46) *Transpiration* adds water to the air.

tropical rain forest A biome distinguished by lush vegetation, abundant rainfall, and plentiful sunlight. (D50) The *tropical rain forest* supports the greatest variety of life of any biome.

tropism (trō′piz əm) A growth response of a plant to conditions in the environment, such as light or water. (A50) Growing toward a light source is an example of a plant *tropism.*

trough (trôf) The long narrow hollow between two waves. (F57) A *trough* occurs between two wave crests.

tundra (tun′drə) A biome characterized by cold temperatures and low precipitation. (D51) The *tundra* blooms in summer.

universe (yōōn′ə vʉrs) The sum of everything that exists. (B70) Our solar system is part of the *universe.*

vacuole (vak′yōō ōl) A cell part that stores water and nutrients. (A24) Some plant cells have large *vacuoles.*

vacuum (vak′yo͞o əm) A space that is empty of any matter. (F17) Light waves can travel through a *vacuum*.

vibration A back-and-forth movement of matter. (F56) It is the *vibration* of the guitar strings that produces sound.

visible light A form of electromagnetic energy that can be seen. (F8) The eye responds to *visible light*.

volume The loudness or softness of a sound. (F78) Please turn up the *volume* on the radio.

water cycle A continuous process in which water moves between the atmosphere and Earth's surface, including its use by living things. (B87, D36) The *water cycle* is powered by energy from the Sun.

wave A disturbance that carries energy and that travels away from its starting point. (F17) The experiment measured how quickly light *waves* travel.

wavelength The distance between one crest of a wave and the next crest. (F17, F57) Red light has a longer *wavelength* than does blue light.

weathering The breaking up of rocks into sediments by such forces as wind, rain, and sunlight. (E62) Through *weathering*, igneous rock can be broken down into sediments.

wetland Any one of three ecosystems—marsh, swamp, or bog—where land and fresh water meet. (D53) *Wetlands* help purify water.

wheel and axle A simple machine made of two wheels of different sizes that pivot around the same point. (C58) A doorknob, along with its shaft, is an example of a *wheel and axle*.

white dwarf A very small, dying star that gives off very little light. (B65) When the Sun's fuel runs out, it will collapse into a *white dwarf*.

work The movement of a force through a distance. (C28) *Work* is done in lifting an object.

xylem cell (zī′ləm sel) A plant cell that, when joined with other similar cells, forms a transport system throughout a plant. (A11) The wood of a tree is formed mainly of *xylem cells*.

INDEX

* Activity

* Activity

CREDITS